Mac Answers!

Tech Support at Your Fingertips, Second Edition

**Bob LeVitus
and Shelly Brisbin**

Osborne/**McGraw-Hill**

Berkeley • New York • St. Louis • San Francisco
Auckland • Bogotá • Hamburg • London
Madrid • Mexico City • Milan • Montreal
New Delhi • Panama City • Paris • São Paulo
Singapore • Sydney • Tokyo • Toronto

Osborne/**McGraw-Hill**
2600 Tenth Street
Berkeley, California 94710
U.S.A.

For information on translations or book distributors outside the U.S.A., or to arrange bulk purchase discounts for sales promotions, premiums, or fundraisers, please contact Osborne/**McGraw-Hill** at the above address.

Mac Answers! Tech Support at Your Fingertips, Second Edition

Photos for the icons courtesy of Apple Computer, Inc. and Hunter Freeman, photographer.

1234567890 AGM AGM 019876543210

ISBN 0-07-212399-0

Publisher
Brandon A. Nordin

Associate Publisher and Editor-in-Chief
Scott Rogers

Acquisitions Editor
Megg Bonar

Project Editor
Patty Mon

Acquisitions Coordinator
Stephane Thomas

Technical Editor
Christopher Breen

Copy Editor
Andy Carroll

Proofreader
Linda Medoff

Indexer
David Heiret

Computer Designers
E.A. Pauw
Dick Schwartz
Roberta Steele

Illustrators
Robert Hansen
Beth Young
Brian Wells

Series Design
Michelle Galicia

This book was composed with Corel VENTURA™ Publisher.

For Frank

About the Authors...

Bob LeVitus, popular Mac columnist for *MacHome*, the *Houston Chronicle*, *MacCentral*, and *Current Technology*, has written 33 computer books that have sold over a million copies worldwide, including *Mac OS 9 for Dummies*.

Shelly Brisbin is the author of six books, including *Adobe GoLive for Macintosh and Windows: Visual QuickStart Guide*, and has been writing about Mac technologies for the past 11 years. She is a frequent contributor to *Macworld Magazine*.

Contents

Part Two　Mac Peripherals and Connectivity

Part Three **Getting Online with Your Mac**

Part Four   **Living with Your Mac: Troubleshooting, Upgrading, Tips, and Toys**

Foreword

Do you remember *MacUser*'s "Help Folder" column? *Mac Answers! Tech Support at Your Fingertips* is like Help Folder on steroids. Bob LeVitus managed to reassemble the old Help Folder team. Shelly Brisbin, the coauthor of this book, was *MacUser*'s editor in charge of Help Folder, and Chris Breen, the book's technical editor, was the coauthor of Help Folder. Together, they've put together a book that is, in many ways, better than Help Folder ever was.

This book is extremely complete and yet it's also easy to use because of its quick, at-a-glance descriptions and comprehensive, cross-referenced index. From page 1, you'll see why Bob and Shelly are as knowledgeable about Macintosh as anyone I know.

I know you're going to love this book as much as I do. Because of this book, I may not need to ask for help anymore— maybe I can even provide help to others!

Guy Kawasaki
CEO, garage.com, and author of *Rules for Revolutionaries*

Acknowledgments

- Megg Bonar, Patty Mon, Stephane Thomas, Andy Carroll, and all of the other folks at Osborne who we have not met and who deserve recognition for keeping us on schedule and insisting on and supporting our attempt to produce a high-quality book.

- Christopher Breen, our technical editor, colleague, and friend, whose broad knowledge and breathtaking speed give us the confidence to put our names on this book.

- Guy Kawasaki, for his kind words. Having the Kawasaki seal of approval means a lot to us.

- The folks at Apple who maintain the Tech Info Library, the indispensable source for obscure and not-so-obscure Macintosh technical information.

- Sarah Elizabeth Campbell for helping us check all of those links.

- Our agents, Carole McClendon of Waterside (for Bob) and Claire Horne of Moore Literary Agency (for Shelly), for their tenacity and fairness.

Shelly would like to thank all of the people who, during the course of this project, offered their own Mac questions. Thanks to Sarah Elizabeth Campbell for the joy that is Bummer Night at Artz Rib House, and for her speedy link checking. Special thanks, as always, go to Frank Feuerbacher and the cats (Gremlin, Ivar, and Weasel) for their love and support. I'll come out of my office now, I promise.

Bob would like to thank Keri Walker, Tim "Shortstop" Holmes, Nathalie Welch, and even Steve Jobs (not to mention all the other fine folks at Apple who somehow helped us get this book written). Thanks. We couldn't have done it without you. Also, thanks to the nice folks at Iron Works BBQ, Saccone's Pizza, and Chuy's for feeding my belly and soul during this

book's gestation. And last but not least, thanks to my family, Lisa, Allison, and Jacob, for putting up with my all-too-frequent absences. I'll come out of *my* office now, I promise.

Bob LeVitus and Shelly Brisbin

Introduction

We have each spent more than 13 years around Macs, most of that time peering under the hood, consulting, reviewing new software, playing games, writing articles and, yes, answering questions. (Our "Help Folder" column mailboxes at *MacUser Magazine* filled up each month with questions from readers about workarounds, upgrades, troubleshooting, and lots more.) And we're still answering questions.

Each new generation of Mac and each new version of Mac OS comes with its own set of opportunities and problems. The amazingly successful iMac, iBook, and Mac OS 9 are just the latest sources of joy and (a little) heartache for us. We have examined and used each Mac and have spent lots of time listening to and reading what others have had to say about them. We've found all sorts of ways to use Mac OS 9's new navigation and searching features and have discovered that the iMac is just like other Macs . . . mostly.

The book is divided into four parts: Mac Basics, Mac Peripherals and Connectivity, Getting Online with Your Mac, and Living With Your Mac: Troubleshooting, Upgrading, Tips, and Toys. In Part One, we offer a detailed look at how the Mac operating system works and at ways you can use its tools to be more productive. You'll also find lots of information about how Mac files and software are organized, as well as information about how you can prevent problems before they happen. In Part Two, we turn our attention to hardware, both inside and outside the Mac. You'll learn about storage devices, printers, scanners, monitors, and networking, including both practical information about using these devices and guidance in choosing and buying equipment. Part Three explains how to get connected and how to use the Internet. Finally, Part Four helps you troubleshoot problems, choose a new Mac or get the most from your *existing* Mac, and have fun with your Mac.

Within these sections, you will find chapters that divide the Mac universe into manageable chunks. We begin each chapter by laying the groundwork—defining terms,

describing tools available within Mac OS, and explaining how your Mac works with other hardware and software. Next, we get more specific, answering important questions about how to use your hardware and software with stops along the way for special cases that relate to certain Mac models. Finally, we help you understand how problems develop and what you can do to find and solve them. Though each chapter in the book is organized a bit differently, depending on the subject matter, we've used this general outline to walk you through the process of working with the components of your Mac.

Besides questions and answers, each chapter includes note, tip, and caution sections that help you get the most from your Mac. The "Bob Speaks" and "Shelly's Scoop" sidebars get down to the real world, nitty-gritty of using the Mac, told from our own points of view.

CONVENTIONS USED IN THIS BOOK

We have included some icons and guides to help you navigate through this book, as follows:

- Small capitals (for example, COMMAND and OPTION), indicate the names of keys you should press to perform a command.

- Menu commands are separated with vertical lines, as in File | Print.

- *Italic* type indicates a new term. We'll define each term following its italicized name.

- The icon that looks like an iMac™ indicates a paragraph or question that deals specifically with the iMac. Same goes for the Only in iBook™ icon.

- The Mac® OS 9 icon indicates a paragraph or question that is specific to Mac OS 9.

 Note: *Notes point out unusual features, functions, and capabilities.*

 Tip: *Tips are shortcuts or workarounds that make it easier to get things done.*

! ***Caution:*** *Cautions suggest that you take care when working with the tools or following the steps described. Ignoring a Caution could result in damage to your Mac or its files.*

We hope that you find this book helpful and that it answers most of the questions you have about using your Mac. We think there's something here for everyone, whether you are just getting started or have been using Macs since the dark ages . . . like us.

Part One

Mac Basics

Chapter 1

Top Ten Frequently Asked Questions

Anwers Topics!

Top Ten FAQs @ a Glance

 This chapter contains the ten questions we hear most often from Mac users.

1. What does a flashing question mark at startup mean?

It means your Mac doesn't recognize a startup disk. In other words, it can't find a valid System Folder on any of the available disks. You will not be able to boot the Mac from that disk until you solve the problem. If you're pretty sure that your hard disk *should* work—it worked last time you restarted, and/or you know that it contains a valid System Folder—try restarting with the same startup disk. If you are successful, rebuild the desktop to eliminate desktop databases as a source of the problem. If you are unable to boot with the current startup disk, insert a bootable floppy or a Mac CD-ROM (one probably came with your Mac; all retail Mac OS upgrade CDs are bootable). If you use a CD-ROM, hold down the C key during startup. When the desktop appears, run Disk First Aid, repair your startup disk, and restart.

 Tip: *Use Sherlock to locate the copy of Disk First Aid on the CD.*

If that doesn't work, the next thing to try is installing new hard disk drivers. If your hard disk is an Apple-brand disk—it is if it came with your Mac—restart your Mac from a CD-ROM as described previously. Then follow these steps:

1. Launch the Drive Setup application on the Mac OS CD-ROM.
2. Choose Functions | Install Driver.
3. Update your startup disk.
4. Restart your Mac.

3

If your hard disk isn't an Apple-brand drive, follow the manufacturer's instructions for installing new driver software. You'll usually find the appropriate program on a floppy that came with your drive.

If installing new software doesn't work, the next thing to try is zapping the PRAM (parameter RAM). The PRAM is a little bit of memory that stores information like printer selection, sound level, monitor settings, and menu flashing. PRAM is not erased when you restart or shut down your Mac. It sometimes becomes scrambled, though, so you may need to reset it. To zap or reset your PRAM, follow these steps:

1. Hold down COMMAND+OPTION+P+R during startup.

2. Continue holding down all four keys until you hear your Mac reboot itself two times.

3. Release the four keys.

 Note: *If you have a PowerBook, there is a special reset option that is intended as a last resort. See Chapter 11 or your PowerBook owner's manual for details.*

2. What sort of hardware can I use to make my Mac go faster?

Elsewhere in this book, we address upgrades and peripherals for your Mac. Here is a comprehensive list of the parts of your computer that can be replaced or made faster.

● **A new processor** The processor (also called the CPU or Central Processing Unit) is the brain of your Mac, and it ultimately determines how fast your computer runs. Even the most powerful processors have their limits, and if your processor is too slow for your taste—and if your Mac can accommodate a faster one—you might want to upgrade to a faster CPU. Processor upgrades come in the form of third-party accelerator cards and are available from companies including Newer Technologies, PowerLogix, and Sonnet. These cards can contain either a faster version of the processor you currently have—say a 400MHz G3 or 450 MHz G4—or a newer and faster type of processor than the one that now lives in your Mac. In the old days of 680x0 Macs, you sometimes had to pry out your original processor and replace it with a faster chip. These days, processors are mounted on cards that can be easily removed and replaced. Some Power Mac models have a special slot designed to hold an accelerator card.

● **Accelerate your current processor** We mention this only because it's possible, not because we think it's a swell idea. Most processors can actually run a little faster than the speed they're set to at the factory. For example, a processor rated at 400 MHz may actually be able to go as fast as 433 MHz. By adjusting DIP switches on the processor card, you can attempt to boost your processor's speed beyond its current setting. Although this works most of the time, the degree to which you can accelerate a CPU varies from processor to processor, and running a processor at accelerated clock speeds causes the chip to work harder and generate more heat. Excess heat can shorten the life of the processor and strain your power supply, which means you may be buying a new Mac before you would normally care to. Boosting your processor's clock speed is not recommended.

● **A faster hard drive** The faster a hard drive can transfer data to your Mac, the zippier your Mac will seem. With a fast hard drive installed, you'll notice that applications launch more quickly and files open in an instant. In addition, a fast hard drive will play audio and QuickTime movies more smoothly—adding to the impression that your Mac is one hot little number. The *AV* label is usually slapped on high-performance hard drives that spin at 7200 RPM or faster. RAID (redundant array of independent disks) systems—a group of hard drives configured to impersonate a single drive—are faster still.

● **A fast SCSI card** Another way to move data more quickly between your hard drive and Mac—and, therefore, speed up performance—is to buy a SCSI card that supports faster transfer rates. With a SCSI card and hard drive that support Fast and Wide SCSI, data will move like the wind

(see Chapter 5 for more information about fast hard drives and SCSI options).

● **A faster CD-ROM drive** Although a faster CD-ROM drive won't make your games run more quickly, it will certainly send data to your Mac in a sprightlier fashion. That's helpful when you're installing very large applications or copying lots of files from a CD-ROM disc to your hard drive. Of course, if the rest of your components— hard disk, the Mac itself, and so on—are old and tired, a faster CD-ROM drive won't do much for you.

● **A graphics accelerator** If you've purchased a Mac in the past four or five years, your Mac probably includes all the video power you'll need to work with a large-screen monitor. If, however, you need more video performance to develop QuickTime movies, work in Photoshop, or perform other professional graphics tasks, adding a graphics accelerator can give your system the kick in the butt it needs. Accelerated video cards blast pixels to your screen more quickly than the Mac's onboard video can, and the added VRAM (video RAM) they include gives your Mac access to more, and richer, color.

● **More RAM** For general computing, additional RAM won't do a thing to speed up your Mac. But in very specific circumstances, such as when you're using Adobe Photoshop or other memory-hungry graphics and 3-D applications, you'll see significant speed improvements in certain operations when the Mac has been outfitted with lots of RAM. Adding RAM can also speed up your Mac by eliminating the need for virtual memory, which is slower than real RAM.

3. How do I know whether to buy a new Mac or upgrade the old one?

For some people, Macs are like cars or clothes; only the newest, fastest, or prettiest ones on the market will do, whether they need them or not. For others, money and plain old common sense dictate that the old Mac stays in service until Mac OS, software, and the old age of the hardware conspire to make it unusable. It is to the latter group of

people that we're talking, because the rest of you already have an iMac or a Power Mac G4 Series on your desk.

Deciding when to buy a new computer is really a question of math. It boils down to this: can I upgrade my Mac for substantially less than it would cost me to buy a new one? There's a follow-up question: if I buy a new Mac, will I lose the investment I've made in stuff that works with my old one?

We try to give partial answers to these questions in Chapter 15. We suggest ways to get the most out of your old Mac and tell you some of the upgrade options that are available. In Chapter 16, we move beyond retrofitting the old Mac and offer suggestions for making your Mac purchase painless.

Some clues that your Mac may be past its prime are listed here:

- Mac OS updates and new versions of software no longer support your Mac. Every version of Mac OS, and every software tool released, include a list of system requirements. The most important of these is the Mac models or processors supported. In the days when there were only a few Mac models, vendors often listed them in the system requirements; but these days, most requirements are expressed in terms of processor speed. Mac OS 8.5 and later, for example, require a PowerPC processor. Software products sometimes state system requirements in terms of the processor supported, but also by the minimum Mac OS version supported.

- Upgrades are no longer available. Even if old Macs can be physically upgraded, new processors are often no longer available because the market isn't large enough. You can't get an upgrade for most 680x0-based Macs anymore, because there just aren't enough people out there who want them.

- Accessories or expansion options are no longer available. For the same reason you can't upgrade a Mac LC's processor—the price would be too high for too little gain—you can't easily buy expansion products to support very old computers. Fortunately, the most important accessories for a Mac (memory; SCSI peripherals; and,

for PowerBooks, batteries) are easily available. But finding PDS expansion cards for that SE, or even NuBus products for a lot more Macs, is getting harder with every passing year.

For those of you who would rather have a rule of thumb than a whole lot of bullet points, try this one. If your Mac doesn't have a PowerPC processor, it's time to get a new one. All Macs released in the past four or five years have had PowerPC processors, and almost all software is designed to work with the PowerPC. Many applications and current versions of the operating system do not work with 680x0 Macs.

4. I can't seem to get a SCSI device to show up on the desktop. How do I troubleshoot a SCSI chain?

Follow these steps to locate problems with a SCSI chain:

1. Use Drive Setup or another SCSI tool, such as the shareware SCSI Probe, or a diagnostic tool you received with your SCSI drive. If the drive you're interested in isn't on the list, click the Scan or Update or other similarly named button. If the drive appears in the software, but not on the desktop, select it and click Mount.

2. Note the SCSI IDs of all the devices you see in the list. Is anything missing?

3. Check to see that all connectors fit tightly to their drives. External SCSI connectors can easily come loose, especially if you haven't tightened the clips on the connectors.

4. If the problem is with an external drive, or if your Mac has one SCSI bus, check the IDs of any external devices connected to the Mac. With the Mac shut down, change the ID of the problem device to a number that is not in use, and restart. Repeat step 1.

5. On the SCSI chain containing the problem device, check each device for termination. If there are terminators on the first and last devices, but nowhere else, the problem lies elsewhere.

6. Replace the SCSI cables connected to the problem device. You can temporarily disable other devices in the chain and use cables you know to be good to perform your tests.

7. Move the terminator from the end of the chain to somewhere in the middle. This is a long shot, but it has worked for us on occasion when nothing else did.

8. If you can, test the problem device with another Mac. If all is well, return to the original Mac. You may have a hardware problem.

5. I'm getting an error that says the printer can't be found. Now what?

If you get an error message telling you that the Mac can't find the printer, chances are that something's wrong with the network, or with the printer itself. If you don't print very often, it's possible that your Mac's printer setup is outdated. If you've recently installed a new version of Mac OS, everything may be fine: simply set print options for the first time. If you're not using a networked printer, check your cabling, and check that the port selected in the Chooser matches the cable plugged into your Mac.

To determine where the problem lies in network situations, narrow down the list of suspects, as follows:

1. Open the Chooser from the Apple menu and click the appropriate printer icon. If you don't see the icon for your printer (or the LaserWriter 8 icon, for most laser printers), close the Chooser and check the Extensions folder for the printer driver you need. If you don't find it there, look in the Extensions (Disabled) folder. If you are still unable to find the file, reinstall printer software from the Mac OS CD.

2. If the driver is present and selected, but the printer doesn't appear in the right pane of the Chooser, check to see that AppleTalk is active. The Active radio button should be selected. If you have to reactivate AppleTalk,

you may need to restart the computer to complete the process.

3. If AppleTalk is active and no printer appears, open the AppleTalk control panel (the Network control panel under older versions of Mac OS) and check to see that the network setup you're using is correct. If you print over an Ethernet network, the selected item on the AppleTalk menu should say Ethernet, as shown in the following illustration. Otherwise, you'll probably see Printer, Modem, or Serial port, depending on your configuration. In any case, make sure that the AppleTalk choice matches your network.

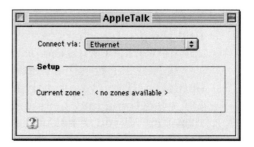

6. How can I conserve battery power when using my PowerBook?

Batteries are both an essential ingredient in PowerBooks and the bane of many a user's existence. Batteries are expensive. Batteries stop working. Batteries even get old and useless. Here, we'll concentrate on how you can keep a battery running as long as possible. Here are some suggestions:

● Put the PowerBook to sleep when you're not using it.

● Use the battery conservation settings in the Energy Saver control panel. Decrease the amount of time your PowerBook remains awake when it's idle. That way, you won't have to put the computer to sleep manually if you don't use it for 5, 10, 20 minutes, or more. You can also adjust the intervals at which your hard disk spins down, and the brightness of the display. If you don't want the computer to sleep after 5 minutes of inactivity, consider

allowing the display to dim, and then allowing the computer to sleep when it has been idle for 10 minutes or so.

● Even while you're working, keep the screen as dim as you can; lighting the screen uses precious battery power.

● Turn off virtual memory, AppleTalk, and File Sharing, all of which require battery power, and two of which you won't need unless you're connected to a network. Though you can use virtual memory with a PowerBook, the fact that it is slower than RAM, and that accessing your hard disk will consume power, make it a good idea to do without it while using your battery.

● Put your System Folder on a diet. Booting a PowerBook with lots of extensions and control panels takes time, and that wastes battery power. And you probably have a large number of extensions installed that you won't need while flying or when checking e-mail from a hotel room.

● Avoid power-hungry applications. The software you use on your desktop Mac may work on your PowerBook, but launching and using it can take a toll on your battery. Try installing a minimal version of the application you use or substituting a simpler tool. For example, you can use a text editor like Bare Bones Software's BBEdit to type that report, and then format it in Microsoft Word when you get back to your desktop Mac.

● Try installing and running that simpler application from a RAM disk.

● Don't use the floppy, Zip, or CD-ROM drive, or remove the disks from it when you have finished. The PowerBook will try to access the drive even when you aren't opening or moving files stored there. If your PowerBook's drive is housed in an expansion bay, consider removing it before you boot up with the battery. Similarly, keeping the PowerBook's ports free of external devices will conserve some battery power.

● Plan your work. If you are moving directly from an area with AC power to one where you will only be able to use the battery, boot the PowerBook while connected to AC, put it to sleep, and wake it up when you're ready to use

the battery. You can even launch applications while plugged in (but don't open documents, which could be lost if your PowerBook crashes), and use them when you're dependent on the battery.

Tip: *You can follow our advice about disabling unneeded extensions and turning off tools you don't need by using the Location Manager. Besides disabling things you don't want, Location Manager lets you turn file sharing and AppleTalk on and off (turning them off saves battery power) and enable a set of Internet and dial-up options.*

 ### 7. Someone just handed me a floppy disk with an important file on it, but I have an iMac or other Mac with no floppy drive. What should I do?

There are four ways to get files onto an iMac without a floppy drive. They are a network, a modem connection, a CD-ROM, or an external removable-media drive.

If your Mac is on a network, or can be added to one, ask the person who gave you the floppy to copy the files onto a Mac or PC, and share the folder containing the files. You can then retrieve them by locating the shared computer in the Chooser and copying files to your Mac's hard drive. For more on file sharing, see Chapter 9.

Files can also be sent to you as e-mail attachments, or stored in an FTP directory, from which you can download them while connected to the Internet. Or you can use software like Global Village's Global Transfer to connect two computers directly via modem and transfer files from one to the other. For more information about e-mail attachments and FTP, see Chapter 13.

If the files you need are actually applications or other software, see if they are available on CD-ROM. If the person providing files to you has a CD-ROM burner, which can create CDs for use with a Mac, he or she can copy the files to a disc. For more information about CD-ROM recorders, see Chapter 5.

Each of the solutions described above requires someone else to help you out by uploading, copying, or burning information so that you can get it into your Mac. But you can take matters into your own hands with an external floppy drive. Newer

Technologies and iMation both offer these drives; the iMation product supports both standard floppies and the SuperDisk format.

8. How can I share my Mac files with PC users over the network?

To use or copy Mac files over a network, a PC must be able to see the Mac's shared folders, or you must transfer and store Mac files on a PC. For this to work, the PC must normally support AppleTalk; you'll need to add AppleTalk support to the PC, since it's not built in, as it is on the Mac. Miramar Systems' PC MACLAN and Cooperative Printing Solutions' COPStalk do this. We like MACLAN's implementation. With MACLAN installed on a Windows 95, 98, or Windows NT PC, shared Mac volumes become visible in the PC's Network Neighborhood window. You'll need to install the software on each PC that needs access to Mac resources.

There are a couple of non-AppleTalk ways to achieve the same goal. If your network uses TCP/IP (it does if you have network access to the Internet), you can install Thursby Systems' DAVE on any Mac whose folders or disks you want to share with PC users. To share folders on the Mac, you must use DAVE's Sharing control panel, shown in Figure 1-1, to share Mac items via TCP/IP. That's in addition to any AppleTalk sharing privileges you set for Mac users. Just like an AppleTalk server, PC users see your shared folders in Network Neighborhood. By the way, Mac users with AppleShare client software 3.7 or later, shown in Figure 1-2, can connect to folders or volumes you've shared via DAVE and TCP/IP, too.

We'll have more to say about configuring and using both PC MACLAN and DAVE in Chapter 10.

9. How can I get faster access to the Internet?

Unless you had your very own leased telephone line in your home or office, modems were the only way to get onto the Internet a few years ago. It's probably not a coincidence that faster ways of getting online became available to consumers at just about the same time the World Wide Web became

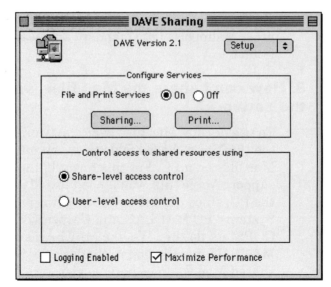

Figure 1-1 Enable sharing in the DAVE Sharing control panel, and then click a folder to share it with PC users, using DAVE

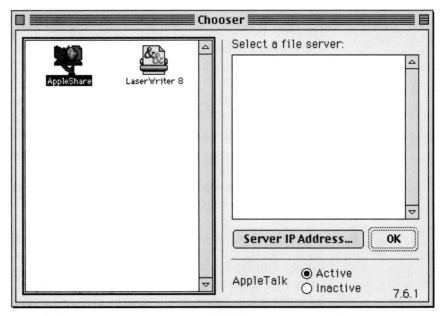

Figure 1-2 You can connect to a TCP/IP-based server if your Mac is connected to a TCP/IP network and if the Chooser shows the Server IP Address button when you click the AppleShare icon

popular, and its content made a speedy connection necessary to get anything out of the Internet. Home users have four choices when it comes to high-speed access:

● *Dual-modem devices* combine the data streams of two modems to double the speed of your connection. You'll need two phone lines, and so will the Internet service provider (ISP) on the other end. Dual-modem equipment is available, but it's unclear whether it will become popular, given the cost-to-speed ratio. ISPs are likely to charge hefty fees for tying up two phone lines for a single connection, and by the time you pay for your own pair of lines, you will be well on your way to affording one of several faster alternatives.

● *ISDN (Integrated Services Digital Network)* is a lot like the phone line you're used to using. In fact, ISDN is a digital version of traditional analog lines and is sold by the telephone company in your community. To use it, you'll need a device that's often called an ISDN modem or router. Actually, it's not a modem at all. ISDN does not convert analog signals to digital, but conducts the whole data transaction in digital mode. You'll also need to buy ISDN service from the phone company. It's like adding a phone line, but a bit more complicated to install and configure. When you get an ISDN line, you're actually getting two 64 Kbps data channels that can be used separately or together, for a top speed of 128 Kbps, a little more than twice the (theoretical) speed of the fastest modem.

● *Cable modems*, which do modulate digital and analog signals, transmit data over cable television lines and usually require that you use the local cable company as your ISP. Unlike an analog or ISDN phone line that serves only your home, cable modems share the data channel (the cable) that connects your computer to the Internet. For that reason, it's hard to say exactly how fast your connection will be. Cable modems can move data at a maximum of 27 Mbps. It is estimated that individuals on a cable data network could see data rates of 1–1.5 Mbps, which is still much faster than modems or ISDN.

● *DSL (Digital Subscriber Line)* is, like ISDN, a phone company service. Actually, it's a group of services, sometimes called xDSL because there are several flavors. The most popular at the moment is ADSL—the A stands for Asynchronous. Like a 56 Kbps modem, ADSL modems move files at different speeds, depending on whether you're uploading or downloading. Maximum ADSL download speed is around 1.5 Mbps, while upload speed is 384 Kbps. ISPs often sell several ADSL packages, charging more for greater maximum speed. Either way, it's much faster than ISDN, and you don't share an ADSL line as you must with a cable modem. DSL service is not universally available, and service at the highest speeds is pretty pricey, but DSL is fast and is gaining in acceptance from ISPs and business users—the surest road to cheap access for all.

If you're seeking Internet access for a business, you have another option—using part or all of a high-speed, dedicated phone connection. With a frame relay connection, you get your Internet access from another company or organization that has purchased a leased line from the phone company. This kind of piggyback arrangement is a great way for a mid-sized business to get fast access without the expense of a leased line. To use frame relay, you'll need a router that supports frame relay, as well as the AppleTalk and TCP/IP protocols you use on your own network.

10. How do I search the Internet with Sherlock?

Your Mac should be configured for Internet access before you use Sherlock's Internet search features. To use Sherlock to search the Internet, follow these steps:

1. Choose Apple Menu | Sherlock (or press COMMAND+F).

2. Click the Internet button (or press COMMAND+H). A list of search engines appears.

3. Choose search sites from the list in the middle portion of the window. Uncheck those you don't want to search.

4. Type your search text in the search field. To search for a phrase or full proper name, place quotes around the words you want to search for.

5. Click the magnifying glass or press ENTER. If your Mac is set up to log onto the Internet automatically, Sherlock connects to the Internet, if you aren't already online.

6. When Sherlock presents the results of its search, click an item to see a summary (in the lower pane of the Sherlock window, above the banner). Figure 1-3 shows the results of our search for Austin singer/songwriter, Sarah Elizabeth Campbell.

7. Double-click an item to open the Web page associated with the item. If it's not already open, your default Web browser will be launched.

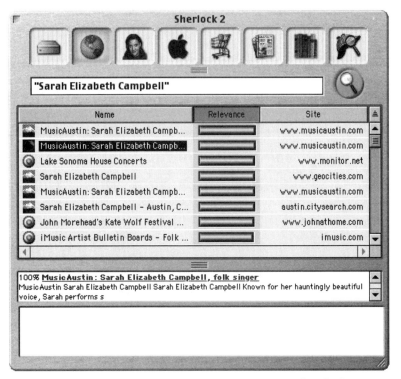

Figure 1-3 Single-click an item to see a summary of a site's contents; double-click to go there

Chapter 2

Finder and Desktop Basics

Answer Topics!

Finder and Desktop Basics @ a Glance

Opening Files and Folders shows you several different ways to open files and folders.

Getting Information About Files and Folders explains the Mac OS tools available for learning more about your files and folders.

Saving and Storing Your Work includes tips on organizing your files and folders.

Copying and Moving Files explains how to manage files.

Organizing Your Desktop helps you figure out what should go on your desktop.

Customizing Your Mac's Look and Feel describes tools you can use to make the Mac desktop look just the way you want it to.

OPENING FILES AND FOLDERS

 Are there different ways to open a file or folder?

You can open a file or folder in four different ways using the Finder. (There's also a fifth way that applies to folders.) They are listed here:

- Double-click the icon to launch the application that created it (in the case of a file) or to reveal the contents in a new window (folder).

- Click the icon once to select it, and then choose Open from the File menu.

- Click a file or application icon once to select it. Hold down the CONTROL key to reveal a contextual menu. Choose Open.

- With the icon selected, press COMMAND+O.

If your icon is a folder, you can view the contents by clicking the triangle to the left of the folder icon once. To see the triangle, you'll need to view the current window as a list. Do that by choosing List from the View menu. When you click it, the triangle points downward, and the contents appear in a list below. Unlike other folder-opening methods that display the folder's contents in their own window, this method lets you look inside the folder without opening a new window. Figure 2-1 shows a window with open folders.

 Why does a particular program open when you double-click a document?

Every file has two identifiers—type and creator—that help the Finder locate an application that can open the file. Each identifier is a three or four-character code. A file's *type* tells the Finder whether the file is an application (with type APPL), a control panel (CDEV), or a document (TEXT, ttro, ttxt, W6BN, and many others). If the file is a document, the type will determine whether the file should appear in an application's Open dialog box.

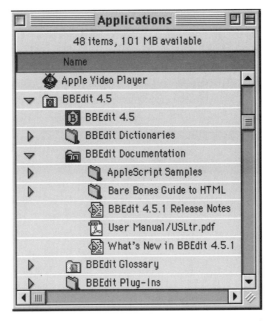

Figure 2-1 Click the triangle next to a folder's icon to view its contents

System files, such as extensions or fonts, behave differently than document files when you double-click them. Extensions, for example, don't open, and font files, when clicked, open a window that displays all of the available font sizes and a sample of how the font will look on screen or in print.

The file's *creator* code tells you what application created the file. Documents have the same creator as the application that created them. When you double-click a file, the Finder looks for the application that created it. If that program isn't there, the Finder may display an error, display the File Exchange "Choose a Program to Open This Document" dialog box, or it may just choose another application to open the file (if you've opened this type of file before using File Exchange).

If you're using Mac OS 8.1 or earlier, this dialog box is known as the Mac Easy Open "Choose a Program to Open This Document" dialog box. The functions that *were* called Mac OS Easy Open in OS 8.1 and earlier are part of File Exchange in more recent versions of Mac OS.

The Finder and the Desktop

Think of the Finder as the master control for your Mac. The Finder controls the way menus, windows, files, and folders appear on screen. It also includes the tools you use to copy, rename, and move files, and to launch or quit applications.

The Finder works just like any other application, with a few exceptions. Like other programs, the Finder uses its own portion of memory, and there's a Finder item on the menu at the upper-right corner of the screen. (That menu is usually referred to as the Application menu.) This means that you can easily switch from an open application to the Finder and back again. Unlike other programs, the Finder is always open; you can't quit the Finder, because if you did, there wouldn't be any way of interacting with your Mac. Of course, to every rule there are occasional exceptions—when something goes terribly wrong, for example, or if you install a shareware substitute. However, the Finder is, for most folks, a constant companion.

Many people use the terms "desktop" and "Finder" interchangeably. It's really not important that you be able to recite precise definitions, since the Finder and desktop work together, but one way of understanding the difference is to think of the desktop as the visual part of the Finder, the part that displays the Mac's background screen and the icons on it. The desktop also includes a database of all the files, folders, and icons on the disk or disks available. You'll learn later that good desktop health is important to smooth Mac operation, and that decorating the desktop with color and pictures can make your Mac screen more fun to look at.

 What does "The document 'x' could not be opened because the application that created it could not be found" mean?

When you double-click a document, the Finder looks for the program that created it. If you get the "application could not be found" error, it means (like it says) that the program isn't on any disk that's currently mounted. It also means that you don't have File Exchange installed or that it's turned off. If

you have File Exchange installed, you'll find it in the Control Panels submenu of the Apple menu.

File Exchange locates applications that may be able to open a document even if the program that created the file isn't available, in which case File Exchange will present you with a list of available programs that may be able to open your file. Be aware, though, that sometimes the list may contain programs that won't actually open the file. In that case, use trial and error in the File Exchange dialog box to find an application that works.

If you want to change File Exchange settings, feel free, but the default settings are generally just what you want.

Follow these steps to use File Exchange:

1. Click the File Translation tab in the File Exchange control panel.

2. Check the Translate Documents Automatically check box.

   You can change the File Translation settings, but the default settings are generally just what you want.

What should I do if File Exchange can't find an application that will open my file?

Sometimes, either because the file in question has problems or because the desktop's internal database is corrupted, a file won't open, even when its application is available. In this case, the thing to do is to open the file from within an application.

To open a file within an application:

1. Launch the application you want to use.

2. Choose Open from the File menu (you can also press COMMAND+O; most applications support that keyboard shortcut).

3. Use the Open dialog box to navigate to the file you want to open.

4. When you find the file, click Open.

If you don't see the file, it may be because the application doesn't recognize the file as one it can open. If the application you're using includes a list of file types in its Open dialog box

(Adobe Photoshop, Microsoft Word, and others do), choose a different one. The dialog box should now display more files. If you can choose All Available, you'll see all of the files in the folder. Open your file.

In some cases, this approach still won't work. At that point, it's time to choose another application, or seek the answer in Chapter 14, where we tackle troubleshooting issues.

GETTING INFORMATION ABOUT FILES AND FOLDERS

How can I find out when a file was created or changed last?

Click the file's icon once. Choose Get Info from the File menu (or press COMMAND+I). The Info window appears, as shown in Figure 2-2. The actual window title is the same as the file,

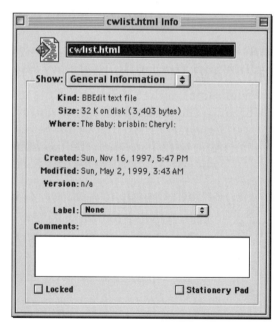

Figure 2-2   The Info window for a word processing document

with "Info" added at the end. Here you'll see the file's icon, name, size, and location, along with the name of the application that created it. Below that are the creation and modification dates. You can even write comments in the Comments field at the bottom of the Info window.

You can get info about any file, including applications and system files. If you choose an application, you'll see the version number and how much memory the application uses.

In older versions of Mac OS, the Get Info window didn't tell you much more than the creation and modification dates of the file. The current version is much improved. For one thing, you can rename a file or folder just by typing a new name in the Name field. If a folder or volume is shared, the Sharing pop-up menu lets you look at a folder or volume's owner and privileges. Also, you can now change the label of an item from within the Info window.

How can I find out which files belong to which applications?

The Info window tells you which application created the file and shows the application's icon. The file in Figure 2-2, for example, was created with our favorite text editor, BBEdit. You can usually use the document's icon to determine the application that created it. That's true in the Info window and on the desktop.

How do I find a file I've misplaced?

Choose Sherlock or Sherlock 2 from the Apple menu or, if you're in the Finder, type COMMAND+F. The Sherlock 2 window will open. Type all or part of the file's name in the blank field provided. If you have multiple disks (hard disks, floppies, or removable media), click the check box next to the name of each one you want to include in the search. Click the magnifying glass button. The results are displayed in a new window. To open one of the files listed, double-click it, or select it and press COMMAND+O. If you click the file once, its

folder path appears in the lower pane of the window. You can also copy or move files by dragging them from the file list, just as you can from any other Finder window.

How can I find a file I created yesterday in Microsoft Word, whose name I've forgotten?

You can search for files and folders by one or more criteria, using Sherlock 2.

To find a file by multiple criteria:

1. Open Sherlock 2 as described in the previous answer.
2. Make sure that the Files button is active. It's the one at the upper-left corner of the window, with a disk drive icon on it.
3. Click the Edit button.
4. In the window (More Options) that appears, click the Date Created check box. When you change search criteria, the options for that search light up.
5. To locate a single date (yesterday's), leave Is selected. To choose yesterday's date, click the day portion of the date that appears, and use the arrows to locate yesterday's date.
6. To narrow your search, click the Creator check box.
7. Type MSWD in the blank.
8. Click OK to close the window.
9. Click the Magnifying Glass button. Sherlock searches for all Microsoft Word files created on the date specified (see Figure 2-3).

Sherlock 2 does a lot more than locate your lost résumé. You can index the contents of your hard drive and have Sherlock search the contents of files (not just filenames and dates) for what you want. With Sherlock's collection of Internet search tools, you can find what you're looking for on the Web just by typing in keywords and choosing sites to search from one of several categories in the Sherlock window. Figure 2-4 shows Sherlock's main window with Internet search options visible.

Figure 2-3 Sherlock 2 will find all Word files that were created on the date specified

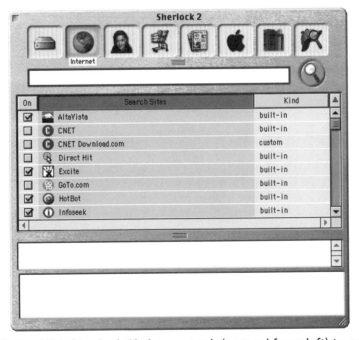

Figure 2-4 Click Sherlock 2's Internet tab (second from left) to see a list of search engines

 How do I search the Internet with Sherlock?

Your Mac should be configured for Internet access before you use Sherlock's Internet search features. To use Sherlock to search the Internet, follow these steps:

1. Choose Apple Menu | Sherlock (or press COMMAND+F).
2. Click the Internet button (or press COMMAND+H). A list of search engines appears.
3. Choose search sites from the list in the middle portion of the window. Uncheck those you don't want to search.
4. Type your search text in the search field. To search for a phrase or full proper name, place quotes around the words you want to search for.
5. Click the magnifying glass, or press ENTER. If your Mac is set up to log onto the Internet automatically, Sherlock connects to the Internet, if you aren't already online.
6. When Sherlock presents the results of its search, click an item to see a summary (in the lower pane of the Sherlock window, above the banner). Figure 2-5 shows the results

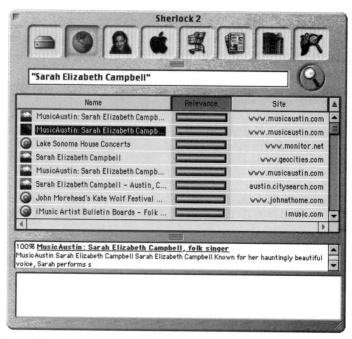

Figure 2-5   Single-click an item to see a summary of a site's contents; double-click to go there

of our search for Austin singer/songwriter, Sarah Elizabeth Campbell.

7. Double-click an item to open the Web page associated with the item. If it's not already open, your default Web browser will be launched.

How do I use Sherlock's indexing feature?

Indexing makes it much easier to search the contents of a local hard drive or removable media cartridge. Sherlock builds an index containing most or all of the keywords you're likely to search for, and adds pointers to the files that contain them. When you search, it's a simple matter for Sherlock to refer to the index and deliver the file you need.

The catch is that your disk must be indexed ahead of time—a very time-consuming process. Fortunately, you can schedule indexing to take place in the middle of the night, so that the process doesn't slow down your work. Once you have created an index, you can tell Sherlock to update the index at intervals you choose.

To index a local disk drive, follow these steps:

1. In Sherlock 2, choose Find | Index Volumes.

2. Choose a volume or volumes from the list that appears, by clicking the check box.

3. Click the Schedule button to set up your first indexing session.

4. Choose a time and day of the week, and click OK.

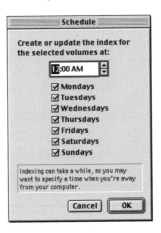

5. Choose Edit | Preferences to view more indexing options that control what is indexed, and how much of your Mac's processing power Sherlock will use to create and update the index.

Once you have an index, feel free to perform searches that use the "Contents Include" option in the More Search Options window. You can do such a search without indexing, but it will be pitifully slow.

? How can I sort files within a folder so that the ones I want come to the top of the window?

With your folder's window open and selected on the desktop, choose Arrange from the View menu, and pick a sorting option from the submenu. You can sort by name, modification date, size, kind, and so on.

If you're viewing the folder as a list (choose As List from the View menu), you can sort the folder (for example, by Name, Date Modified, Size, and so on) by clicking the appropriate label at the top of the window. To see all of the options, expand the window to the right.

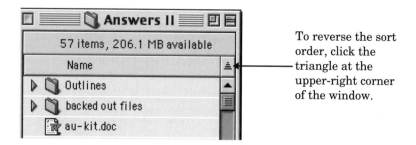

To reverse the sort order, click the triangle at the upper-right corner of the window.

SAVING AND STORING YOUR WORK

When I'm working within an application, I sometimes want to rename a file or save it to a different folder. Can I do this without returning to the Finder?

Most applications include a Save As command on the File menu. When you're ready to rename or copy your file, do this:

1. If you have changed the file and want to update the existing copy, save the file as you normally would (with the Save command, or by pressing COMMAND+S).

2. Choose Save As from the File menu.

   - To rename the file, replace the current name by typing a new name in the dialog box.

   - To copy the file elsewhere, use the Save dialog box to navigate to the folder where you want to save the file.

3. Once you have specified the name and location for the file, click Save.

Where should I save my files?

The Macintosh doesn't really care where you save your documents. You can save them in the same folder as the application that created them, file everything in a Documents folder, or create folders for each project you work on, or for each member of the family.

The main questions to consider when choosing places for your files are as follows:

- *Where will you be most likely to find the file when you need it?* If you create folders for documents, projects, or people, your chances of finding what you're looking for (without resorting to Sherlock) are much greater. Make this choice based on how you like to work.

● *Do you need to work on several files at once?* If you open two or three files at the same time, it probably makes sense to store them together, especially if they were created by the same application. That way, you can open the files without having to dig through lots of windows or navigate to several folders from the Open dialog box.

● *Do you share your Mac?* If the whole family creates files on the same computer, it's a good idea to give each person a folder of his or her own. Besides the organizational benefits this provides, it also makes it possible for Mom and Dad (or even Big Sister) to password-protect files and folders so that they aren't accessible to the younger members of the family.

● *What's the easiest way to back up your data?* If your idea of a backup is copying files to a floppy disk or Zip cartridge, storing all of the documents you want to protect in a central location makes copying that folder to the backup disk a piece of cake. And the easier it is to back up your data, the more likely you are to do it.

How do I rename a file or folder?

In the Finder, click the *name* of a file or folder. Don't click its *icon* or this trick won't work. The item's name is now surrounded by a border, as shown here:

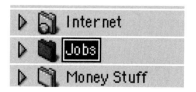

Typing a new name will overwrite the old one. When you've finished typing the name, press the ENTER or RETURN key, or just click the desktop. Your file or folder has a new name. If you click the icon instead of the name, just press the ENTER key once to activate the name field.

Can I rename applications, or the System Folder?

You can rename application files, though you should exercise caution when you do. Changing Microsoft Word to Word so that the label takes up less room in a window full of icons is okay, but don't get carried away, especially if you share your computer with others.

Do not rename the System Folder, or items within it. The Mac expects the System Folder to have that name, and that goes for most of the files inside.

Why can't I rename certain items?

If you have File Sharing turned on, and you are sharing a folder that contains the items you want to change, the steps listed above will not work. You also won't be able to change the name of an item that lives on a shared disk that is mounted on your desktop. To change the name of a shared item on your hard disk, stop File Sharing, change the name, then start File Sharing again. To turn off File Sharing, click the File Sharing control strip item and choose "Stop Share File" from the menu, or choose the File Sharing control panel and click Stop.

You also won't be able to rename items stored on a locked disk.

COPYING AND MOVING FILES

How do I copy multiple files?

To copy several files at once, click the first file you want to copy and hold down the SHIFT key as you click a second file, a third, and so on, until you've selected all of the files you want to copy. Then release the mouse button. Or, if the files are all in a group, you can click and drag the selection rectangle around all the files you want to copy and then release the mouse button.

Whichever method you use, finish the copy by clicking any of the selected items, and dragging the group to your destination.

 ## How do I copy an item to a new location on the same disk?

If you want two copies of an item on the same disk, hold down the OPTION key when you drag the file or folder from the old location to the new.

If you want to make a duplicate copy in the same folder, choose File | Duplicate, or use the keyboard shortcut COMMAND+D.

 ## How do I move a file or folder?

Moving a file or folder is just like copying it except that you don't leave the original behind. When you drag an item to another folder on the same hard disk, the file is moved, not copied. To move a file or folder to a new disk, make the copy, and then throw the original in the Trash.

There's another way to use the Finder to copy and move folders: title bar icons. Finder windows include folder or disk icons to the left of the item's title. You can copy or move a folder (using the procedures we've already described) by dragging the title icon to the desired destination.

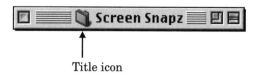

Title icon

✚ *Tip:* *You can also use contextual menus with title icons.*
CONTROL+click the icon to see the menu.

 ## Is there a way to disable the message box that asks if I'm sure I want to empty the trash? I know what I'm doing.

Hold down the OPTION key as you choose Empty Trash. The trash can empties with no dialog box or warning.

To turn the warning off permanently, select the Trash icon and then the Get Info command (select File | Get Info or

press COMMAND+I), and uncheck the Warn Before Emptying check box.

ORGANIZING YOUR DESKTOP

 ## How do I store icons right on my desktop?

The short answer? Just drag any icon you like onto the desktop. When you do, the file or folder is moved from its current location. If you want to put the file back where it came from later, select it and then choose File | Put Away, or press COMMAND+Y.

 ## What are aliases and how do I use them?

An alias is a pointer to a file or folder. Double-clicking an alias to open it achieves the same thing as double-clicking the original file or folder; the Finder locates the original using the path specified by the alias. Alias files are much smaller than their parent item (unless they point to tiny originals).

You can use aliases in many ways—to get at frequently used items from the desktop without moving the originals, to speed up the process of logging onto file servers, to make the system think a required file is stored somewhere it isn't, to have an item in your Apple menu, and so on.

 ## How do I create an alias?

Click the file, folder, or application you want to create an alias for. Choose Make Alias from the File menu, or press COMMAND+M. An alias appears near the original item. It has the same name as the original with "alias" at the end, and its label is italicized. Move the alias to the desktop, or to any other location on your hard disk. When you double-click the alias, the original file, folder, or application opens.

The shortcut for creating aliases is to hold down the COMMAND and OPTION keys, click the item you want to make the alias of, and drag to another location. An alias will be automatically created in the new location.

 How do I add an alias to the Apple menu?

You can quickly locate frequently used items by placing aliases on the Apple menu. To do this:

1. Create an alias for a file or application.
2. Open the System Folder.
3. Drag the alias to the Apple Menu Items folder icon, to move it there.
4. Click the Apple menu. Your alias will appear on the menu.

You can store aliases to files, Internet bookmarks, or folders in the Favorites folder, on the Apple menu. You can drag an alias to the Favorites folder, or better yet, use a contextual menu to create one there. CONTROL+click the item you want to add to Favorites. From the contextual menu that appears, choose Add to Favorites. The original remains right where it was, and an alias appears in the Favorites folder on the Apple menu.

 Tip: *When you create an alias, its name consists of the original filename followed by "alias." You can change the alias's name to anything you like without disturbing the alias's relationship to the original.*

The reverse is also true, if you're using Mac OS 8.1 or later. You can move or rename the original file or folder without breaking the alias's connection to it. If you're using an older version of Mac OS, however, the alias will stop working if you alter the original item.

 What items should go on my desktop?

Besides icons for your hard disk and CD-ROM drive (when the drive has a CD in it), most people will want to have a Desktop Printer icon. You can print a document by dragging it onto the printer icon. You'll learn more about this in Chapter 6.

You may also want to keep a few other aliases on the desktop—perhaps your word processing application, your Internet browser, and other items that you use every day. Be careful not to overdo it; some folks believe that a too-crowded desktop slows down the Mac. If you like to leave items on the desktop, work for a while without them, and judge the speed hit for yourself.

What can I remove from my desktop?

The Mac OS installer puts a number of items on your desktop. Most of them can be moved or thrown away. For example, you don't need the Mac OS Setup Assistant once you have your system up and running. The Browse the Internet and Mail icons are aliases to your Web browser and your e-mail software, respectively. Keep 'em or ditch 'em; it's up to you. If you use multiple printers, you may have several desktop printer icons. Unless you use the different printers often, you can throw away the excess icons and pick a different printer from the Chooser or control strip when you need it. You may also choose to remove the Sherlock 2 icon (just press COMMAND+F to open it in the Finder). Finally, the QuickTime Player icon can go, unless you really need immediate access to the player. You may also find an icon labeled QuickTime Pro on your desktop. That's an Apple sales pitch for the commercial version of QuickTime. It can go too—don't worry, you'll have a chance to purchase each and every time you open the free player. To remove an item from your desktop, just drag it to the Trash.

How do I keep my desktop neat and tidy?

Two things mess up a desktop: icons and windows. We've just covered the icon issue, now let's look at windows. By default, Mac windows are horizontal rectangles that display icons with lots of space between them. This arrangement works well if you only have a couple of windows open and a few icons in each window, but things get more complicated if you need to work with files in several locations, or if you have lots of files.

First, you can resize windows with the resizing box at the lower-right corner of any window. Click in the box and drag horizontally and/or vertically to resize.

You can expand the whole window to its largest possible size by clicking the zoom box, which is the second one from the right in the title bar of most windows. The zoom box is shown here:

The Zoom box

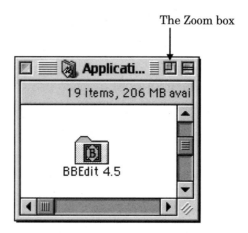

You can get windows out of the way without changing their size (some people like their windows just so) by collapsing them. By clicking the collapse box or double-clicking the title bar, you can leave only the title bar visible, as shown here:

The Collapse box

Click the collapse box again and the window reappears.

This function was called Windowshade in Mac OS 8.0 and earlier. Though the Windowshade name is gone in more recent versions of the Mac OS, the feature is very much alive. Select Apple Menu | Control Panels | Appearance and click

the Options button. Check the Double-click Title Bar to Collapse check box to activate the shade. Uncheck it to disable it.

 ## How can I organize my desktop with the application switcher?

With the application switcher, you can "tear off" the application menu that appears in the upper-right corner of your screen. The result, shown here, is a Finder window with a list of open applications:

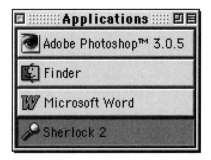

Just click an icon to move to that application. Click the zoom box (second button from right) to change the display from names to icons.

To display the application switcher, click the application menu in the upper-right corner of your screen, and drag all the way down the menu, past the end. As you drag, the menu will "tear off." When you let go, the switcher window will appear. Close it just as you would any other window.

There are a number of ways to customize the look of the application switcher. Many of these are tucked away in the Mac OS Help system. To dig deeper into the application switcher, choose Mac OS Help from the Finder's Help menu, and search for the words *application switcher*. You'll learn how to make the switcher display horizontally, list applications in the order you opened them, and lots more.

 Tip: *You can drag documents over application switcher icons to open them.*

Bob Speaks: Pop-up Windows

You may have noticed that we didn't mention pop-up windows as a way of keeping your desktop tidy. That's because neither Shelly nor I use them. But, in the interest of completeness, our editor asked me to include them.

Pop-up windows are an alternative to regular windows. When closed, they appear as a tab at the bottom of your screen. They pop open when you click their tab or drag an item onto their tab.

To create a pop-up window, make any window active and then choose View | As Pop-up Window. An alternative way to create pop-up windows is to click a window's title bar and drag it to the very bottom of your screen, where it will turn into a tab.

To move a pop-up window, click its tab and drag it to a new location along the bottom of your screen.

Finally, you can change a pop-up window back into a regular window by dragging its tab upward, away from the bottom of the screen and toward the menu bar.

 On my PC at work, I can switch among open applications with a keystroke. Is there any way to do this on the Mac?

Well, if you haven't upgraded to Mac OS 8.5 or later, do it. You can now move between open applications on your Mac by pressing COMMAND+TAB. This shortcut cycles through your open applications. SHIFT+COMMAND+TAB cycles backward through your open programs.

CUSTOMIZING YOUR MAC'S LOOK AND FEEL

 How do I change the Finder's appearance?

Mac OS includes several tools for customizing the look of the Finder. The Appearance control panel lets you set a color scheme for Finder windows. You can also choose a highlight color, and even change the system font—the typeface Mac OS uses in all of its menus and windows.

The desktop, too, can become more colorful. You can change the Mac OS desktop pattern that appears behind your icons and windows, or replace the pattern with a picture. The Mac OS CD-ROM contains a selection of pictures you can copy and use on the desktop.

Once you've selected a group of settings you like, you can gather them into what Apple calls a theme. A Mac OS theme is a group of Finder appearance (and sound) preferences that you can save as a single unit. You can save and switch themes in the Appearance control panel. Here are some of the Finder features you can include in a theme:

- **Appearance** The look of windows, icons, and buttons
- **Color** Colors for menus and highlighted text
- **Fonts** System fonts used in menus, windows, and dialog boxes
- **Desktop pattern** An image or color pattern displayed on the desktop
- **Sounds** Noises associated with actions such as pulling down menus or closing windows

A selection of themes is included with Mac OS, and you can create your own from scratch, or vary the canned ones. Figure 2-6 shows the default appearance settings for one of the included themes.

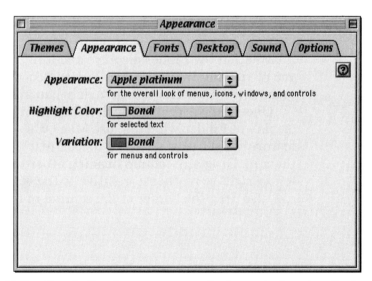

Figure 2-6 Here's the Appearance control panel, showing the look of the Bubbles theme

 ## Can I create my own patterns and pictures?

To create your own desktop picture, you'll need a PICT or JPEG file. You can create PICT or JPEG files with most Mac graphics programs, and PICT clip art is available from numerous locations, including the Internet and America Online.

Open the Appearance control panel and click the Desktop tab. Click Place Picture, and locate the PICT or JPEG file you want to use as your desktop background. With the picture visible in the Desktop Pictures window, you can choose from the positioning options and click Set Desktop to set the file as your desktop picture. To change the picture, just repeat the process and choose a new file.

 ## How do the Finder's Preferences and View Options affect the look of the screen?

You use the Finder's Preferences to control the spacing of icons within windows, and to select a few other settings related to the way icons relate to their windows. Change these options in the Finder by selecting Edit | Preferences. The View Options control the size of icons and tell the Finder whether to require that the icons snap to an invisible grid when dragged, or not. These options can be changed by selecting View | View Options. The options vary slightly, depending upon whether you're viewing by icon, list, or button.

Finder Preferences is also where you choose what information the Finder displays about files and folders when you're viewing them as a list. You can choose whether or not to display a file's creation date, label, or size, for example.

Once you've decided which informational columns to display in Finder windows, use Mac OS's nifty customization features to get your windows to look just the way you want them to. Drag any column heading other than Name to the left or right to reorder it, relative to the other columns. You can also drag the border of the column to resize it.

Can I change the highlight color of selected text?

When you select text, the Finder highlights it with a color you select in the Appearance control panel (under the Appearance tab). You can change it by picking a new color from the pop-up menu. While you're at it, you can change the color of menus and controls with the Variation pop-up menu.

Can I have my favorite program launch automatically when I turn on my Mac?

To have a program (or programs) launch automatically when you start your Mac, create an alias for each item you want to open at startup, and put them in the Startup Items folder, located inside the System Folder. When you boot your Mac, the programs (or documents, if you like) will open after the Finder and desktop have completed their startup process.

Keep in mind that launching items at startup means that it will take longer to boot your Mac.

How can I display the date and time on my Mac screen?

You can use the Date & Time control panel to display the date and/or time on the menu bar. Open the control panel and click the On button under the Menubar Clock label. You can also use the control panel to choose the font and size of your menu bar display, as well as numerous other menu clock options, such as chiming on the quarter hour or hour. Click the Clock Options button to adjust these.

My Mac's clock seems to lose/gain time. Is there any way to keep the clock accurate?

Computer clocks, like most timepieces, tend to lose time—over time. If you're connected to the Internet, though, you can keep your Mac's clock up to date.

The Date & Time control panel includes an option that allows you to periodically connect to one of several network

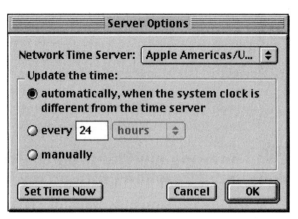

Figure 2-7 Schedule regular connections to a time server to keep your Mac up to date

time servers around the world. A time server is an extremely accurate clock, that's linked to the Internet. When you log in to the time server, its clock passes the correct time to your Mac.

To keep your clock ticking right, click the Use Network Time Server check box in the Date & Time control panel. Then click Server Options (Figure 2-7) to schedule clock updates.

If you are not connected to the Internet when it's time for a scheduled update, your Mac will connect for you. If unscheduled connections are a problem for you, don't select one of the automatic update options. You can manually update the time by clicking the Set Time Now button.

Can I change the Welcome to Mac OS screen that appears when I start up my Mac?

You can use a custom startup screen by naming a PICT resource file StartupScreen and copying it into the System Folder. When you restart, the picture will display, instead of the Welcome to Mac OS screen.

To prepare a PICT file for use as a startup screen, you'll need to save it as a PICT resource, using a graphics program like Adobe Photoshop or Thorsten Lemke's GraphicConverter. The latter is shareware. You'll find it on the Internet or on America Online.

Tip: *If startup screens you create or convert look funny, try lowering the resolution of your Mac screen before converting the image in Photoshop. To do this, open the Monitors & Sound control panel, and choose 640 × 480, for example. Now, convert your image to a PICT resource as previously described.*

What tools does Mac OS include for disabled users?

There are several Mac OS features designed to assist people with visual or motor-skills disabilities. Visually impaired users can magnify the Mac screen with CloseView, a control panel that is included, but not installed, with Mac OS.

Once you have installed CloseView, look for it in the Control Panels folder after you reboot. You can magnify the screen from 2 to 16 times normal size, and you can reverse the screen's video, changing from black text on white background, to white text on a black background.

Tip: *Another way to magnify the screen is to lower your screen's resolution. To do this, open the Monitors & Sound control panel, and choose a lower resolution. For example, if your screen is currently set to 800 × 600 pixels, change to 640 × 480. Unfortunately, not all monitors and Macs support resolution switching. Your Monitors & Sound control panel won't allow you to change it if yours happens to be one of them.*

Easy Access is useful for those who have difficulty manipulating the mouse. Instead, you use keyboard commands to perform mouse functions.

To install CloseView or Easy Access, follow these steps:

1. Run the Mac OS Installer from the Mac OS CD.

2. Proceed through the installer's introductory screens. When you are asked whether you want to reinstall or add/remove software, click Add/Remove.

3. In the Custom Installation and Removal window, click the Mac OS 9 check box. The customization menu will light up.

4. Choose Custom Installation from the menu.

Select Mac OS 9 features to install.

Selection: | Recommended Installation | ◆ |

Feature	Size	
☑ Core System Software	18,557K	ⓘ
▷ ⊟ Assistance	5,365K	ⓘ
▷ ☑ Compatibility	948K	ⓘ
▷ ☐ Mobility	3,899K	ⓘ
▷ ⊟ Multimedia	15,407K	ⓘ
▷ ⊟ Network & Connectivity	17,640K	ⓘ
▷ ☐ Printing	9,964K	ⓘ
▽ ⊟ Universal Access	45K	ⓘ
☑ Close View	33K	ⓘ
☐ Easy Access	12K	ⓘ

Selected size: --   [Cancel] [**OK**]

Figure 2-8 You must use the installer to add Easy Access and CloseView to Mac OS

5. From the list of system components, click the triangle next to Universal Access, as shown in Figure 2-8.

6. Choose CloseView and/or Easy Access and click OK. Installation will proceed. When you restart, the control panel(s) will be available.

Chapter 3

Inside the System Folder

Answer Topics!

Inside the System Folder @ a Glance

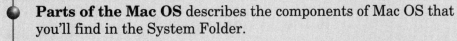

- **Parts of the Mac OS** describes the components of Mac OS that you'll find in the System Folder.

- **Fonts** explains fonts and font management in Mac OS.

- **Sound and Speech** shows you how to use sound and speech to pump up the volume.

PARTS OF THE MAC OS

 ## What is the System Folder?

All computers depend upon a group of special files, collectively called the operating system. These files start the computer up and keep it running. In a Mac, the operating system is Mac OS, and the files that keep things humming along reside in the System Folder. In the early days of the Mac, the System Folder contained little more than a file called System, the Finder, and a few files to support printing, networking, and so on. Today, most System Folders are many megabytes in size, and contain, in addition to the bare essentials, a whole slew of preferences, fonts, tools, libraries, and other files that your Mac itself and the applications you use need to run properly.

The first rule of thumb for the System Folder is be careful! There are lots of files in there, and some of them aren't needed to run your particular Mac. But, unless you know what you're doing, moving things around, deleting them, or renaming them is a bad idea. You'll learn more about maintaining and trimming your System Folder in this chapter, so take some time to read it before you change things.

Be careful with the folder itself, too. Don't rename it or move it around on your hard drive. It should live at the drive's *root level*. The root level is the window that appears when you double-click your hard drive's icon to open it.

 ## What is a control panel?

You'll find the Control Panels folder in the System Folder. A control panel is a tool that is loaded at startup. You can get to control panels from the Apple menu, or by opening the Control Panels folder and double-clicking the control panel icons. Some control panels are stand-alone applications, while others act as "front-ends" to other system tools. Either way, most control panels allow you to configure a very specific system-related function. Control panels that are part of Mac

OS let you adjust the behavior of your keyboard, mouse, memory, screen, and much more.

To install a new control panel, simply drag and drop it on the System Folder. In most cases, you'll have to restart the Mac to use the control panel.

What is an extension?

Like control panels, extensions are loaded at startup, and have their own folders within the System Folder. Unlike control panels, extensions don't have a user interface; you don't open or configure them, but they're running all the time. Some extensions use a control panel as an interface, while lots of them simply do their work without an interface. Extensions make it possible to print, use certain peripherals, and control other system tasks.

You'll find several types of files in the Extensions folder: most are system extensions, others are Chooser extensions (they used to be called CDEVs). There are also plenty of files in the Extensions folder that support system extensions. For example, Apple Guide is a system extension, but the many guide documents in the Extensions folder contain context-sensitive help for applications and the system. Chooser extensions include AppleShare and LaserWriter, among others. If you have a fax modem, there's probably a Chooser extension to go with it.

Applications sometimes come with extensions, too, especially if they need to interact with Mac OS.

Do I need all of the control panels and extensions in my System Folder?

No. Most extensions and especially control panels have a specific function, and if you don't use the function, you can do without the file. Removing unnecessary extensions is a great way to save RAM and (a little bit of) disk space. Control panels can be easily removed, but the benefits of doing so aren't nearly so great, since they don't use very much memory.

Be very careful when removing extensions; while most are named logically—Color Picker, Speech Manager, and so on—and can therefore be zapped if you don't use these tools, others are essential to the system and have names that don't roll trippingly off the tongue. Woe to the unsuspecting CD-ROM user who deletes High Sierra File Access, for example. You'll need this extension to mount certain CD-ROMs. If you're on a network (that includes a single Mac with an AppleTalk printer), you'll want to leave all of the Open Transport extensions (OpenTptAppleTalkLib, Open Transport Library, and so on) right where they are, or risk losing your ability to connect with the network.

How do I manage extensions and control panels?

You could just drag extensions and control panels out of the System Folder, into the Trash, but that's not the easy way to do it. Besides, there's more to managing system files than adding and removing them.

Extensions Manager is a control panel (it works with an extension called EM Extension) that lets you create and keep track of sets of extensions, control panels, startup items, and shutdown items.

Open Extensions Manager control panel to see what's currently installed in your system. You can sort the items by name, location, memory use, or whether the item is installed and active. The Package heading tells you where the file comes from (Mac OS or a third party), making it easier to figure out where each item actually comes from. To find out what the extension or control panel does, click it in Extensions Manager and then click the Show Item Information triangle at the bottom of the window, which changes to Hide Item Information when the information is displayed, as shown in Figure 3-1.

Extensions Manager's pop-up menu lets you save sets of system files. For example, if you use a PowerBook and want to keep the system footprint low when using battery power, create an Extensions Manager set that includes a minimal group of tools. You don't, for example, need networking

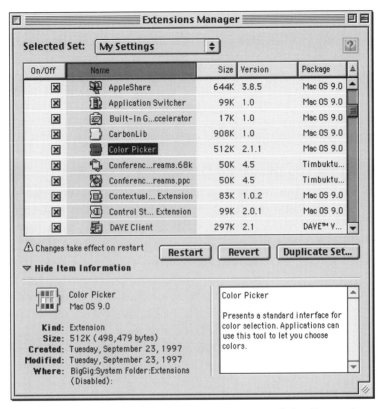

Figure 3-1   The information pane at the bottom of the Extensions
Manager window tells you what the file does, where it
comes from, and more

software like AppleShare, or the LaserWriter driver if you
are using the PowerBook on an airplane. When you get back
home, open up Extensions Manager and choose a set that
includes the networking tools you'll need to connect the
portable to a network.

Having memory trouble? Assuming it's the computer
kind, you can free up a bit of RAM by disabling some
extensions. To choose extensions to disable:

1. Choose Control Panels | Extensions Manager.

2. Click the Size label at the top of the list of files to bring
   the largest extensions to the top of the list.

3. Take a look at the list; if you see an item that you're sure you don't need, uncheck the check box to deselect it. In many cases, QuickTime and its associated files (QuickTime PowerPlug and QuickTime Musical Instruments) will be right at the top of the list. You *could* disable QuickTime, but many CDs and some applications require it. Of course, you won't be able to play QuickTime movies without it.

You'll have to make decisions like this for each extension you want to remove. Fortunately, you can easily enable files you've turned off by returning to Extensions Manager when necessary. When you finish making changes to a set of extensions, you must restart the Mac before the changes will take effect.

Extensions Manager also keeps track of Startup Items and Shutdown Items—files that load when the Mac boots or shuts down. Just enable or disable these items as you would a control panel or extension.

If you're having problems with extensions and control panels and you suspect that the trouble lies with one of the third-party extensions you have installed, use Extensions Manager to get back to an Apple-only system:

From Extensions Manager's pop-up menu, choose Mac OS Base or Mac OS All. Extensions Manager will disable all items that are not part of Mac OS and will ask you to save your previous settings. When you restart, Mac OS will load only the system-related items. If this eliminates the problem, you can gradually enable your third-party extensions again, starting with the most important and taking care to note when the problem returns. The most-recently added extension will probably be part or all of the cause. To return to your previously saved settings, open Extensions Manager and select your configuration in the pop-up menu.

What happens to control panels and extensions when I disable them?

Extensions Manager moves disabled control panels and extensions to folders called Control Panels (Disabled) and Extensions (Disabled). These folders live in the System

Folder. When you enable a file and restart, it is moved back to the Control Panels or Extensions folder.

Extensions Manager is OK, but I've heard that there are other tools that can manage system files and help diagnose problems. What are they?

Casady & Greene's Conflict Catcher is one of our all-time favorite Mac utilities. Like Extensions Manager, Conflict Catcher allows you to create and save sets of system files. You can also use Conflict Catcher to test for extension conflicts, and to help you preserve the contents of your previous system files and preferences when you reinstall Mac OS. One of Conflict Catcher's coolest features is the ability to manage groups of extensions and control panels. Some system features, such as QuickTime and CD-ROM software, involve a number of related extensions. Conflict Catcher allows you to enable or disable all of the files related to a particular system feature at once. Figure 3-2 shows both individual extensions and several Conflict Catcher groups.

Figure 3-2 Conflict Catcher gives you the flexibility to enable individual system extensions and control panels, or groups of related files that support individual system features

 ## What are preference files?

The files that are stored in the System Folder's Preferences folder contain all sorts of data that applications and system files need. Serial numbers, passwords, and application settings all live in the Preferences folder. Most of the time, you can ignore preferences, confident in the knowledge that they're doing their jobs. But preferences can occasionally be the source of trouble.

Preference files, like all files, can become corrupted. Depending on the contents of a preference file, this may mean that you have to re-enter an application's serial number, or re-enter the settings that tell the application which windows to open at launch time. Sometimes, a corrupted preference file prevents an application from opening.

The first line of defense is to back up your preferences. If you regularly back up your Mac's startup disk, you're safe. If you only back up the documents you create, consider adding the Preferences folder to your routine. If you haven't done that and something gets corrupted, try opening the application. Doing this will often create a new preference file, replacing the corrupted one (though you'll lose any customized settings you may have set up for the program). If you have trouble opening an application (and you're pretty sure the trouble isn't related to a lack of free memory or some other general system problem), copy the application's backup preference file into the Preferences folder in the System Folder, and try again. If replacing the application's preference file doesn't do the trick, you may need to reinstall the application.

What are libraries?

Lots of system items have library files associated with them. Library files have names like File Sharing Library, AppleScriptLib, and so forth, and live in the Extensions folder. They support extensions with similar names, and should be kept or deleted along with those extensions, depending on whether you use the extensions or not.

If you've been fiddling with your Extensions folder and find that something stops working, chances are that it's because you've deleted a library file.

What's all that stuff on the Apple menu?

The Apple menu is a great way to get at the things you need quickly. The Apple menu puts control panels, the Chooser, Sherlock/Sherlock 2, Note Pad, Calculator, and a number of other items at your fingertips. You can also add your own items, and use special Apple menu tools to locate frequently used files and applications. Best of all, you can use the Apple menu from within any application or the Finder. Here are some of the items you'll find on the Apple menu, and what they do:

- **Apple System Profiler**   This tool gives you a quick look at your Mac's hardware and software. The Profiler tells you about the processor, hard disk, installed memory, video system, operating system version, and lots more.

- **Apple CD Audio Player**   Think of this tool as a remote control for your Mac's CD player. With it, you can play individual CD tracks and do all of the other things you would expect a CD player to do.

- **Calculator**   A staple of the Mac OS since its earliest days, the calculator is a very simple number-cruncher.

- **Key Caps**   Have you ever wondered how to create a bullet (•) or a trademark symbol (^{TM})? Key Caps shows you a map of your keyboard, and what happens when you combine a modifier key, such as OPTION or SHIFT, with other keyboard keys.

- **Network Browser**   Use this tool for connecting to file servers and Internet sites. You can save URLs and server pathnames here and reach them directly from the browser's window.

- **Remote Access Status**   The quickest way to get on or off the Internet is to choose this item.

- **Scrapbook**   Store graphics, text, or even a QuickTime movie in the Scrapbook. Add an item by opening and pasting it into the Scrapbook. Use your image or text by copying it from the Scrapbook to a document.

- **Sherlock/Sherlock 2 (formerly Find File)**   It's usually quicker to press COMMAND+F, but going the Apple menu route lets you look for files without switching to the Finder first. Sherlock can also locate Web pages and other resources on the Internet, and search inside files on your hard disk for words or phrases.

- **Stickies**   Stickies lets you take notes. Drag the little windows anywhere onscreen. Here's a tip: if you want to make notes but don't want to see the Stickies all the time, double-click a note's menu bar to collapse it.

 Tip: *Pre-Mac OS 9 users will notice that we've omitted some items, including Jigsaw Puzzle, Note Pad, and SimpleSound. That's because Apple omitted them first. If you're still using Mac OS 8.x, you'll find these useful tools (well, useful except for Jigsaw Puzzle) on your Apple menu, along with the rest. Jigsaw Puzzle is not included on the Mac OS 8.6 CD.*

How can I use the Apple menu to find or store files, programs, and servers I use frequently?

First things first. To get on the Apple menu, a file (or its alias) must reside within the Apple Menu Items folder, stored in the System Folder. The Apple menu is hierarchical, meaning that you can add a folder (or alias) and get to its contents by selecting them from a submenu. Here are some cool Apple menu options that can help you find and use your favorite files and applications.

- **Control Panels**   Control panels are stored in this folder, which lives at the root level of the System Folder. When you install new software that includes control panels, they appear here.

● **Favorites** This folder is intended as a storage place for URLs you want to connect to quickly and easily. You can also use a contextual menu to add aliases for local files or folders to the Favorites folder.

● **Recent Applications and Recent Documents** When you open an application or document, Mac OS puts an alias of the file into the Recent Applications or Recent Documents folder, within the Apple Menu Items folder. When you choose one of these items from the Apple menu, you'll see your files on the submenu. By default, the folders keep track of the most recent ten items you've opened, trashing the oldest aliases as it adds new ones. You can change the default number in the Apple Menu Options control panel, shown in Figure 3-3.

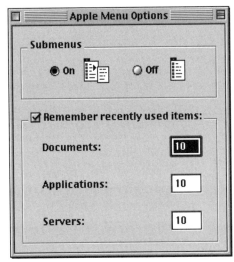

Figure 3-3 The Apple Menu Options control panel lets you choose the number of items that appear on the Recent submenus. You can also turn all hierarchical menus on or off

● **Recent Servers** If you use the Chooser to mount remote volumes (via AppleShare or File Sharing), aliases to your most recent choices will appear on the Recent

Servers menu. The aliases include the user name and password information you supplied when you logged onto the remote server, making the Recent Servers menu an especially quick way to get back to networked volumes you've used before.

 ## What is the control strip?

Like many things in Mac OS, there's more than one way to change your screen resolution or turn on File Sharing. The control strip is a quick way to get at a number of useful tools. Most of them are also available as control panels, but it's usually quicker to use the control strip—a row of icons with menus that you can add to the desktop.

To use the control strip, follow these steps:

1. Locate the control strip icon, shown here, at the bottom left corner of your screen:

2. If you don't see the control strip icon, open the Control Strip control panel (Apple menu | Control Panels | Control Strip), and click Show Control Strip.

3. Click the control strip icon once to extend the strip.

4. Each control strip item has a menu associated with it. Click and hold down the mouse button on an item to show its menu. This illustration shows the Monitor BitDepth control strip menu:

You'll find the following items on the control strip:

Item	Function
AppleTalk Switch	Turn AppleTalk networking on and off
CDStrip	Control an audio CD in your CD-ROM drive
File Sharing Strip	Turn Personal File Sharing on and off, and view users connected to your Mac
Keychain	Lock or unlock the keychain, and permit access to the Keychain control panel
Location Manager	Open Location Manager, and choose from available locations
Monitor BitDepth	Control the number of colors your monitor displays
Monitor Resolution	Change your monitor's resolution
Printer Selector	Choose from a list of available desktop printers
Remote Access Control Strip	Connect to a server, or open Remote Access control panel
Sound Volume	Control the volume of your Mac's beep sound
SoundSource Strip	Choose the Sound In, CD, or another sound monitoring source
Web Sharing CS	Turn Web Sharing on or off, or open the Web Sharing control panel

PowerBooks and iBooks have their own set of control strip modules. For more information about using the control strip with your PowerBook or iBook, see Chapter 11.

 ## Can I add items to the control strip?

Again, like most things Macintosh, the control strip has inspired shareware and freeware developers. You'll find lots of control strip modules on the Internet and on AOL. Some provide access to Internet tools; others create custom clocks, calculators, and other functions.

To add a new control strip module, just drag it to the closed System Folder or to the Control Strip Modules folder, inside the System Folder. As you may have guessed, you can get rid of a control strip module by moving it out of the Control Strip Modules folder.

I added an item to the control strip, but its icon doesn't show up. Why?

Adding an item to the control strip does not extend the strip. To do that, drag the end of the control strip in the direction that the arrow is pointing. Icons for your new control strip modules should appear. If they don't, check the Control Strip Modules folder to be sure that the item you're looking for is in the right place.

I don't like the control strip at the bottom of my screen, but I want to use it. Can I move the control strip?

To move the control strip, hold down the OPTION key and click the right end of the strip. Drag up or down to change its location.

If you want the control strip to collapse to the right side of the screen instead of the left, drag to the right while you hold down the OPTION key.

What are startup and shutdown items, and how can I use them?

The System Folder contains folders called Startup Items and Shutdown Items. Items you place in these folders will be launched when you boot or shut down the Mac. You can put applications or individual documents—or their aliases—in these folders.

One good use for startup items is launching your e-mail application, or any other application you always load, first thing in the morning. You can have the Mac launch multiple applications if you like, as long as memory holds out. The more you add to the startup process, though, the longer your Mac will take to get up and running. Another way to use Startup Items is to add desktop organization tools like James Thomson's shareware gem, DragThing. DragThing, which lets you put icons representing your favorite files and applications in panels right on the desktop, greets at least one of your authors each morning when the Mac starts up.

When you shut down, try launching a backup program or a diagnostic tool set to perform regular maintenance on your hard drive. These are great ways to get things done that you might otherwise forget to do.

My System Folder has lots of folders in it. What's Claris, for example?

A number of applications add their own folders to your System Folder. Apple's former subsidiary, Claris, made the ClarisWorks, Emailer, and FileMaker applications that are still on a lot of Macs. Installing any of these tools creates a folder called Claris in the System Folder. Likewise, installing Adobe applications, such as PageMaker and Photoshop, creates a folder called Adobe in the System Folder. Most vendors use these folders to store dictionaries, translators, and help files. If you use several applications from a vendor who uses this folder arrangement, all of the programs can use the same set of files. ClarisWorks and Claris Home Page, for example, both use the same dictionary file, stored in the Claris folder.

What's in the Appearance folder?

The image and preference files associated with Mac OS themes (discussed in Chapter 2) and their individual elements are stored in the Appearance folder, inside the System Folder. To add a picture, sound, or theme, just drag it into the appropriate subfolder, within the Appearance folder.

FONTS

 ### How do I manage fonts?

Mac OS includes two kinds of fonts: TrueType fonts and printer fonts, also called Type 1, or PostScript fonts. Actually, what most folks call fonts are typefaces—families of fonts. But we won't quibble. TrueType fonts display on the Mac screen and print to low-resolution printers (like inkjets), while PostScript fonts download themselves to high-resolution printers when you print a document, producing high-quality text. Both TrueType fonts and printer fonts are stored in the Fonts folder, inside the System Folder.

TrueType fonts, like the old bitmapped screen fonts used in earlier versions of the operating system, are stored in font suitcases. Double-click a suitcase and you'll see the different font weights (bold, italic, and so on) included in the font family. Double-click an individual font to see a sample, as shown in Figure 3-4.

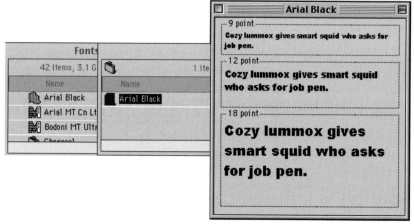

Figure 3-4 Double-click a font suitcase, and then an individual font, to see a sample of how the font will look onscreen, and an approximation of how it will look on the printed page

Printer fonts are not stored in suitcases, and you can't open them. When you print a document that contains a certain font, your printer uses the font file. Mac OS includes both TrueType and PostScript versions of some fonts so that you can print to both laser and inkjet printers.

 ### How do I install new fonts?

Just drag TrueType suitcases or Type 1 fonts to the System Folder. They'll be installed in the Fonts folder automatically. Removing fonts is as simple as quitting the application you're in and dragging the fonts into the Trash.

SOUND AND SPEECH

How can I add sounds to the Finder?

Macs have included sound since the earliest days. From a custom sound at startup that welcomes you to your Mac, to the beep sound that gets your attention when something goes wrong, you can change the sounds the Mac makes, and add your own sounds, too.

Bob Speaks: Mac OS Sound Sets

There are already several neat third-party sound sets available for OS 8.5 and later. I'm currently using one that's based on the sounds from the video game Myth: The Fallen Lords, which makes my Mac sound like a video game all the time. I tried another set that mimics the sounds you'd hear on a Silicon Graphics (SGI) workstation, which was pretty slick, too. These sets are kind of dorky, and I usually end up turning them off, but they're fun to experiment with. Search your favorite shareware site, or search AOL for Mac OS sound sets if you want to give it a try.

When you find some sounds you like, drop them into the Sound Sets folder, which you'll find in the Appearance Folder in the System Folder.

You control most sound functions in the Sound control panel—it's the Monitors & Sound control panel in Mac OS 8.*x.* Here you can set the Mac's volume, choose sound input and output devices, and pick an alert sound from a selection of built-in beeps. To have the Mac chime on the hour, half-hour, or quarter hour, open the Date & Time control panel, click the Clock Options button, and choose your preferred sound and interval.

The Appearance control panel's name is a bit outdated in Mac OS 8.5 and later; there's a Sound tab that lets you add sounds to all sorts of Finder actions, like opening windows, dragging files, and pulling down menus. You can include a set of sounds as part of a Theme, and you can choose your own set of sounds to use from the pop-up menu under the Sound tab. Mac OS includes a set called Platinum Sounds, but you can add others. Figure 3-5 shows your sound options.

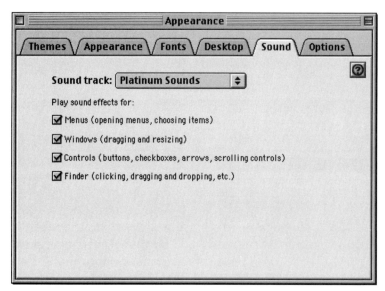

Figure 3-5   You can add sound to some or all of these Finder actions in the Appearance control panel

 ## How do I add new alert sounds of my own?

Assuming that you've made or downloaded Mac OS–
compatible sound files, or created your own, all you
have to do to use them is drag them to the System Folder.
Unlike fonts, control panels, and extensions, sound files
are not stored in their own folders. To see what sounds are
available in your system, open the System Folder and
double-click the System file. Figure 3-6 shows a System
file with sound files and keyboard layout files. Double-click
a sound file to hear it.

Mac® OS 9

 Note: *Mac OS 9 includes a few new sounds. Play them by
double-clicking their icons in the System file, or check them
out in the Sound control panel.*

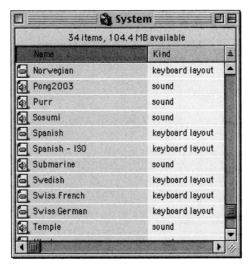

Figure 3-6   By default, Mac OS includes several sound files and a whole
lot of keyboard layouts

 How do I get my Mac to talk to me?

Open the Speech control panel. Here, you can tell the Mac to speak those annoying dialog boxes that pop up when you do something wrong, or when the Mac needs your attention for some other reason. You can choose to have the Mac speak alerts as they are written onscreen, or use a custom phrase. There's also a large selection of voices to choose from.

To enable talking alerts, follow these steps:

1. Open the Speech control panel.

2. Choose Talking Alerts from the pop-up menu. Figure 3-7 shows the Talking Alerts options in the Speech window.

3. Click the Speak the Phrase check box to select a pithy phrase from the list, or have the Mac speak the alert text, just as it appears in the dialog box.

4. Click the Options pop-up menu again to view the list of voices. Choose one, and click the sound icon to hear how it will sound.

5. Adjust the slider to speed up or slow down the voice.

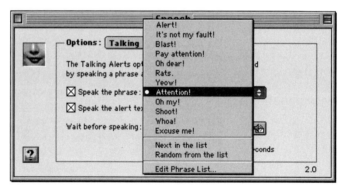

Figure 3-7 Choose a phrase to use, or have the Mac read alert boxes to you

 What is speech recognition, and how do I activate it on my Mac?

Speech recognition means that your Mac can hear and respond to spoken commands. You can use speech recognition to open documents and applications, pull down menus, and navigate in the Finder. With third-party software, you can even use speech recognition to open hyperlinks in a Web browser. To use speech recognition, you need the following items:

- A PowerPC-based Macintosh
- Text-to-speech software
- English Speech Recognition software (included, but not installed, with Mac OS)
- A Macintosh that includes a microphone, a 16-bit microphone, or a microphone-equipped monitor

The standard Mac OS installation includes text-to-speech software, including the Speech control panel, but not speech recognition. You will need to perform a custom install, using the Mac OS CD, to add it. To install English Speech Recognition software, follow these steps:

1. Launch the Mac OS Installer from the CD.
2. Choose the disk you want to update and click Select.
3. When the installer asks whether you want to reinstall or Add/Remove software, click Add/Remove. You're not replacing system software, just adding to it.
4. The installer displays a number of options. Choose English Speech Recognition by clicking the check box next to that item. You don't need to install Text-to-Speech because it is already in your system (unless you have altered your System Folder in some way). If you're not sure, install Text-to-Speech, too.
5. Click Install. When installation is complete, restart your Mac.

The English Speech Recognition package you installed adds some features to the Speech control panel and places a new folder of AppleScripts on your hard drive. We'll introduce you to the new stuff as we go through the process of configuring your Mac to listen to and obey your commands. To set up speech recognition, follow these steps:

1. Choose Apple menu | Control Panels | Speech.

2. Choose Listening from the Options pop-up menu. Notice that the Options menu contains extra items when speech recognition software is installed, as shown in Figure 3-8.

3. Click the Listen Only While Key(s) Are Pressed option to tell the Mac to respond to your spoken commands only when the designated key (ESC, by default) is pressed. If you leave the Key(s) Toggle Listening On and Off option selected, the Mac will listen to find out whether keys are pressed or not.

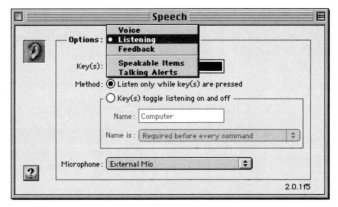

Figure 3-8 The first step in configuring speech recognition is to choose Listening from the menu. If you don't see this option, English Speech Recognition isn't installed

4. Instead of pressing a key to initiate a command, you can tell the Mac to listen when it hears its name. Type a name you'd like to use in the Name field, and use the Name Is pop-up menu to tell the Mac when to respond to its name. Figure 3-9 shows the completed Listening window.

5. Choose Feedback from the Options pop-up menu.

6. Choose a character, if you like. Characters' faces appear onscreen when speech recognition is activated. The character you choose makes no difference in the way speech recognition works.

7. Click Speak Text Feedback to tell the Mac to respond to your spoken commands. If you'd rather have a simple sound to indicate that the Mac understood you, choose one from the Recognized pop-up menu.

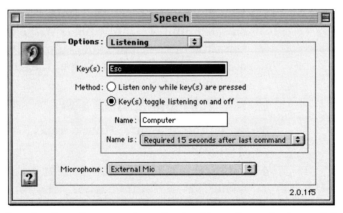

Figure 3-9   Setting these options in the Listening window of the Speech control panel tells the Mac to listen when it hears its name spoken

8. Choose Speakable Items from the Options pop-up menu.

9. Turn Speakable Items on to activate the folder of the same name. The Speakable Items folder contains AppleScripts that the Mac executes when you give it a spoken command. You can view the contents of the folder by choosing Apple menu | Speakable Items. When the Mac is ready to speak, a small window with the face of your chosen character appears, telling you that speakable items are ready. Another window shows speakable items you can use. If you've told the Mac to speak responses to your commands, it will say "speakable items is ready."

10. Make sure that your microphone is plugged in before you begin using speech recognition.

Now, you're ready to use speech recognition. In this example, we've set up the Mac to respond to its name—*computer*—and a command from the Speakable Items folder. To have your computer do your bidding, follow these steps:

1. In a normal tone of voice, with no background noise, say "Computer, what time is it?" The Mac will display the time in the Speakable Items window, and if you've configured the system to speak its responses, it will tell you the time aloud.

2. Say "Computer, tell me a joke."

3. When the Mac says "Knock, knock," respond "Computer, who's there?"

4. When the Mac answers, repeat what it says and add "who?" as in, "orange who?" The computer completes the joke.

5. With a Finder window open on your screen, tell the Mac to "close this window." See the Speakable Items window in Figure 3-10, complete with responses to spoken commands.

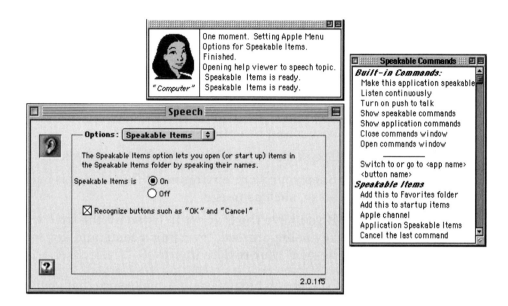

Figure 3-10 When you issue commands to the Mac, the results appear in the Speakable Items window, which appears in the foreground of all of your applications. The window appears when you turn on Speakable Items in the Speech control panel

❓ How can I add new speakable commands?

Speakable items are simply AppleScripts that respond to your voice. If you launched the scripts in the traditional way, they'd work just fine. You can write AppleScripts that perform specialized commands, but you can also use aliases to add more basic capabilities, like opening applications and files. To create a speakable item that will open Microsoft Word, just click the application and say "Computer, make this speakable." The script creates an alias to the application and drops it into the Speakable Items folder. You can change the name of the alias to "Word" to shorten the command that you'll speak to launch the application.

 I'm having trouble getting the Mac to respond when I talk to it. What's wrong?

It's likely that the Mac's microphone didn't hear you. When you talk to your Mac, use these guidelines to improve your results:

- Position the microphone a little bit above eye level, for best sound reception.
- Speak clearly, and in a normal tone of voice.
- Keep your work environment free of excess background noise, such as music.
- If you have the Mac set to listen all the time without a key being pressed, try using a command key for awhile to see if your results improve.

If you're still having trouble, make sure that your setup is complete. Check to make sure that your software is configured and ready to go. Next, check the external microphone connection to your Mac to see that the plug fits snugly into the Sound In port. Open the Sound control panel (the Monitors & Sound control panel, if you're using an older version of Mac OS), and check that the Input Source (Sound Monitoring Source if you're using Monitors & Sound) displays either Sound In or External Microphone. You can also check sound settings with the SoundSource control strip.

 How can I use speech recognition with my Web browser and other applications?

Several commercial and shareware speech recognition add-ons are available. Check out the nifty ShockTalk and ListenUp Web browser plug-ins that allow Web authors to build speech recognition into their pages. If you have a browser equipped with plug-ins and a page that has been coded for them, you can talk your way through a Web site without ever raising your mouse.

There's a downside to talking to your Mac: Apple announced in 1997 that it would no longer develop upgrades

for its Speech Recognition package, though the company has upgraded the underlying PlainTalk engine that is used by both Speech Recognition and Text-to-Speech. Fortunately, the most recent version of PlainTalk is stable and is still included in Mac OS. To learn everything there is to know about Apple Speech Recognition, or perhaps even to let Apple know that you'd like to see it back in development, visit http://speech.apple.com/.

Do any third-party developers offer tools that work with Apple's speech recognition software?

We're sorry to say that several developers who offered speech products, including collections of speakable items and tools for navigating the Web with speech, no longer sell these tools. Apple's Speech site, described in the preceding question, includes links (some live, some dead) to tools and demonstrations of speech technology. The good news is that two companies—IBM and Dragon Systems—have announced continuous speech recognition programs for the Mac, supposedly to ship by the end of 1999. Watch for them.

Chapter 4

Mac Housekeeping: Organization, Backup, and Maintenance

Answer Topics!

Mac Housekeeping @ a Glance

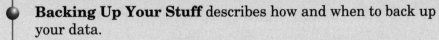

- **Backing Up Your Stuff** describes how and when to back up your data.

- **Cleaning Up Around the Desktop** discusses deleting files.

- **Preventive Maintenance** explains how to keep your Mac running smoothly, to avoid potential problems.

BACKING UP YOUR STUFF

 ### Do I really need to back up my stuff?

If you want to be sure that the term paper, financial plan, Girl Scout newsletter, or resume you just spent hours working on won't become just a memory, you better believe you need to back up your stuff.

All of your files are stored on your hard drive or on a removable disk, such as a floppy or Zip disk. While hard drives are really quite reliable, and even floppies and Zip disks can hold up for years, there's always the chance that something will go wrong. And, if it does, your data is probably a goner unless you've backed it up.

Even if you don't create documents that will stand the test of time, you should still back up your Mac. You have a CD-ROM for Mac OS and disks or CDs for your applications, but what about those control panels and shareware applications you worked so hard to configure just right? If your hard drive gives out, the preference files that know your ISP's phone number, and which desktop pattern you like will be history.

 ### How much should I back up?

Ideally, you'll back up your whole hard drive. That way, if anything goes wrong, you can re-create the contents of the drive with minimal hassle. If that's not possible (usually because you don't have another large hard drive or a high-capacity backup device, like a Jaz drive or tape drive), set some priorities. The most important items to back up are your documents; anything you've created and saved on your hard drive. For lots of people, this includes e-mail—messages you've written and received. Next, back up the System Folder's Preferences folder. If you have a Zip or other removable drive, such as a Jaz or SyQuest drive, back up your entire System Folder onto a cartridge. This way, you'll have an up-to-date backup as well as a bootable startup disk, in case of emergency.

What will backup cost me?

Backup devices and media (disks, cartridges, and tapes) vary in price by capacity and convenience. Floppies cost practically nothing, but they don't hold much data, and many newer Macs don't even include a floppy drive. At the other end of the spectrum, DAT (Digital Audio Tape) drives cost several hundred dollars and tapes go for about $10 apiece. But you can put the entire contents of your hard drive on one tiny DAT cartridge much more quickly than you could copy the same information to floppies.

Somewhere in the middle are cartridge media, like Zip, Jaz, and SyQuest. They hold from 100MB to 2GB (typical hard drives are 4 to 10GB, and you can get a drive for $200 to $500 and additional cartridges from $7 to $100).

As we write this, a new backup option is becoming available to Mac users. The Orb drive, from Castlewood Systems, is a removable-media drive that uses 2.2GB cartridges that cost about $30 each. The drive itself costs around $200 and is available for SCSI and USB Macs. We haven't had a chance to test the Orb ourselves, but we're excited about the aggressive price and high storage capacity. Orb may be a great replacement for your old Jaz drive.

How reliable are the different kinds of backup media?

Not all backup media are created equal. DAT tapes are probably the most reliable media you can find, while Jaz disks—especially considering their high cost—are a pretty big gamble. In general, disk-based media, which are written on by moving heads, are less robust than tape or CD-R. The latter uses a laser to burn your data onto a compact disc.

When we talk about reliability, we mean the risk that a cartridge, tape, or compact disc will become corrupted, thus destroying its contents. The more you use a piece of media, the more likely it is to go bad, though there is no guarantee that it will. If you're very concerned about the chance of your backups going bad, make a second set of backups.

How often should I back up?

Think about the way you work: do you use the Mac all day, creating lots of documents? Or do you dust off the old machine a few times a week to read your e-mail? Daily backups might seem like overkill, but they're worth it if you constantly add or change the documents on your Mac. Home users may find that weekly backups are enough. After all, even if you use the Mac every day, it's not necessary to back up after you surf the Web or play a game.

Bob Speaks: Three Backups Are Better Than One

If it's worth backing up, it's worth backing up three times. I recommend you alternate three sets of backups, keeping one of them off-site.

Since I have a lot of data—several gigabytes—I choose to back up to DAT (Digital Audio Tape) tapes, which hold from 2 to 8GB of data (more, with compression) and cost around $10 to $20 each. A DAT tape drive—an external SCSI device—costs about $600.

I created three different backup sets on three different DAT tapes. On Monday, Wednesday, and Friday, I use Tape 1. On Tuesday, Thursday, and Saturday, I use Tape 2. On Sunday I use Tape 3, which is then stored in my safe deposit box. (You could just take it to a neighbor's house. The point is, it shouldn't be in the same building as the computer, in case of fire, theft, flood, or other bad stuff that could happen.)

Every week I move each tape up one position in the rotation. So next week, Tape 2 will be swapped with Tape 3 off-site, and I'll use Tape 3 on Monday, Wednesday, and Friday, and Tape 1 on Tuesday, Thursday, and Saturday. The following week Tape 1 would be the off-site tape, and I'd use Tapes 2 and 3 all week.

I use Retrospect software from Dantz Development to automate this whole process. Initial backups (the first time) take about an hour to back up almost two gigabytes of data. Incremental backups usually take no more than five or ten minutes. I have Retrospect configured to launch itself and perform my daily backup automatically every evening at 5 P.M. All I have to do is make sure the right tape is in the drive.

I rarely lose data. When I had a total hard disk crash that wiped out everything on my drive, I got a new drive, restored the data from my backup, and was back at work in a couple of hours.

I guess my point is that at some time in your life your hard disk will crash completely, taking with it all the bits and bytes you've accumulated over the years. So, either develop good backup habits before the fact, or be ready to live without all your "stuff."

One last thing: if you do have a catastrophic disk crash without a backup, you might try DriveSavers. They specialize in recovering data from crashed disks, and they're very good at it. Of course, they're going to charge you more than a DAT tape drive and a ten-year supply of tapes. And even then, they may not be able to recover all your stuff. But if you need them, you need them. Their phone number is (415) 883-4232 and their URL is http://www.drivesavers.com.

What are incremental backups?

Incremental backups—which can be performed by backup applications like Retrospect or Retrospect Express, both from Dantz Development—are backups that only include those files that have changed since the last complete backup. Backing up only the changed files is much faster than backing up the entire hard drive, and it is much less stressful for your backup media, which will wear out more quickly if you erase them every time you back up.

What is data archiving, and why would I do it?

If you want to save the contents of a folder or volume, but would like to remove the files from your hard drive, use the archiving feature of your backup software to move the files to a backup disk or tape, removing the originals from your hard drive.

Archiving is useful if you want to store old files someplace safe, or simply need the room on your hard drive.

Caution: *Since archiving data removes it from your computer, you may want to back it up, too. As we pointed out earlier, backup media varies in reliability, and it is usually much more difficult to recover data from cartridges or tapes than from a hard drive.*

I need to back up several Macs, and maybe even a PC or two, in my office. Do I need a backup device for each computer?

There's no need to break the bank buying Zip or DAT drives. Using Dantz's Retrospect, you can set up a backup server—a single Mac that manages backups for networked computers, including both Macs and PCs. To back up multiple machines, you need Retrospect Remote, client software that lives on each computer to be backed up. Dantz sells Retrospect Remote in packages for 5, 10, and 50 users. With the remote software (a control panel) installed, the Retrospect server software polls each networked computer to see if it needs to be backed up. Remote users can also request a backup from the server.

That's a great way to back up a PowerBook when you return from the road.

To use network backup, you'll need a tape drive because only tape can store enough data to back up several machines at once. Some companies use tape loaders—devices that automatically switch DAT tapes into and out of a tape drive, and can therefore support many more users than a standard DAT drive.

If you have a TCP/IP network, you can back up PCs as well as Macs with Retrospect. Dantz sells a Windows version of its Remote software, which interacts with the Mac server just as Mac clients do.

CLEANING UP AROUND THE DESKTOP

 ### Does emptying the trash really delete my files?

It takes several steps to get rid of a Mac file. First, you drag it into the Trash, removing it from its place in your work folder, but *not* from your hard drive. The Trash is, basically, a folder, just like any other.

When you choose Empty Trash from the Special Menu, the Mac removes the contents of the Trash folder and tells you that there's more space on your disk. In fact, what has happened is that the Desktop database has been updated. The files are actually right where you left them, and they will stay there until other files are written over them. This means that it's often possible to retrieve files that you have thrown into and emptied from the Trash, unless you've added lots of new stuff to the disk. It also means that those files you thought you kept away from prying eyes by throwing them away may be vulnerable, assuming a snoop knows how to recover them.

To recover a file, get a file recovery tool like Norton Utilities for Macintosh, and search for the missing file by name or by some other parameter that the recovery tool supports, such as date or file type. If the file hasn't been overwritten, you'll get it back.

 ## Does it help my Mac's performance if I get rid of old files?

As long as you have room on your hard drive (or drives) there's no reason you *have* to delete old or unused files, but it does save disk space and can help your Mac run at tip-top speed.

Each file on a disk has an entry in the Desktop database. So, the more files you have, the larger the database is. Since the Mac uses the database to find and launch files, it stands to reason that a lean, mean database will make your Finder operations run faster. If you can't bear to delete files, try archiving them, as described in an earlier question in this chapter.

What can I safely delete from my hard drive?

When you get a new Mac or install a new version of Mac OS, you'll find plenty of files on the hard drive that you don't really need. Some files are intended for specific Macs (not the one you have) and some support peripherals you don't have (such as other printers). There is also lots of helpful documentation that can be removed once you've read it.

A good place to look for unneeded files is the Extensions folder, inside the System Folder. Here, you'll find lots of printer drivers and modem scripts for devices you don't have or don't use. If you have a desktop Mac, you can get rid of files that pertain to PowerBook portables. Users of older PowerBooks can delete CD-ROM software, but be careful. If you ever anticipate connecting an external CD-ROM or adding an internal one, don't delete CD-ROM software; instead, disable it with the Extensions Manager.

Extensions Manager is a great way to temporarily disable control panels and extensions that you aren't sure whether you need or not: if you disable it, you can get it back easily if problems arise. See Chapter 3 for more about using Extensions Manager.

When you remove old applications from your Mac, you may find that their preferences have stayed behind. Preference files are usually tiny; but some applications, like those from Microsoft, can leave folders full of dictionaries, cache files, and

so forth. When you're sure that a file's application no longer exists on your Mac, trash the preference files and other support files.

The ColorSync Profiles folder (in the Preferences folder under older Mac OS versions, and at the root level of the System Folder in more recent versions) contains more than 2.5MB of profiles for specific monitors and types of displays. You don't need most of them. Even if you delete one you need later, you can reinstall it from the Mac OS CD-ROM.

PREVENTIVE MAINTENANCE

What's the easiest way to keep my Mac running right?

The first step to good Mac health is common sense. When you're ready to turn the Mac off, shut it down from the Special menu or by pressing the Power Key on your keyboard and then clicking the Shut Down button. Proper shutdown allows the system to put everything away before it shuts itself off. On the hardware front, make sure the Mac is turned off before you connect or disconnect peripherals. This rule is absolutely crucial unless you have an iMac or other Mac with USB ports. Plugging in or unplugging SCSI, ADB, and/or serial devices while your Mac is powered up can cause fatal hardware damage. The safest course is just to shut down before plugging in or unplugging anything.

You should also consider installing antivirus software. Even if you don't download files from strangers, you probably do install new applications. Virus software will scan disks as you mount or insert them, and can also check files for problems as they are downloaded from the Internet.

I've heard that Macs aren't as susceptible to viruses as PCs or other computers. Is that true?

Macs can and do become infected with computer viruses. Though many of the viruses that cripple PCs and Internet servers (most of them running the Unix operating system) don't infect Macs, plenty of other viruses do. Macs are also susceptible to some viruses that are transmitted via e-mail

attachments and within document files, such as Microsoft Word documents.

The solution is to install antivirus software and keep up with updates that inoculate your system against new viruses. Virex, from Dr. Solomon's Software; VirusScan, from Network Associates; and Norton AntiVirus for Macintosh, from Symantec can scan for viruses when you tell them to, or automatically when a disk is inserted or a new file downloaded.

Because new viruses are being created constantly and spread quickly, virus software makers publish updates, usually available for download from the vendor's Web site. It's a good idea to check for updates frequently and keep an eye out for virus alerts in publications or on the Web.

What tools does Mac OS include that can help with maintenance?

Disk First Aid examines and repairs the directory structure of disks: floppies, hard drives, or mountable cartridges. You can also verify the condition of (but not repair) CD-ROMs. It's a good idea to run the Disk First Aid application periodically, just to check the status of your hard drive and other important disks. Figure 4-1 shows Disk First Aid after verifying a disk that is in good shape.

Disk First Aid works in two steps: first, you verify the condition of a disk. If Disk First Aid finds problems, you will see an error message in the list of "instructions and results." Then, click Repair to fix the disk. Though Disk First Aid can repair some problems, you may need a full-fledged disk repair tool, such as Norton Utilities or Tech Tool Pro, to solve serious problems.

What is rebuilding the desktop, and why should I do it?

The Desktop database, which stores information about each file on the disk, becomes fragmented or corrupted over time. A corrupted Desktop database can prevent files from opening or cause the Finder to lose track of which files belong to which application.

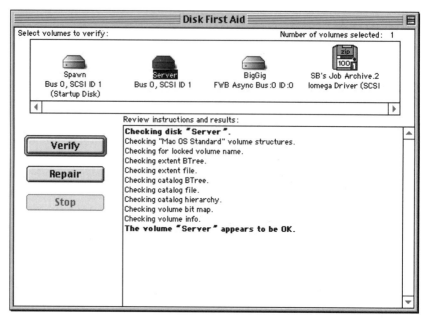

Figure 4-1   Disk First Aid shows that the selected disk doesn't need repair

The solution to a damaged desktop is to rebuild it. It's a good idea to rebuild the desktop once a month or so, even if you aren't having any problems. It's a fairly quick way to keep the Mac running smoothly.

To rebuild the desktop, follow these steps:

1. Restart your Mac.

2. Hold down the COMMAND and OPTION keys as the Desktop screen appears, but before your startup disk icon appears (just after the extensions and control panels finish loading).

3. When the "Are you sure you want to rebuild the Desktop?" dialog box appears, let go of the keys and click OK. The Desktop database rebuilds, and a window shows you its progress. If you have multiple disks mounted, the Mac will ask whether you want to build each disk's desktop in turn.

How can I keep my hard drive running right?

When you add or save files to disk, the Finder drops them wherever it can find free space, even if that space is not contiguous. When you delete a file, the space it took is freed up in the same way. The result is that if you create, save, copy, or delete files, over time the disk becomes fragmented: files are spread out and the Finder has to search more of the disk to assemble files for launch. In short, fragmented disks run less efficiently. Periodically defragmenting your hard drive keeps things running better.

To defragment a disk, you need a utility like Norton Utilities Speed Disk or Alsoft's DiskExpress. These defragmentation applications will bring together the pieces of your files that are scattered around the disk and make all of the data on your disk contiguous.

Tip: *It's a good idea to back up your disk before you defragment it. Backups are discussed in the first section of this chapter.*

What is disk optimization, and how is it different from defragmenting?

Software (including Norton Utilities) that optimizes a disk actually moves the contents of the disk so that system files, applications, and documents are all grouped together on the disk, while defragmenting simply reconnects disjointed files and makes the data contiguous.

How often should I defragment or optimize my hard drive? Or should I bother?

It's not necessary to defragment the disk regularly, and fragmentation varies a great deal by the way you use your drive. Do it when the drive seems slower than normal, or if Disk First Aid finds problems but cannot solve them by itself.

If your drive is full, and if you often delete lots of files to make space available for new ones, you may need to defragment the drive more often. The reason for this is that with little free space available, deleted areas will be overwritten more regularly.

Part Two

Mac Peripherals and Connectivity

Chapter 5

Storage Devices

Answer Topics!

Storage Devices @ a Glance

All About HFS+ describes the new Mac OS Extended format for file storage.

Storage Basics describes the components of Mac OS that you'll find in the System Folder.

Setting Up a SCSI Chain details the steps and pitfalls of chaining SCSI devices together.

IDE describes how the Mac uses IDE storage devices.

USB Storage describes the use of the new USB connection standard.

FireWire explains FireWire technology, and how to get it.

Hard Drives explains the installation, use, and care of hard disk drives.

CD-ROM Drives and Recorders explains CD-ROM drive speed, caching, and care.

DVD Drives and Technology describes DVD options and formats.

Floppy Drives discusses the care and availability of floppy drives.

Removable-Media Drives explains how to choose and use a removable-media drive.

ALL ABOUT HFS+

 ### What is HFS+?

Apple introduced Mac OS Extended format—also called HFS+—in Mac OS 8.1. HFS+ takes its name from the Hierarchical Filing System that Mac OS computers use to identify folders and files, and to allocate space for them on disk. Each hard disk is divided into a given number of equal-sized blocks, and each file that is stored on the disk takes up one or more blocks of space. HFS+ makes it possible to get more data onto a disk because it divides the disk into many more blocks, each of which is smaller. This means that small files still take up one block on the disk, but the blocks are smaller than in regular HFS format, so less space is wasted. In other words, when you create a disk as a Mac OS Extended format volume, the disk is the same size, but it can store more data.

But upgrading to HFS+ is not simply a matter of installing Mac OS 8.1 or later. You have to re-initialize each disk that will use the Mac OS Extended format. That also means that HFS+ disks can't be used with pre-Mac OS 8.1 machines, because the older OS does not recognize the new format. Fortunately, you can mount non-HFS+ disks on a Mac OS 8.1 or later machine. You don't have to reformat every hard disk you own—just those you want to squeeze the most space from (and, of course, these disks will only be usable with Mac OS 8.1 or later once they've been reformatted). You can also use PlusMaker from Alsoft (http://www.alsoft.com) to create an HFS+ volume without completely reformatting the drive. The utility keeps the data intact, and through some voodoo of its own, makes HFS+ happen.

HFS+ benefits large disks more than small ones, because large disks waste more space under standard HFS. (Larger disks divided into the given number of blocks end up with larger block sizes and more wasted space, such as when a 4K file occupies a 64K block.) The most productive way to use

Mac OS Extended format is to update one or more hard disks and leave your removable cartridges in the standard format. Floppies can't be converted to HFS+, and disks under 640MB in size don't benefit much from HFS+.

How do I upgrade to HFS+?

Upgrading to HFS+ requires that you erase the disk completely. It is essential that you back up your data before you proceed. If you're smart, you'll back it up twice, just in case.

To use HFS+ on a disk that is not your startup disk, follow these steps:

1. If it isn't already up-to-date, upgrade the operating system on your startup disk to Mac OS 8.1 or later. You must be using a PowerPC-based Mac to upgrade to Mac OS 8.1.

2. Back up the entire disk you wish to upgrade to HFS+, either onto another hard disk or to removable media.

3. Click on the icon of the disk to be upgraded.

4. Choose Erase Disk from the Special menu.

5. Select Mac OS Extended from the pop-up menu, as shown here:

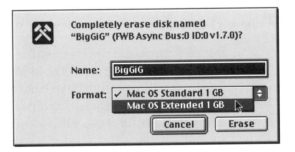

6. Click Erase.

7. When the disk is initialized, restore the backed-up contents of your disk to the newly prepared HFS+ disk.

As we mentioned earlier, there is an easier way, but it'll cost you about $30. Alsoft's nifty PlusMaker will update HFS disks to HFS+ without reformatting. We have used it

successfully on half a dozen disks, and it works as promised. Note that you should still back up the entire disk first, just in case. And again, if you're smart, you'll back it up twice, just in case the first backup somehow goes bad.

How can I upgrade my startup disk to HFS+?

To add the HFS+ format to your startup disk, you'll need to boot from another disk, like the Mac OS CD, or your Disk Tools floppy. Once again, be sure to completely back up the startup disk before you make the change. The CD or floppy you use to boot from must have Mac OS 8.1 or later installed.

Can I use Drive Setup to format my disk as HFS+, instead of using the Erase Disk menu option?

Yes. Drive Setup will format a disk. The Erase Disk command initializes disks (not as thoroughly as formatting does) and will work on both disk partitions and physical disks. Drive Setup only works on physical disks, and can only be used with Apple-branded disks—those that ship with Macs. To format a non-Apple drive you purchased, you'll need a utility like FWB's Hard Disk Toolkit. See the question, "What's the difference between formatting and initializing a disk?" later in this chapter for more about formatting and initializing.

Are there any other caveats for using HFS+?

Besides up-to-date system software, you'll want to be sure that there is either a bootable Mac OS CD or a DiskTools floppy readily available, in case of emergency.

To use disk diagnostic software, including Disk First Aid and Drive Setup, with HFS+ volumes, you'll need the latest versions. Check the vendor's Web site for updates. You may find that some shareware tools no longer work once you've converted to HFS+.

STORAGE BASICS

I've heard of SCSI, IDE, and USB. What do these acronyms mean, and how do they affect the storage devices I use with my Mac?

Every Mac has at least one SCSI, IDE, or USB port that you can use to connect internal or external storage devices. In the case of SCSI and USB, you can connect other kinds of devices, too, but we'll discuss those in later chapters. The portion of the motherboard that contains the connectors is referred to as the *bus*. All storage devices inside and outside the Mac are connected to a bus that supports SCSI, IDE, or USB.

iMac™

Most Macs since the Mac Plus (released in 1986) include an external SCSI (Small Computer System Interface) port. SCSI, pronounced *scuzzy,* also connects the internal hard disk drives and CD-ROM drives to the Mac. The exceptions are the iMac, which was the first Mac not to have SCSI; G3 and G4 Power Macs, and iBooks don't have it either.

Only in iBook™

The drives inside most recent Macs, like most PCs, are IDE (Integrated Device Electronics) devices. Current Macs, including the iMac and iBook, support USB (universal serial bus) devices. The internal hard drives in these machines are IDE devices. Like IDE, USB is a PC standard that has been transplanted to the Mac. USB is used to connect all sorts of peripherals, including high-speed Internet devices, printers, keyboards, and mice. You can also use USB to connect external Zip, SuperDisk, or floppy drives to an iMac.

Do any Macs use more than one kind of connector?

All current Macs, some Mac clones, and Performas use internal IDE drives. Most older Power Macs, clones, and Performas have a SCSI port on the back. Some of these IDE-using Macs include an empty internal IDE connector, meaning that you can choose either an IDE or SCSI disk drive when it's time to expand your Mac's storage. Each kind of connector is on a separate bus, which means that you can use the different devices simultaneously, and that they don't compete with one another for system resources. You can also

use PCI SCSI cards to add external SCSI drives to any Mac with a PCI slot.

SETTING UP A SCSI CHAIN

 ### What is a SCSI ID?

Each SCSI device you connect to your Mac has a SCSI ID—a number that is unique among the items on the SCSI bus. A SCSI bus supports IDs ranging from 0 to 6 (the Mac itself is 7). Since no two IDs can be the same, it's important to know a device's SCSI ID before you install or connect it. Though using devices with duplicate IDs won't harm the Mac, the drives simply won't be recognized. By default, the internal hard drive shipped with your Mac is set to SCSI ID 0. The internal CD-ROM drive has an ID of 3. That leaves five slots available for additional devices.

 ### How do I check a device's SCSI ID?

To check the ID of devices already connected to or installed in your Mac, open Apple Drive Setup, shown here, and note the names and IDs of the devices.

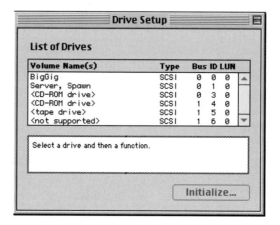

To check the SCSI ID of an external SCSI device, look at the back of the device. On most SCSI devices, a small window or dial displays the ID number, and push buttons or some other simple mechanism will allow you to adjust the number

up or down. Though some ID selectors allow you to choose numbers above 6, the 0–6 rule of SCSI IDs still applies.

To determine and change the SCSI ID of an internal drive, refer to the instructions that came with the drive. In many older drives, you'll be setting several jumper switches on the bottom of the drive, according to a table provided in the drive's documentation. Most modern drives use bare pins with plastic jumpers that you put on the pins to set the SCSI ID.

What is a SCSI chain?

When you connect SCSI peripherals to a Mac, you use cables to create a link, leading from the Mac to the first device, from the first device to the second, and so on. This arrangement is called a *SCSI chain*. Since each device communicates through the chain, rather than each directly with the Mac, any trouble along the chain can prevent all devices on the far side of the problem spot from working. In other words, SCSI chains are very delicate creatures.

What is SCSI termination?

All SCSI chains live by one important rule: the chain must be terminated at each end, and no device except the first and last ones should be terminated. Termination closes the electrical loop on which all devices in a chain operate. To terminate a chain, you need a terminating resistor (also called a terminator). Internal devices use tiny resistors that you can add or remove on the bottom of the drive. External terminators are rectangular blocks that fit into the extra SCSI port on the last device in your SCSI chain.

When you buy a Mac with an internal SCSI hard disk and CD-ROM drive, the two devices are terminated because they are the only ones in the chain. If you add a new device, you must either insert it in the middle of the chain, or move the terminator to the new device at the end of the chain.

Experience has proven to us that sometimes this advice doesn't work and you may have to move the terminator to the middle of the chain or remove it completely to get your SCSI chain working properly. With that said, try it the proper way first, as described previously. If (and only if) that doesn't

work, try moving the terminator to the middle of the chain or removing it completely. Keep experimenting with the SCSI chain until you find a combination that works. Remember, though, not to plug in or unplug SCSI devices while the Mac is running.

What does it mean that my Mac has multiple SCSI buses?

Some older Power Macs have two SCSI buses: one internal and one external. Unlike other Macs, where devices installed inside the computer and those connected to the external SCSI port all rely on the same SCSI chain, multiple-bus Macs support two chains of devices. That means that you can connect more devices, and that you must terminate each chain independently. Each chain has its own SCSI IDs, too. You can give an external drive an ID of 0 (the same ID used by your internal startup disk) without fear of conflict.

To find out if your Mac has multiple buses, and what they're being used for, open Drive Setup. The Type column tells you whether your drives use SCSI or ATA (used by IDE and USB devices). If a drive's entry in the bus column is 0, the bus is internal to the Mac. Bus 1 is external.

Tip: *If you really need a second SCSI bus for your PCI Mac, and don't have one, you can add a SCSI expansion card to your Mac. Adaptec (http://www.adaptec.com) is among the leading vendors of SCSI cards.*

How do I terminate the SCSI chain in a single-SCSI bus Mac?

Single-bus Macs with both internal and external SCSI connectors (all non-Power Mac desktop systems; most PowerBooks; and the Power Mac 6100, 7100, and 8100) should have a terminator on the internal startup disk and one on the last external device connected. Since the Mac's disk drive comes terminated from the factory, you only need to worry about the other end of the chain. If your single-bus Mac has an internal SCSI CD-ROM drive, you may need to

remove a terminator from the drive before you add another
SCSI device.

To terminate an external device, you'll need a block
terminator (often supplied with external drives). Connect the
terminator to the unused SCSI port on the last SCSI device
in the chain, and you're in business. Block terminators work
on all external SCSI devices. Some SCSI device vendors have
eliminated the need for a block terminator by including a
switch that turns termination on and off.

 Note: *If you have a Mac IIfx, you'll need a special terminator,
sometimes called a black terminator because—you guessed
it—it's black.*

How many SCSI devices can I connect to my Mac?

If your Mac has a single SCSI bus, you can connect a total of
seven devices, including both internal and external ones. If
you have two SCSI buses, you can theoretically connect 14
devices, but most Macs don't have that many internal drive
bays. Usually, you'll be able to add one to three new devices
inside your Mac, assuming you already have an internal hard
disk and CD-ROM drive.

I know that I need to have unique IDs for my SCSI devices, and that the first and last device in the chain must be terminated. Do the devices have to be connected in numerical order, too?

No. The Mac doesn't care whether ID 1 comes before or after
ID 5 in your SCSI chain.

I can't seem to get a SCSI device to show up on the desktop. How do I troubleshoot a SCSI chain?

Follow these steps to locate problems with a SCSI chain:

1. Use Drive Setup or another SCSI tool, such as the
   shareware SCSI Probe, or a diagnostic tool you received
   with your SCSI drive. If the drive you're interested in isn't
   on the list, click the Scan or Update or other similarly

named button. If the drive appears in the software, but not on the desktop, select it and click Mount.

2. Note the SCSI IDs of all the devices you see in the list. Is anything missing?

3. Check to see that all connectors fit tightly to their drives. External SCSI connectors can easily come loose, especially if you haven't tightened the clips on the connectors.

4. If the problem is with an external drive, or if your Mac has one SCSI bus, check the IDs of any external devices connected to the Mac. With the Mac shut down, change the ID of the problem device to a number that is not in use, and restart. Repeat step 1.

5. On the SCSI chain containing the problem device, check each device for termination. If there are terminators on the first and last devices, but nowhere else, the problem lies elsewhere.

6. Replace the SCSI cables connected to the problem device. You can temporarily disable other devices in the chain and use cables you know to be good to perform your tests.

7. Move the terminator from the end of the chain to somewhere in the middle. This is a long shot, but it has worked for us on occasion when nothing else did.

8. If you can, test the problem device with another Mac. If all is well, return to the original Mac. You may have a hardware problem.

I've heard that the Mac can't recognize drives larger than 9 gigabytes. Is that true, and is there a way around the limit?

Actually, Macs using system software earlier than version 7.5.2 are stuck with a 2 gigabyte volume limit. If your Mac has PCI slots (most Power Macs do) or uses Mac OS 7.5.2 or greater, the volume size limit is 2 terabytes (2,000 gigabytes).

Can I use PC SCSI devices with my Mac and vice versa?

SCSI is SCSI is SCSI, as far as the connections and drives are concerned. Unfortunately, there's more to connecting a storage device than the hardware. To work with a Mac, a SCSI device must have Mac drivers, and the Mac OS must be able to recognize it. Since PC users tend to buy IDE drives (you need to add a special card to a PC to use a SCSI drive), there's no real advantage to buying a "PC" SCSI drive. If you have a drive you'd like to try, consider purchasing a copy of FWB's Hard Disk Toolkit driver software. You can play it safe by checking the FWB Web site (http://www.fwb.com) to find out if HDT supports the drive you want to use.

I'm confused. What's the difference between SCSI-2, Fast SCSI, Wide SCSI, and UltraSCSI?

SCSI is not just one standard; it comes in several flavors. The Mac primarily uses the original and slowest kind of SCSI, SCSI-1. In Macs with two SCSI buses, the internal one is almost always SCSI-2, as are most modern drives. You can use a SCSI-2 drive with a SCSI-1 connector, but you won't get the full speed benefit from the fast drive when using a slower, external port.

SCSI-2 makes it possible to modify the SCSI standard further, to get increased speed. The speedier variations of SCSI in common use on the Mac are

- **Fast SCSI** A version of SCSI-2 that doubles SCSI's maximum throughput to 10MB/second. In multi-bus Macs, most internal SCSI buses use Fast SCSI.

- **Wide SCSI** Adds an additional cable inside the SCSI connector and can achieve a maximum throughput of 20MB/second or 40MB/second, if combined with Fast SCSI. No Macs include Wide SCSI ports; to use it, you need a Wide SCSI adapter card that plugs into a Mac's PCI or NuBus slot.

- **UltraSCSI** Provides twice the speed of SCSI-2. That means that if you use Fast SCSI-2, at a maximum throughput of 10MB/second, an Ultra Fast system would

provide a theoretical speed of 20MB/second. The fastest SCSI combination is Ultra Wide SCSI, with a rated speed of 40MB/second. Like Wide SCSI, UltraSCSI devices require an accelerator card (only available for PCI Macs).

IDE

Do Macs support EIDE?

The original version of the Integrated Device Electronics (IDE) standard was severely limited. The most notable limitation for end users was the 525MB limit on the size of disk drives. By the time Apple began using IDE, Enhanced IDE (EIDE) was already available, and Mac IDE buses have always adhered to that standard.

How do I know if I have IDE drives in my Mac?

Open Apple System Profiler from the Apple Menu, and click the Devices and Volumes tab to see details about your hard drive. You can also use Drive Setup to see if the drive type is ATA or SCSI. ATA drives use the IDE bus.

I have multiple IDE devices in my Mac. Which should be the master, and which should be the slave device?

Apple's 1998 generation of G3 Power Macs have multiple IDE buses, and they also allow you to daisy-chain drives on the same bus. To do this, one drive must be the master, and one the slave. The best rule to follow when deciding which IDE device will rule is that the faster ones (hard drives) should be the masters, while CD-ROM and Zip drives, which can't use the bus's full speed, should be slaves. To configure your IDE drives, you'll need a current version of Drive Setup, or another formatting utility that supports this arrangement.

USB STORAGE

How do I add additional storage devices to my iMac?

All iMacs include at least one available USB port, as do all current Mac models. The new, slot-loading iMacs have two. You can use it to add a Zip drive or other USB storage device. By adding a USB hub—a small device with several USB ports—you can add additional devices.

iMac™

Can I use PC USB devices with my iMac?

Like IDE and other standards that are used in both Mac and PC environments, the answer (from the hardware point of view) is definitely yes. But to use a USB device, the device must have Mac drivers and be supported by Mac OS. Most major printer, scanner, and removable media vendors include Mac and PC drivers with their USB products. If you're not sure, check the package for a Mac OS logo, or contact the manufacturer. Do not take the word of salespeople in retail stores. They are often uninformed.

✚ ***Tip:*** *If you have a USB device that doesn't include its own Mac drive, get yourself a copy of USB Overdrive. It's a shareware tool from Alessandro Levi Montalcini. USB Overdrive is a generic USB driver, meaning that you can use it with any USB device.*

FIREWIRE

What is FireWire?

FireWire is a high-speed storage technology that many experts agree will eventually replace SCSI. While SCSI is a parallel standard, FireWire is one of a group of fast serial transfer media types. Storage and consumer-electronics vendors have been choosing up sides in the battle between FireWire, SSA, PC-AL, and others. Apple's horse in this race is FireWire.

 Can I get FireWire on my Mac?

All current PowerMacs include FireWire ports, and current PowerBooks support an optional FireWire card. Some of Apple's new slot-loading iMacs have FireWire ports, too. Apple has indicated that all Macs will eventually support the standard.

HARD DRIVES

 Are internal hard drives better than external ones?

Since you can add internal storage devices to most Power Macs, you usually have a choice (inside or outside) when adding a new hard drive to your system. An internal drive saves desk space, and will probably be about $75 cheaper than the external kind, since external drives come with a case and power supply of their own. If your Mac includes an IDE controller, internal drives are even cheaper. Internal drives are also a better choice if you're doing graphics or multimedia work, where fast disk access is essential; the internal SCSI ports of modern Macs are faster than the external SCSI-1 ports. External drives have the advantage of being portable, however, which makes them an easy way to share files with other Macs. It's also more convenient to have an external drive repaired or replaced if something goes wrong with it.

If you have a blue-and-white G3 PowerMac, a G4 PowerMac, an iMac, or an iBook, keep in mind that you will have difficulty finding external hard drives, since these machines do not include external SCSI ports, and USB vendors have not yet shipped many external hard drives for the Mac. Your only option is to get a USB-SCSI adapter.

 What's the difference between formatting and initializing a disk?

When you initialize a hard disk, you erase all of its data; that's what happens when you choose Erase Disk from the Special menu. Formatting, on the other hand, not only removes data, but also re-creates the disk's contents completely, including the partition that is set aside for Mac

files. Besides completely obliterating anything that may once have been on the disk, the formatting process allows you to re-create one or more partitions, and to ignore bad blocks or sectors on the disk by having your formatting software leave them out of your partition.

You can use one of several utilities to format a drive: each application installs its own drivers. Drive Setup, Hard Disk Toolkit, or the software that came with your hard disk can all format your drive.

Does it matter which driver I use?

Hard disk drivers themselves are all pretty much the same to an end user. The choice you make depends on what software package you prefer. Formatting software often includes drive testing and other features. Drive Setup, for example, is pretty minimalist, while Hard Disk Toolkit (a *lite* version is bundled with a number of third-party drives) is chock full of features that help you evaluate your drive's condition and let you set a variety of partitioning options.

Should I partition my drive? How do I do it?

If you have a large drive (more than 2GB), partitioning it is a good way to organize your stuff, and can actually save space. Under Mac OS Standard format, a file takes up more space on a large drive than it does on a 1GB or smaller disk. Partitioning a big drive keeps file sizes down by creating several volumes from a single disk. You can also use partitions as an organizational or file sharing tool. Finally, some people partition drives so that different sections of the drive support different operating systems. You can create both Mac OS and Windows 95 partitions on the same drive, for example.

To partition a drive, use Drive Setup or the driver software that came with your hard drive.

 Tip: Plan your drive partitions carefully, making sure to leave enough room on each for growth. You won't be able to partition the drive again unless you reformat the drive.

 Should I buy drive management/diagnostic software?

If you can't do what you want with Drive Setup, or if your third-party drive came with software you don't like, consider a commercial drive management package. If, on the other hand, you have no interest in tuning or tinkering with your hard disk, don't bother.

 What's an AV drive?

An AV (audio/visual) drive has a much faster data transfer rate than a typical hard drive. Multimedia authors need the faster drive to play audio and video without the fits and starts that normal folks often notice when playing QuickTime movies. Because AV drives are faster, they are also significantly more expensive than standard hard drives.

AV drives can also suspend something called *thermal recalibration*—a process whereby the drive pauses for an instant to check on itself. This thermal recalibration can cause havoc when you stream data off your drive uninterrupted—when burning a CD, for example.

I want to replace my hard drive with a bigger one. How do I transfer data from my old drive to my new one?

The simplest way to do this is to back up the contents of the old drive onto a DAT tape, external hard disk, or removable-media cartridge(s); replace the drive; and then copy the old stuff onto the new drive. The other simplest way, assuming your Mac has a spare internal drive bay, is to install both the old and new disks (being careful to check their SCSI IDs and termination, as described in the "Setting Up a SCSI Chain" section, earlier in this chapter) and make your copy directly.

Even if you have the copying part figured out, there's still the little matter of transferring your system files from the old to the new disk. You can't simply replace the old System Folder with a Finder copy, and you probably don't want to use the new drive's System Folder, because it doesn't include your special set of control panels, extensions, and preferences. Here's how to get everything you need moved over.

If you're copying directly from an old hard disk to a new one, follow these steps:

1. Decide which System Folder you want to use. It's possible that the new hard drive contains a version of Mac OS that's newer than the one you've been using. If you're comfortable with moving to the next version (be careful; new system software might introduce incompatibilities with some of your software), open the Startup Disk control panel and choose the icon for your new hard drive. Close Startup Disk.

2. Restart the Mac. It will boot from your new disk.

3. Do a clean install of system software from a Mac OS CD-ROM or from the Net Install disk images on the new hard disk. When you've finished, you'll be asked to restart the Mac again.

4. Now comes the tedious part: open the System Folders for your old and new hard disks. Arrange the windows so that you can see both folders' contents.

5. Copy any control panels, extensions, preferences, and other items that appear in the old System Folder from the old disk to the same location in the new System Folder. Be careful to copy only items that aren't already in the new System Folder. You don't want to replace new control panels with old ones.

6. When you've finished updating the new folder, double-click the system file from the old disk. If you have stored custom sounds in the old system, now's the time to drag these files over to the new System file to install them.

7. Restart the Mac. Now, you're in business. But don't remove or erase that old hard drive just yet. Keep it installed and running for a few days, just to make sure that nothing you've done to the new System Folder causes problems.

Tip: *Casady & Greene's Conflict Catcher 8 can manage your clean install with its System Merge feature. CC takes the old non-Apple extensions and control panels from your previous System Folder and adds them to your new System Folder.*

 Note: *If you haven't customized your old System Folder very much, you can skip steps 4–7, but you may need to reinstall applications that include System Folder items.*

CD-ROM DRIVES AND RECORDERS

CD-ROM drive speeds keep going up and up. How important is it to have the fastest drive available?

CD-ROM drive speeds are measured in comparison to the speed of the original CD-ROM drives: the second generation of drives, twice as fast as the first, was said to be 2x. As of this writing, 32x CD-ROM drives are commonplace.

Though getting the fastest drive possible sounds like a no-brainer, the benefits are limited. That's because the CD-ROM titles you buy—even the games and multimedia titles—don't usually take advantage of the hardware's full speed. To work with a variety of drives, CD-ROM–based content is often mastered at a speed slower than the fastest drive available at any given time. That doesn't mean that a 16x CD will run slowly on a 32x drive. You just won't get the full benefit of the hardware when playing the disc.

With that said, it's important to note that you won't save a lot of money by purchasing a slower drive, assuming you can find one. At any given time, there are only a couple of drive speed choices available, and the prices don't vary greatly.

What are the benefits of internal as compared to external CD-ROM drives?

Since just about every current Mac includes a CD-ROM drive, and the older ones that do not can't take an internal one, this may seem like an odd question. But in the event that your internal drive dies, you might find it helpful to consider both of your options.

Internal drives don't take up space on or under your desk, and they're not much trouble to install. An internal drive may be slightly cheaper than an external one, especially if you have an IDE Mac. On the downside, you may have trouble adding an internal drive to your Mac if the Mac didn't come with a CD-ROM drive to begin with. The drives are easy enough to find, but the brackets you need to mount them are Apple-only parts that must be installed by an authorized dealer. That will add significantly to your cost.

External drives, on the other hand, are flexible; you can connect them to any Mac you have (as long as it has the needed SCSI port), including a PowerBook or older system that doesn't have an internal CD-ROM drive. That comes in handy when you need to install software on a PowerBook. You can also use an external CD-ROM drive along with an internal one, to mount two CDs at the same time. Many reference works come on multiple CDs, and it's useful to be able to mount two disks at the same time.

Tip: *If you need to replace a CD-ROM drive, consider a CD recorder (CD-R). With it, you can archive your files on a CD, make a backup copy of your hard disk, or create your own audio CDs. CD-R drives are significantly more expensive than CD-ROM players (under $500), but think of what you get for that extra money. By the way, you can use the CD-R drive to play CDs, too.*

 ## Should I buy third-party CD-ROM driver software?

Mac OS includes software that supports almost any SCSI CD-ROM drive you can find on the market, and Apple updates its drivers with each new Mac OS release. Most folks don't have to buy any new software to add or upgrade a CD-ROM drive. Under the 7.*x* versions of Mac OS, some Mac clones did not use the included CD-ROM software because of a licensing flap with Apple. Clone makers, and most CD-ROM drive makers, bundle a CD-ROM driver with their drives. FWB's CD-ROM Toolkit and CharisMac's Anubis are popular choices.

These, and a few other similar tools, are also available in commercial versions: they're designed to squeeze more performance from your drive by caching the contents of the CD-ROM titles in RAM and on your hard disk. This speeds things up because both RAM and hard disks are faster than a CD-ROM drive. But, for the same reason that a faster CD-ROM drive won't necessarily make Quake run faster

(the software can't keep up with the hardware), third-party caching software is no guarantee of faster playback.

In other words, in most cases you're better off sticking with the driver that came with your Mac or your replacement CD-ROM drive.

! **Caution:** *CD-ROM Toolkit will not cache your CDs if your startup disk is formatted with Mac OS Extended format (also known as HFS+). We're not sure why, but that's the way it is.*

Can I play music CDs on a CD-ROM drive?

Apple's CD-ROM software and all of the third-party driver packages include controllers for audio CDs. Some offer better optics than others, but all will play your discs.

How do I care for a CD-ROM drive and for the CDs themselves?

Like floppy drives (discussed in a later section), CD-ROM drives are susceptible to dust. Keeping the computer covered and away from excess dust is the first line of defense. You can also buy CD-ROM–cleaning CDs. Use one if you have trouble reading several of your CDs.

CDs, themselves, should be kept in jewel cases or the envelopes they came in. The discs are pretty sturdy, as long as they are kept away from dirt, heat, and cold.

DVD DRIVES AND TECHNOLOGY

What is DVD?

DVD stands for digital video disc (or digital versatile disc). It's a high-capacity version of CD-ROM technology that is already available to television watchers, and will probably replace the CD-ROM drive within a couple of years. Like a CD-ROM drive, DVD uses a laser to read the contents of a coated disc. In fact, DVD-ROM drives can read CD-ROM discs.

Capacity is DVD's great advantage. CDs can hold up to 650MB of data, while DVD discs, depending upon which of several available formats is used, contain 2.6GB to a

whopping 17GB of information. You can also play DVD movies on your computer, if you're so inclined.

How can I add a DVD drive to my Mac?

The easiest way to get DVD for your Mac is to buy a Power Macintosh G4 iMac DV, or a PowerBook G3, with a DVD drive. If you want to add DVD to an existing Mac, you need both the drive (which will replace your CD-ROM drive), and an MPEG-2 decoding card that the drive uses to stream MPEG video and digital audio content. You need the card because your Mac isn't peppy enough to manage the tremendous stream of audio and video data that pours forth when you play a DVD movie. Macs with built-in DVD drives have everything you'll need to play MPEG video.

You can buy a DVD Kit for older PowerBooks in the G3 series. The kit consists of a DVD-ROM drive and a PC card for MPEG decoding. Adding a DVD drive to an existing Mac is a bit tricky, because very few third-party drives are currently available. You can do it, though, since external DVD drives connect via SCSI, just like other storage devices. DVD-ROM drives from Pioneer (http://www.pioneerusa.com) and E4 (http://www. e4.com) include both the drive and the MPEG-2 PCI card.

Can I use a consumer DVD drive with my Mac?

You can use any DVD-ROM drive with your Mac, but you'll need to buy the PCI card to play video on your Mac. E4 is the only vendor we know of who sells the card separately, as well as with its own DVD drive. Be careful, though. Most consumer drives are not DVD-ROMs, but DVD-Video, an older, inferior variety of drive.

You can add an external DVD drive to any PCI-based Mac, or to a PowerBook that includes a PC card slot. You'll also need Mac OS 8.1 or later, which includes DVD driver software.

 ## Can I add a DVD drive to my iMac or iBook?

iMac™

Because the iMac or iBook has neither a SCSI port nor expansion card slots, there is currently no way to add DVD to an iMac. Two of Apple's three current iMac models include a DVD drive.

 ## I know that there are several DVD drive types and formats. What are the differences between the formats?

Most current DVD offerings for the Mac are DVD-ROM drives. Like CD-ROMs, you can read discs with these drives, but you can't record your own DVD information. DVD-ROMs hold up to 4.7GB per side.

The top-of-the-line Power Macintosh G4 includes a DVD-RAM recordable drive. At this writing, it's the only Mac with a DVD-RAM, but it probably won't be for long. Here's a breakdown of DVD standards and capacity.

Standard	Description	Capacity	Comments
DVD-Video	Consumer, read-only format.	2.25 hours of video	Not intended for computers. Video-only format.
DVD-ROM	Read-only data and video.	4.7GB per side	Currently the only DVD format available for the Mac.
DVD-R	Write-once format. Drives can also read DVD-ROM discs.	3.95GB per side	Drives exist, but are very expensive.
DVD-R/W	Rewritable version of DVD-R.	3.95GB per side	Drives not yet available.
DVD-RAM	Rewritable standard.	2.6GB per side	Discs can't be read by older DVD drives, but can be read by Generation 3 DVD drives. DVD-RAM drives can read CD formats.

DVD discs are available in different capacities. That's possible because DVD discs are thin and can be layered to double the rated capacity of a single side. A two-sided disc quadruples the space available for data on a single disc. A double-sided, double-layered DVD disc can store up to 17GB of data, or more than eight hours of video.

FLOPPY DRIVES

 ### How do I clean a floppy drive?

You can purchase floppy cleaning kits that consist of a cleaning disk, cotton swabs, and a cleaning solution whose main ingredient is usually alcohol. You can also blow dust out of the drive with a can of compressed air, which may be more effective than the cleaning kit anyway.

 ### Can I get a floppy drive for my iMac or other floppiless Mac?

iMac™

Yes. Both Newer Technology and IMation (and several others) have USB floppy drives available for users whose Macs came without a floppy drive. We'd suggest you skip the floppy, though, and get a SuperDisk or Zip drive, unless you absolutely require one—for example, if you have old, beloved files on floppies or use copy-protected software that requires a floppy-disk key install.

REMOVABLE-MEDIA DRIVES

 ### Are removables as fast as hard disks?

The short answer is no. Hard disks deliver data much more quickly than cartridges, and with the price of hard drives plummeting, they're not very expensive. On the other hand, cartridges are portable, and the modern ones (Zip and Jaz) are speedy enough to allow you to launch documents or applications, if need be. You won't notice a significant speed loss unless you're using an old Mac or a very large file.

❓ I have a Mac and a PC. Is there a way to share a Zip drive between the two?

Yes. Get a Zip Plus drive. Iomega has cleverly designed the Zip Plus's cable so that it will fit either a Mac's SCSI port or a PC's parallel port.

If your Mac is an iMac, iBook, G3 PowerBook, or G4 PowerMac, you could choose a USB Zip drive instead. Most current PCs have USB ports. Before you plunk down for the USB drive, though, check to be sure that all the computers you plan to use it with do indeed have USB ports.

❓ DAT drives are expensive, but tapes are cheap, and they hold many gigabytes of data. When should I consider buying a tape drive?

If you have lots of data to store, and you like to back up your files frequently, a tape drive is the right choice. That's especially true if you need to back up several computers. Tape is reasonably fast and efficient, and each one can hold up to 20GB of compressed data if you use data-compression built into tape drives and/or backup software.

Unlike other removable-media formats, tapes do not mount on your desktop, so you can't use them to shuttle files from place to place the way you can with a Zip cartridge. You'll need software, like Dantz's Retrospect, to back up and restore the contents of your hard disk to tape. Fortunately, most tape drives for the Mac include a version of Retrospect, and you can buy additional Retrospect software that will let you back up several computers to the same tape drive, over the network. By the way, those computers need not all be Macs. Retrospect supports PC backup, too, over a TCP/IP network.

Chapter 6

Choosing and Using
Printers with Your Mac

Answer Topics!

Choosing and Using Printers with Your Mac @ a Glance

- **Choosing a Printer** describes several types of printers, methods for connecting them, and how to choose the right one.

- **Connecting and Configuring Printers** explains the process of getting a printer connected.

- **Printing** gives details of how to use the printing features included in Mac OS.

- **Printing Problems** explains common printing problems and how to solve them.

CHOOSING A PRINTER

 What kinds of printers can I use with my Mac?

To work with a Macintosh, a printer must have a compatible connector and must be supported by Apple's system software. That makes almost any major printer brand a candidate for your desktop or network because most printer makers use either industry-standard Ethernet or the serial connectors Macs use to connect to serial devices. On the driver side, vendors such as Hewlett-Packard, Epson, Canon, and others either supply drivers for the Mac, or can take advantage of printer software that is part of Mac OS.

Print quality varies widely. You can choose an inexpensive personal printer, a heavy-duty corporate printer, a high-quality color printer, or even a super-high-resolution dye-sublimation printer. All of them work pretty much the same way with your Mac: connect the printer to the Mac or network, install a little software, and voilà, you're printing. These days, most printers are either ink-jet or laser printers.

The other major distinction between Mac printers is PostScript versus QuickDraw. PostScript printers use Adobe's PostScript page description language to produce high-resolution printed versions of your documents. Fonts are rendered crisply and graphics don't look jagged. On the other hand, you can save money by choosing a QuickDraw printer that prints documents at, or near, the resolution of your Mac's screen. Most ink-jet printers use QuickDraw, while laser printers almost always use PostScript.

 What's the significance of printer resolution?

Resolution, whether on your Mac's screen, or on the printed page, is measured in dots per inch (dpi). The more dots, the higher the resolution and the sharper the image. Fewer dots means that images and text can look jagged. Laser printers provide a minimum resolution of 300 dpi, while consumer inkjets often come in at around 150 dpi. Some laser printers support up to 600 dpi, and high-quality imaging printers can go as high as 1,400 dpi.

Unless you're publishing a book or some other document that needs to be typeset quality, 300 dpi is plenty of resolution for most people, though a 600 dpi printer will produce better-looking halftones (pictures) and other graphics. Even an inkjet's 150 dpi provides plenty of resolution for many home users, but those who want to print high-quality reproductions of digital photos may opt for higher resolution, photo-quality printers.

What's the right kind of printer for me?

The short answer is this: get a PostScript laser printer if you can afford it. Even if you're working at home, a laser printer produces better-quality text and is much faster than an ink-jet printer. If you do a lot of printing, or want to include graphics in your documents, buy a faster laser printer with all the bells and whistles.

If you are on a tight budget, there's good news: most of today's ink-jet printers are pretty good. They're lots better than the old dot-matrix printers that used to be the only choice for home users. Ink-jet printers are much slower than laser printers, not only because they are usually connected to your Mac by a serial cable or by LocalTalk, but because they use a mechanical process to create the printed page. Laser printers, though they vary greatly in speed, do not waste time dragging a cartridge across the page.

There's another advantage to ink-jet printing: it's a very inexpensive way to print in color. The color versions of popular ink-jet printers are only a little more than their black-and-white counterparts, and they're a lot less expensive than color laser printers, which, despite the precipitous drop in printer prices, will still cost you several thousand dollars. On the downside, ink-jet printers go through ink cartridges very quickly, especially if you're doing a lot of color printing. You'll pay at least 30 bucks apiece for most ink-jet cartridges.

You'll note that we recommend PostScript laser printers. PostScript ensures the best results with fonts and with graphics, especially at high resolution, and especially with Macs. Fortunately, most laser printers these days do use PostScript, and their prices have come down considerably in the past few years.

 ## What are the specifications I should look for when choosing a printer?

Once you've decided what type and resolution of printer is right for you, it's time to compare speed and features. Printer speed is measured in pages per minute (ppm). Laser printers range from 4 to 20 ppm, while ink-jet printers are much slower. Pages per minute is a bit misleading; just because the printer claims to print 8 ppm doesn't mean that you will see eight pages after 60 seconds. Ratings are based on the fastest possible print job: a simple text document with no graphics, and nothing else slowing the printer down. A printer that is physically capable of moving eight pages from paper tray to output tray each minute may actually print half that many pages every 60 seconds in practice.

If printing envelopes is part of what you do, or if you need to print on labels, transparencies, or card stock, make sure the printer you're considering can do it. Some printers have envelope feeder attachments that you can add, for a cost of $50–$150. Other printers can accommodate envelopes without an attachment. Because laser printers often use curved paper paths, thick or sticky stock can be a problem unless the printer is designed to work with it. Try to test the printer you're considering with unusual paper, even if the salesperson or the specifications assure you that the printer will work with your paper.

Another aspect of printer shopping that warrants hands-on experience is print quality. Even if the printers you're considering offer the same resolution, the quality of their images can vary greatly. In addition to printing a page full of text, try printing one with a large area of black on it. And if you're buying a color printer, print a continuous tone image like a photograph. A good printer will reproduce black and colored areas faithfully, while a lesser printer's blacks will look washed out, or gray.

CONNECTING AND CONFIGURING PRINTERS

How do I connect a printer directly to my Mac?

You can connect an ink-jet printer to your Mac via a serial or USB cable and port. Most ink-jet printers include the cable you need. If you are not sure that the cable is included, ask for a Mac serial cable with a DB-9 connector, or a USB cable. Macs do use different serial connectors than PCs do, but all USB cables are the same.

How do I connect a printer to a network?

There are two ways to make a physical connection between printer and network, as follows:

● LocalTalk is the networking technology built into older Macs. With LocalTalk connectors on each Mac and printer on the network, you can use twisted-pair phone wire to complete the connection. To use LocalTalk with a printer, you'll need to purchase a connector for it. If your Mac or Macs aren't already using LocalTalk, each one will also need a LocalTalk connector. Keep in mind that, though it is cheap, LocalTalk is very slow. However, it is faster than a plain old serial connection. Use LocalTalk if you're on a budget and only have a couple of devices to network.

● Ethernet can connect almost every printer in an office. Many office-grade printers have built-in Ethernet ports, or support cards that add it. In most cases, you'll use Ethernet with a printer on a network that is already established. Ethernet is much faster than LocalTalk and will allow you to add PCs to your network (assuming you have the proper software).

No current Mac includes LocalTalk connectors. If you have an iMac, iBook, or a G3 or G4 Power Mac, you must connect to an Ethernet network or use a local USB printer.

? I have a LocalTalk laser printer, but all of the Macs in our office use Ethernet. Can I add the printer to the network?

Farallon makes a hardware bridge that allows you to use a LocalTalk printer on an Ethernet network. This small box, about the size of a modem, has both a LocalTalk cable to connect to the printer and an RJ-45 jack for an Ethernet cable. Though a bridge-equipped LocalTalk printer is not as fast as standard Ethernet, this method eliminates the need for a host Mac.

? How do I change the name of my networked printer?

Networked printers are identified in the Chooser by unique names. When you get a printer, it's usually named by manufacturer and model. Most folks like to give their printers a more original name, whether for the sake of convenience (for example, Downstairs Printer is a more descriptive name than LaserWriter IIg) or as a diversion (we know an office where all of the printers are named after famous dogs—Snoopy, Astro, Ren, and so on).

To change the name of an Apple printer as it appears on the network, you'll need a copy of the Apple Printer Utility (APU). This tool should not be confused with the Desktop Printer Utility that comes with Mac OS. To get APU, you'll need to make a trip to Apple's support Web site at http://download.info.apple.com/Apple_Support_Area/ Apple_Software_Updates/English-North_American/Macintosh/ Printing/LaserWriter/. Load the latest version of APU (version 2.2 at this writing). To change your printer's name, follow these steps:

1. Open the Apple Printer Utility.

2. Double-click the name of the printer whose name you want to change. If your network has zones, locate the correct zone and double-click the printer.

3. When the printer window appears, open the printer by clicking the triangle next to Name, to open it.

4. Type the new name in the field provided, as shown in Figure 6-1, and close the window.

5. Click Save to confirm your choice. APU will tell the printer its new name.

If you have a non-Apple printer, it may have come with utility software that will allow you to change the printer's network name. In that case, you don't need Apple Printer Utility.

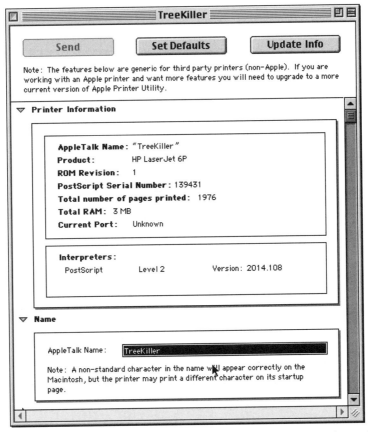

Figure 6-1 Rename the printer by clicking the Name triangle and typing the new name in the field that appears

 Note: *If you have desktop printer icons that are associated with your printer under its old name, you will need to create a new desktop printer or configure the existing one to work with the renamed printer. For more information about desktop printers, see the next section.*

 ### How can I change the name of my desktop printer?

If you're using desktop printing, you can rename the printer icon that appears on your desktop just as you would any file or folder in the Finder. Changing the icon's name does not change the network name of the printer. So go ahead, call your desktop printer Bluto, or Marketing Madness. No one else will be the wiser.

PRINTING

 ### What software do I need to install before printing?

In most cases, the Mac OS includes everything you'll need to print successfully. The exceptions to this rule occur when you use a printer that requires you to use vendor-supplied driver software. Hewlett-Packard, for example, supplies custom driver software for many of its printers. So does Epson. Often, you can print with the Mac OS printer software, but you may not be able to take advantage of special printer features supported by the custom driver.

If your printer came with driver software of its own, read the documentation before installing it. It's also a good idea to make sure that the driver software is compatible with the version of Mac OS you're using. If you're not sure, contact the printer vendor's tech support folks for help or check their Web site.

I have an older PostScript printer. Would I benefit from upgrading my LaserWriter software?

Yes. If you are using Mac OS 8 or later, you already have LaserWriter 8.4 (or later) installed. If not, you can find the upgrade on Apple's Software Updates Web site (http://www.info.apple.com/swupdates/). If you're not sure what printer software you're using, choose Print from the File menu and look for the version number at the upper-right corner of the resulting dialog box.

LaserWriter 8 was introduced primarily to support PostScript Level 2, a new version of PostScript that is included with today's PostScript printers. But older Level 1 printers can also benefit from LaserWriter 8, especially the 8.4 version, which significantly upgraded the features and look of Mac OS printing software.

What is desktop printing?

With desktop printing, you can drag documents you want to print to an icon on your desktop. Each printer you use (if you have access to more than one) can have its own icon on the desktop, and you can assign an icon for special printer configurations, such as printing envelopes, or printing in color. To activate a desktop printer, follow these steps:

1. Turn on your printer.

2. Select Chooser from the Apple menu.

3. In the left pane, click the appropriate printer driver icon. There may be several. If you're using a laser printer, the right choice is almost always LaserWriter 8. If you're not using a laser printer, or if yours came with its own driver software, pick the driver that matches the printer you've got.

4. Choose your printer in the right pane of the window (shown in Figure 6-2). If you're using a serial printer (one that's connected directly to your Mac), you may have to choose the serial port, rather than a named printer. In that case, you'll see labeled icons for each serial port on your Mac (usually, Printer and Modem). Click the one that corresponds to your connection to the printer.

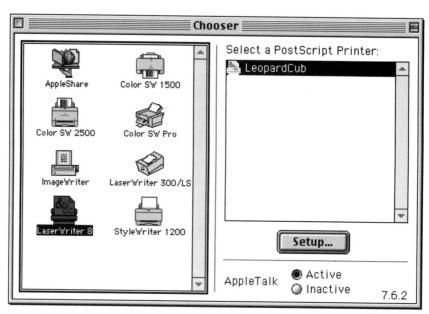

Figure 6-2   Select a printer in the Chooser

5. If you're using a serial printer, you're done. Close the Chooser. If it's a network printer, click the Setup button.

6. Click Auto Setup. The LaserWriter driver will search for a Printer Page Description file (PPD) that matches your printer. If it doesn't find a PPD that matches your printer exactly, Setup will present you a list of PPDs to choose from. If you don't see one that sort of matches your printer (one from the same manufacturer, for example), choose Generic.

7. Close the Setup window. A new printer icon will appear on your desktop, as shown here:

To use the desktop printer, drag a document onto the icon. The application that created the file will open and a print dialog box will appear. When you've clicked OK, the printing job proceeds, and the application quits.

How can I keep an eye on the progress of my print job when using desktop printing?

Once you have sent a print job or jobs to the printer, you can view their progress, change their order, or cancel them. Just double-click the desktop printer icon (you can tell that a job is printing because a page icon appears on top of the active desktop printer icon). The desktop printer window opens (with the printer name in the title bar), showing all of the print jobs that are currently queued for printing, as shown in Figure 6-3. Click an item to select it. The buttons at the top of the window light up, and you can pause, start, schedule, or trash the print job. Your print job appears in the window just below the buttons, and any other jobs you have queued wait their turn in the pane below.

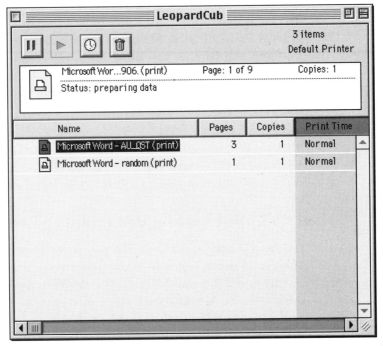

Figure 6-3   Click a document in the desktop printer window to make changes to its queuing

Can I kill a desktop print job once I've sent it to the printer?

Yes. Click a document in the print queue and then click the Trash button. The print job disappears from the list. If you just want to delay the job, leaving it in the desktop printer window, click the Pause button. The print job moves to the lower portion of the window.

Can I change the order in which jobs print, or change their timing?

To change the order of print jobs, drag a document within the desktop printer window, moving it above or below other jobs on the list. You can't move the currently printing job unless you stop it first. Select it and click the Pause button to do so.

To have a document print at a later time, click it, and then click the Timer button and set a print time.

Can I print to a different printer than I normally do?

To change printers, you must pick a new printer before you choose Print in an application. You can create as many desktop printers as you like, or simply choose to use a different printer in the Chooser, assuming that the new printer is on and available on the network, or connected directly to your computer.

   Tip: *When you choose Print, the name of the printer for your job will appear at the top of the dialog box. If you want to choose a different printer, click Cancel and go to the Chooser.*

How do I print several documents at once?

In the Finder, select the files you want to print (click one; then hold down the SHIFT key and click the rest to select them) and drag the group to the desktop printer icon. If the files were all created with the same application, it will open and present one print dialog box. If your files were created by different applications, each one will present its own print dialog box. The rest of the files will then be queued and printed in turn.

Can I print my Mac's screen?

To print the screen or a part of it, you must first take a picture of it. You can do this with a keyboard shortcut in the Finder, or with a screen capture tool, such as Snapz Pro or Capture, that lets you customize the picture. You can then print the resulting file as you would any document.

To take a picture of the screen, press COMMAND+SHIFT+3. The Mac takes a picture and creates a PICT file, called Picture 1 (or Picture 2, Picture 3, and so on, depending on how many you have already created), on your hard disk. To take a picture of part of the screen, press COMMAND+SHIFT+4. Press the mouse button and drag the cross-shaped cursor to select a portion of the screen. When you release the mouse button, the Mac snaps the picture and creates a PICT file. You can open the screen pictures in SimpleText (just double-click the file) or print it immediately by dragging it to the desktop printer (see "What is desktop printing?," earlier in this section, for more information on desktop printing).

You can also print the contents of a Finder window by making the window active and choosing Print Window.

Why does the Page Setup dialog box look different in various applications?

Not only can the Page Setup dialog box, where you can specify parameters such as paper size, page orientation, and PostScript options, look different from one application to another, but so can the Print dialog box itself. Software developers often add panels to the Print and Page Setup dialog boxes that accommodate special features in the software. Adobe Photoshop, for example, includes options in its Page Setup dialog box, shown in Figure 6-4, that address features particular to printing graphics. To find out if an application has special printing options, follow these steps:

1. Choose Page Setup from the File menu (some programs call it Document Setup).

2. Click the pop-up menu near the top of the window, usually labeled Page Attributes.

3. Choose the application's name from the menu.

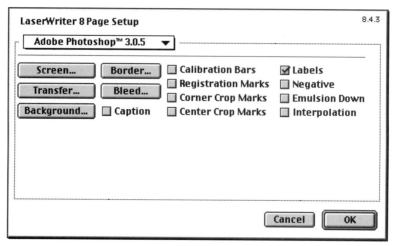

Figure 6-4 Photoshop's Page Setup options

Can I print a document that has been saved as a PostScript file?

The PostScript computer language, which is used to print documents to a PostScript laser printer, describes a document in computer code. When a document is printed from the creating application, it is converted to PostScript and then sent to the printer, which interprets the PostScript code and creates the printed page.

Sometimes, it's helpful to save the document as a PostScript file, either for transfer to another location, or for printing from a machine that does not contain the application that created the file. To save a file as PostScript, follow these steps:

1. With the file you want to save open, choose Print from the File menu.

2. From the destination pop-up menu, choose File.

3. Choose printer options as you normally would.

4. Click Print.

5. You will be asked to name the PostScript file. The default name is *filename*.ps. Click Save. The printer driver spools the file to disk, just as if it were being printed.

6. Open the Apple Printer Utility.

7. Double-click the printer you want to use.

8. Choose Utilities | Send PostScript File.

9. Locate the file you want to print and click Send, or click Add if you want to print several files. When you've chosen all of the files you want to print, click Send. The PostScript files will be queued for printing.

Tip: *You can use Adobe's Downloader or the shareware utility DropPS to print a PostScript file. The advantage to DropPS is that you can drag and drop your PostScript file onto its icon to print it.*

Can I print using TCP/IP?

TCP/IP is the *protocol*, or language, of the Internet. Many printers in corporate environments now use TCP/IP to communicate with computers on the network. To make that possible, printers must be connected to the network by Ethernet, and they must support TCP/IP (that is, they must be able to have a numeric IP address of their own). Apple printers that support TCP/IP include the LaserWriter 8500, 16/600 PS, 12/640 PS, and Color LaserWriter 12/600 PS. Many other printers support TCP/IP. Check your printer's documentation to see if yours does.

To print via TCP/IP from a Mac, you must be using LaserWriter 8.5.1 or later, included with Mac OS 8.1.

To configure your Mac for TCP/IP printing, follow these steps:

1. Open the Desktop Printer Utility application. You'll find it in the Apple Extras folder that was installed with Mac OS. If it's not there, search for it on the Mac OS CD, and copy it to your hard drive.

2. Select Printer (LPR), as shown in Figure 6-5, and click OK.

3. In the Printer Page Description (PPD) pane, click Change and select your printer's PPD.

4. In the Internet Printer pane, click Change.

5. Enter the IP address of your printer, and the queue name, if there is one.

Figure 6-5 The Desktop Printer Utility lets you configure printers, including those that support TCP/IP

6. Click the Verify button to locate the printer on the network.

7. Click OK to close the window.

8. Click Save, and name the new desktop printer. Quit Desktop Printer Utility. You're ready to print.

PRINTING PROBLEMS

 How can I troubleshoot general printing problems?

Before you panic, or even begin troubleshooting, try a little repetition. If you're using PrintMonitor or desktop printing, remove the old document from the print queue and print the file again. Also, try turning the printer off and then on again, or pressing the Reset button, if your printer has one. If the problem remains, it's time to search for the cause.

Like most troubleshooting tasks, finding printing problems is a matter of going through the process step by step, eliminating one potential cause after another until you find the culprit. When you describe the problem, be as specific as you can: it won't print is not specific. I can't find the printer in the Chooser is specific.

I'm getting an error that says the printer can't be found. Now what?

If you get an error message telling you that the Mac can't find the printer, chances are that something's wrong with the network, or with the printer itself. If you don't print very often, it's possible that your Mac's printer setup is outdated. If you've recently installed a new version of Mac OS, everything may be fine: simply set print options for the first time, as described earlier in this chapter. If you're not using a networked printer, check your cabling, and check that the port selected in the Chooser matches the cable plugged into your Mac.

To determine where the problem lies in network situations, narrow down the list of suspects, as follows:

1. Open the Chooser from the Apple menu and click the appropriate printer icon. If you don't see the icon for your printer (or the LaserWriter 8 icon, for most laser printers), close the Chooser and check the Extensions folder for the printer driver you need. If you don't find it there, look in the Extensions (Disabled) folder. If you are still unable to find the file, reinstall printer software from the Mac OS CD.

2. If the driver is present and selected, but the printer doesn't appear in the right pane of the Chooser, check to see that AppleTalk is active. The Active radio button should be selected. If you have to reactivate AppleTalk, you may need to restart the computer to complete the process.

3. If AppleTalk is active and no printer appears, open the AppleTalk control panel (the Network control panel under older versions of Mac OS) and check to see that the network setup you're using is correct. If you print over an Ethernet network, the selected item on the AppleTalk menu should say Ethernet, as shown in the following illustration. Otherwise, you'll probably see Printer, Modem, or Serial port, depending on your configuration. In any case, make sure that the AppleTalk choice matches your network.

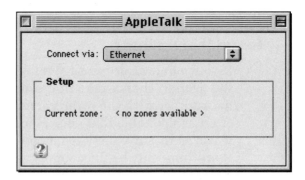

4. Is the printer or network cable plugged in? If you're using an Ethernet network, check to see that the green light on the network adapter in your computer is lit.

5. Is the printer turned on? Is the network cable or serial cable plugged in? Reconnect cables if you're unsure.

6. Is the printer's green Printer Ready light on (or is there a yellow or flashing light indicating some kind of problem? Some printers include an LCD display with information about the printer's status. If the printer says Ready or something similar, the problem lies elsewhere. Messages like Offline, or Not Ready, or a blinking yellow warning light indicate a problem with the printer itself. Try resetting the printer.

Everything looks okay on my network, but I still can't find my LocalTalk printer in the Chooser. What else should I check?

Your network may not be properly *terminated*. A network of LocalTalk devices that is daisy-chained—one device connected to a second device, then a third, and so on—should have a terminating resistor on the first and last connectors in the network. LocalTalk resistors fit in the empty slot on a LocalTalk connector.

After adding resistors on each end of the daisy-chain, open the Chooser and click the appropriate printer driver. If the printer still doesn't appear, remove one and then the other resistor, experimenting with the network until you can see your printer in the Chooser.

My serial printer is connected correctly, but I can't print. I often get the error "serial port in use." What should I do?

If your printer shares a serial port with a modem or other device, or even if you need to change the serial port you use to print on occasion, you are likely to experience serial port problems. One quick way to address the problem is to shut down your Mac, reconnect the serial cable, and attempt to print again after checking the status of the serial port in the Chooser. If problems persist, try resetting the Mac's parameter RAM. This process is usually called "zapping the PRAM." Like restarting the Mac, which clears the system's main block of memory, zapping the PRAM resets a section of memory that controls the operations of the Mac's CPU and motherboard.

To zap the PRAM, press COMMAND+OPTION+PR as your Mac starts up. Keep holding them down until your Mac bongs its startup chime a second time.

A specific document will not print, even though the network, software, printer, and computer all seem to be working properly. What's wrong?

Some printer errors become apparent when a warning icon appears on top of the desktop printer icon, or when a dialog box indicates a printer error. Some dialog boxes are specific (for example, paper jam, insufficient memory, or PostScript error) and some are not. Even error dialog boxes that tell you the source of the error don't always provide the help you need. Once again, you may need to do some sleuthing to solve the problem. If you can't get a document to print, follow these steps:

1. Remove the problem document from the print queue by opening the desktop printer window and trashing the file. Then, try printing again.

2. Change the current PPD file to Generic, in the Chooser. If printing is successful, you may be able to solve the problem completely by replacing the PPD for your printer with a fresh copy.

3. If the problem persists, reinitialize the printer and try printing again.

4. Print the document one page at a time. You may be able to isolate a problem font or graphic if the printer refuses to print a certain page. Next, try printing a different document, preferably a simpler one.

5. Turn off background printing. To do this, choose Print, and then select Background Printing from the options pop-up menu, near the top of the dialog box. Click Foreground (no spool file). The Mac will try to print, displaying a status dialog box in the foreground (and interrupting other tasks) instead of sending the file to a desktop printer. Read the status messages as they appear to get an indication of when the print job runs into problems.

6. It's possible that the problem lies with the printer driver software. Using the Mac OS CD, reinstall the software related to printing. Don't pick and choose files at this point, just reinstall everything that relates to printing (except QuickDraw GX, which has no effect unless GX is your chosen printer driver). If you use a non-Apple printer with its own software, reinstall that, too. Restart the Mac and print again, after checking to be sure that the right printer driver is active and that you've chosen the right PPD file for your printer.

All of a sudden, the pages I print look faded or blotchy. What's wrong?

Your problem is with the ink or toner cartridge. But before you replace it, try a less drastic step. If you're using an ink-jet printer, remove the cartridge and try cleaning the exposed portion with a cotton swab to remove excess ink. If you have a laser printer, remove the toner cartridge and carry it carefully to a sink or large trash can (spilled toner is very difficult to clean up). Gently shake or roll the cartridge from side to side to redistribute the toner powder inside.

Many ink-jet printers have a "blast" or "clean" option that shoots ink through the toner cartridge to dislodge built-up gunk. Read your printer's documentation for more information.

If the problems persist, replace the cartridge. If the cartridge vendor allows you to return spent cartridges for recycling, as Apple does, do so using the cartridge's original packaging.

Chapter 7

Imaging and Input Devices

Answer Topics!

Other Peripherals @ a Glance

- **Keyboards** explains the care and feeding of keyboards.

- **Mice** describes the different kinds of pointing devices, and how to care for a mouse.

- **Scanners** explains how to choose and use a scanner.

- **Digital Cameras** describes cameras that are available, and how to work with them.

- **USB Peripherals** defines USB, and provides details about available hardware.

KEYBOARDS

 Can I use any kind of keyboard with my Mac?

Macs use keyboards with one of two types of connectors: USB (Universal Serial Bus) or ADB (Apple Desktop Bus). All Macs produced between 1987 and 1997 used ADB, while current ones, along with some PCs, use USB. If you have an ADB Mac, you won't be able to use any PC-compatible keyboards with it.

You can replace your Mac's keyboard, either because you don't like yours or because of damage. Early ADB Macs included small keyboards that didn't have the full complement of keys. In those days, you could opt for a 101-key keyboard, sometimes called the Enterprise or "Battleship Saratoga" keyboard because of its resemblance to the expansive deck of an aircraft carrier. In modern times, Apple and clone makers have found ways to squeeze a full set of keys (number pad, function keys, and all) onto smaller keyboards. You can buy these from most computer dealers, and via mail order.

USB keyboards are readily available, too, and are welcomed by owners of all current Mac models.

 What's an ergonomic keyboard?

In an attempt to give users the flexibility to type in a variety of positions, Apple developed an ergonomic keyboard. The ergo keyboard comes in three connected pieces—left, right, and number pad—that can be positioned independently to ease the strain of typing.

 I've spilled liquid on my keyboard. How should I clean it?

It's relatively easy to take apart and clean a keyboard. Follow these steps:

1. Shut down the Mac and disconnect the keyboard from it.

2. Place the keyboard on a clean surface, preferably away from the computer.

3. Use a damp sponge to wipe the exterior of the keyboard.

4. Turn the keyboard over and use a screwdriver to remove the screws that hold the frame together.

5. Use a hair dryer to dry the keyboard.

6. If you spilled something sticky onto the keyboard, use a damp (but not wet) cloth to wipe up liquid that remains between the keys.

7. Dry the keyboard again, with a cloth, and let it dry for several hours before you put it back together.

If your keyboard has truly been inundated by sticky liquid, extreme measures are called for. Remove the circuit board and soak it in a bath of distilled water for a couple of hours. Thoroughly dry the keyboard with a hair dryer set on cool or warm—a hot dryer held too close to the keyboard components could melt them.

Can I use a standard keyboard with a PowerBook or iBook?

Yes. Most PowerBooks have an ADB port on the back. Just shut down the PowerBook and connect the keyboard. If your PowerBook has a USB port, you'll need a USB keyboard, and you need not shut the Mac down to add the keyboard. iBooks and PowerBook G3s have USB ports.

Tip: *You can use both a standard keyboard and mouse with your PowerBook by connecting the keyboard to the ADB or USB port, and the mouse to the keyboard. If you just want to use a standard mouse, connect it directly to the PowerBook's ADB or USB port.*

MICE

Is it true that Bill Gates stole the idea of a computer mouse from Apple?

Much as we would like to spread the rumor that Microsoft did Apple wrong, we can't...at least, not in this particular case. Computer mice first made their appearance in prototype machines at the Xerox PARC facility in the late 1970s. Apple

was the first company to popularize the mouse when it introduced the Lisa in 1983 (ten years ago you had to pay extra for a PC mouse and software to run it).

Why doesn't the Mac mouse have two buttons, like a PC mouse? Put another way, am I missing something because I only have one button on my mouse?

The short answer is that the Mac operating system (and thus the software that runs on the Mac) doesn't support a two-button arrangement, by default. On an IBM-compatible PC running Windows, the second mouse button is usually used to bring up a menu, right where you click. That menu is context-sensitive: it changes with each application and task you use it for. Would it be nice if the Macs included and supported a two-button mouse? Yes, we think so, but you do get most of the two-button functionality with contextual menus. Just hold down the CONTROL key when you click, and it's like having a second mouse button. You'll be able to use contextual menus in the Finder and in most major applications. And, as the name implies, the items on those contextual menus vary, depending upon what you're doing. Click on a file, and you'll find commands for modifying or moving it. The same goes for folders. It even works on the desktop. If you're in Excel, control-clicking on a cell allows you to edit it.

You can also buy multibutton mice for your Mac from vendors like Kensington and Logitech. We know one Mac power user whose mouse has four buttons.

Can I buy alternatives to the mouse that came with my Mac?

There are several kinds of mice on the market. Kensington, Logitech, Datadesk, and others make mice that suit a variety of mousing preferences. You can mouse with a trackball under your palm, or with a wireless pointer. Some mice are shaped to fit your hand, while others are designed to glide smoothly on any surface. Before you buy an alternative mouse, spend some time using it. Not every mouse is right for every hand.

> **Tip:** *When choosing a replacement mouse, make sure that it is compatible with your Mac. Don't buy an ADB mouse for a USB Mac, or vice versa. If you're not sure what you have, take a look at the ports on the side or back of the Mac. USB ports are small and flat. You'll find them on the iMac, iBook, blue-and-white Power Mac G3, Power Mac G4, and some G3 PowerBooks. An ADB port is round, with several small pinholes. You'll find ADB ports on older Macs.*

 ### I don't like the mouse that came with my iMac. What's the cheapest way to replace it?

iMac™

Replacement mice can cost $40 or more. If that seems high to you, and you have an iMac or other Mac that came with a "hockey puck" mouse, check out the Contour Designs (www.contourdesign.com) UniTrap mouse cover. It looks like a standard desktop mouse, but fits over the iMac's round mouse. The shell comes in a choice of iMac colors.

 ### My mouse seems to move sluggishly. What's wrong?

Chances are that your mouse needs cleaning. A mouse's moving parts are susceptible to dirt and dust, which can clog up the works.

To clean the mouse, follow these steps:

1. Disconnect the mouse from your Mac or keyboard.
2. Turn the mouse upside down on your desk or table.
3. Turn the plastic ring that sits around the mouse ball until you can remove the ring from the mouse.
4. Place your hand over the mouse ball, and turn the mouse over, allowing the ball to fall into your hand.
5. Pour some rubbing alcohol onto a lint-free cloth, and clean the mouse ball with the cloth.
6. Blow the dirt and dust out of the mouse itself.
7. Clean the rollers and innards with a Q-tip swab dipped in alcohol. Rollers are notorious for accumulating and hiding gunk.
8. Replace the mouse ball and ring.

SCANNERS

 ## Is it worth the cost to buy a scanner?

When scanners first became available, they were expensive, slow, and not very practical for anyone but desktop publishing professionals. Today, they're inexpensive and much easier to use. Scanners are also more useful to regular folks, today, because of the World Wide Web. With scanner in hand, you can add photos and artwork to your Web home page with ease.

Scanner prices begin at around $150 and reach into the thousands. With a basic scanner, you can scan images at 300 dots per inch and use the included software to edit the image before you add it to your Web page or print publication. Spend a little more and you can up the resolution to 600 dpi and scan text with optical character recognition (OCR). Professional scanners provide higher resolution, as well as sophisticated tools for manipulating images.

 ## What kinds of scanners can I use with my Mac?

Good news. You have a lot to choose from. Most of the scanners on the market today will work with Macs. First of all, most scanners use SCSI or USB, making them compatible with all Macs. Because the Mac is so important to graphics and desktop publishing professionals, most scanner vendors have made sure that their products include Mac software.

Scanners come in two major formats—flatbed and sheet-fed. To use a flatbed scanner, just place your original image on the glass and start your scan. Flatbeds are versatile, because they allow you to scan images of various sizes and don't require you to destroy an original just to put it through the scanning process. Of course, a full-sized flatbed scanner does take more than its share of desk space.

Sheet-fed scanners are usually much smaller than flatbeds. You insert the original artwork into a slot, and the scanner moves it through the mechanism. You can use a sheet-fed scanner in any situation where space is at a premium, and when you don't need the full image area of a flatbed.

What features should I look for in a scanner?

Aside from the scanner's format (flatbed versus sheet-fed), the primary features you should look for when shopping for a scanner have to do with image quality. That's what separates a consumer scanner from a professional one.

First and foremost, look for a scanner with good resolution. We use the term *good* rather than *high* here, because not everyone needs a truly high-resolution scanner, especially if your goal is to scan images for your Web site or other onscreen purposes. No computer screen can approach the resolution of a typeset page. Images on the Web need not be scanned at resolutions above 150 dots per inch, while most laser printers start at 300 dots per inch, moving rapidly up from there. The good news is that most scanners, even low-end ones, can scan at 300 dots per inch.

Scanner resolution is sometimes expressed with multiple numbers, for example 300×600. That means that even though the scanner engine can scan 600 dpi, the machine's optics actually scan 300 dots. In short, look at the first number when comparing scanner resolution.

The other basic measure of scanner quality is bit-depth. Color on a computer screen is measured in bits per pixel. The more bits available, the more distinct colors the screen or page can display. Most low-end scanners support 24 bits per pixel, meaning that they can scan 16.7 million colors. Better scanners, on the other hand, can support 30, 32, or even 36 bits per pixel. Once again, the bit-depth of your home scanner is more than enough to accurately reflect images you intend to display on a Web page, or print on a 300 dpi color printer.

A final important scanner feature is the bundled software. At minimum, your scanner will include an application that performs scans and allows you to set scanning preferences. Some scanners include image-editing software or a plug-in that allows you to use Adobe Photoshop to edit your scans (or both). Many scanners also include OCR software. Some vendors price their products so that you can get a better

software bundle if you're willing to pay a few dollars more for a basic scanner. If you're planning to use the scanner with multiple computers, look for one that includes software for both Mac and Windows on the same CD.

What resolution should I use when scanning?

Resolution should vary based on how your document will be used. If, for example, you're scanning a photo for a Web page, resolution can (and should) be fairly low. First of all, as we mentioned earlier, the computer screen can't display images at high resolution. In addition, file sizes of high-resolution images are larger and, therefore, take longer to download. On the other end of the scale, images to be printed and reproduced in a magazine or other high-quality document should be scanned at the highest resolution your output device (printer or imagesetter) can handle. Table 7-1 provides some guidelines for choosing scanning resolution.

How should I prepare scanned photographs for the Web?

When you scan an image, it is usually saved as a TIFF file. To make the image visible to viewers of your Web site, you'll need to translate the file into a GIF or JPEG file. Several shareware utilities, including GraphicConverter and GIFfer, will convert graphics files to GIF or JPEG format. So will commercial programs, such as Photoshop and PhotoDeluxe.

Document Type	Resolution
Web page graphic	75–150 dpi
Text for OCR	300 dpi
Line art for printing	300 dpi
Photographs/halftones for printing	Same as the resolution of your printer or imagesetter

Table 7-1 Choose the Correct Resolution for Your Scanned Documents

You can also use these tools to compress GIF images for the Web and add a transparent background to the image, making it look crisper onscreen.

I've just added a scanner to my SCSI chain. Now nothing on the chain works. What's wrong?

Scanners, like storage devices, must follow the rules of SCSI. Scanners usually work best when they are the last device on your SCSI chain, but some want to be first. If your scanner has only one SCSI port, you may *have* to make it the last device on the chain. For more details on SCSI troubleshooting, see Chapter 5.

My Mac is short on memory, and the software for my new scanner includes lots of extensions that bloat my system. What can I do?

You could bump up virtual memory in the Memory control panel, or you could do a little trimming. In addition to the software that runs the scanner itself, many bundled packages also include a number of extensions that support the scanning process and graphics display. If you don't already use these extensions, they will be installed for you when you set up your scanner. Unless you use your scanner every day, chances are that you can do without this software most of the time. If you want to disable some scanner software to save memory, you can do so with Extensions Manager.

To create a custom set of extensions for scanning, follow these steps:

1. With your normal set of extensions running, open the Extensions Manager control panel.
2. Click Duplicate Set.
3. Name the new set "Scanner set," or something similar. Note the name of the extensions set, shown at the top of the window.
4. Install the software that came with your scanner. You will probably be asked to restart the Mac.

5. When the Mac has successfully restarted, open Extensions Manager.

6. From the pull-down list at the top of the window, choose the set of extensions you were using before you installed the scanner software.

7. When you're ready to use your scanner, return to Extensions Manager, choose the scanner set, and restart your Mac with the scanner connected.

DIGITAL CAMERAS

 Why would I want a digital camera when I already have a film camera?

Most people usually don't choose digital cameras for their photographic quality or features. Though digital cameras have improved considerably since they became available a few years ago, their primary benefit, especially for amateur photographers, is the ease with which you can use them to create images that will eventually find their way into your computer.

What should I look for in a digital camera?

Digital cameras store their images in memory or on a storage card. Either way, you want as much storage as you can get. Storage is measured by the number of pictures you can store simultaneously. Though they're significantly more expensive, cameras that support storage cards are the way to go. Memory-based units are limited, whereas you can buy additional storage cards.

Many digital cameras use an LCD display as a viewfinder, though it takes a toll on battery life. Look for an LCD display that is bright and large. Look through the displays of several cameras as you move them around. Is the motion jerky? Do the images appear clear?

Photographic features are another important consideration in choosing a camera. If you're used to 35-millimeter outfits, with detachable lenses and variable aperture settings, you'll

be disappointed with the low end of the digital camera spectrum. Most are more like Instamatics. However, even without replaceable lenses, most decent digital cameras do allow you to zoom in on your subject, and some have auto-focus and macro features. Macros (that is, recorded instructions, not the long lenses that you find in traditional photographic equipment) allow you to save a set of photographic settings for future use.

My digital camera goes through batteries like there's no tomorrow. Is there a problem with the camera?

Battery-hungry cameras aren't uncommon. Digital photography and the LCD displays found on many cameras use lots of power and can suck the life out of many kinds of batteries. Aside from using an AC adapter when you can (especially when you're downloading your images to the Mac), try using rechargeable NiMH or Lithium batteries.

I have trouble getting my Mac and digital camera to communicate. What can I do to troubleshoot?

Like SCSI, digital cameras and their connectors can be temperamental. First, read your camera's instructions carefully. You may find that it's necessary to disable AppleTalk or some other software to get the camera and computer to talk to one another. If the documentation doesn't offer specific help, try simplifying your system by disabling several extensions (you can use Casady & Greene's Conflict Catcher to locate software conflicts) before trying to connect the camera.

Cameras use the serial port (a source of some flakiness) to connect to your Mac. Try restarting your Mac and plugging the camera's cable into the port while you're powered down. Another variation on this tactic is to make the connection as we just described, but delay turning the camera on until you've launched the software that you'll use to download your images.

You can avoid the problem altogether by getting a card reader for you camera. Card readers accept the PC card from the camera, and connect to your USB Mac. Like all USB

devices, card readers are hot-swappable, and a lot less flaky than serial connections.

In short, when troubleshooting digital cameras, try everything you can think of. Something unexpected just might work.

USB PERIPHERALS

 ### What is USB?

Universal Serial Bus (USB) was developed by Intel and others looking for a flexible replacement for serial connectors, and one that could be standardized and used in a variety of devices. USB can be used for everything from floppy drives to keyboards to high-speed telecommunications devices.

 ### Does my Mac support USB?

All current Macs include USB ports. Power Macs and PowerBooks released in 1998 or earlier do not.

 ### Can I use ADB peripherals with my iMac?

iMac™

The only way to use an ADB peripheral with an iMac or other USB Mac is to get an ADB-USB adapter. Griffin Technology, sells an ADB-to-USB adapter (dubbed "iMate") to make the connection.

 ### What USB peripherals are available?

You'll find keyboards, mice, digital cameras, removable media drives (Zip, SuperDisk, and floppy), recordable CD-ROM drives, network adapters, and printers readily available for all USB Macs.

 ### There's only one available USB port on my first-generation iMac. Can I connect more than one device?

iMac™

Well, actually, you have two USB ports available to you. In addition to the port on the iMac, there are two on the keyboard: one for the mouse and one that's available for any compatible USB device.

Unlike SCSI or LocalTalk, USB doesn't use a daisy-chain arrangement to connect several devices to the same computer. Like an Ethernet network, you connect USB devices to a *hub*—a box with a number of ports—that then connects to the host computer.

USB hubs usually offer four to seven ports and cost about $100. Vendors include Entrega, Macally, Peracom, and Phillips Electronics.

Apple's newest iMacs, introduced in October 1999, allow you to connect twice the USB devices. Each of the two USB ports is on a separate USB channel, making the two completely independent, and allowing you to connect up to 127 USB devices per channel.

Chapter 8

Video and Display

Answer Topics!

Video and Display @ a Glance

- **Video Basics** includes definitions and explanations of important display-related terminology.

- **Choosing a Monitor** shows how to select and rate a monitor.

- **Using Monitors** provides tips and advice for working successfully with monitors.

- **Monitor Troubleshooting** provides suggestions for dealing with monitor problems.

VIDEO BASICS

 ## What is resolution?

The size of a computer's display is measured in pixels. The greater the number of pixels displayed onscreen, the higher the display's *resolution* is said to be. Resolution is expressed with a horizontal and a vertical pixel measurement—800 × 600, for example. The higher the resolution, the more detail the monitor can display. However, since pixels can vary in size, high-resolution images don't look the same on all monitors. On a large screen, high resolution displays a very sharp but small image. That means that you can see more of an image on a large monitor with high resolution than on the same monitor with low resolution. On the other hand, viewing an image at high resolution on a smaller monitor provides a very clear picture but shrinks the image or text so much that it may be hard to work with.

Today's Macs typically support 800 × 600 or 1,024 × 768 when using a 17-inch monitor. With more video RAM or a third-party video card, you can increase resolution to as much as 1,600 × 800 pixels. Small monitors and older PowerBooks frequently max out at 640 × 480 pixels.

 ## What is bit depth?

Besides resolution, the other important measure of the quality of a screen display is the *bit depth*, or color depth. Within the multimillion-color spectrum, a display can choose from a certain number of colors in creating its screen images. Color depth specifies the number of color choices available to a given pixel. Hence, color depth is measured in bits per pixel. A 24-bit display (very common, today) can choose from 16.7 million colors. By contrast, a 1-bit display chooses between two "colors," black and white.

When you choose a color depth to use onscreen, the options are expressed in terms of the number of colors the display has to choose from. The choices range from 256 colors or levels of gray up to "millions" for 24- or 32-bit displays. Thousands of colors is usually a good choice, unless you're a designer or desktop publisher doing high-quality scanning or

color separation work. Table 8-1 shows the relationship of bit depth to onscreen color display, and how different color settings appear on the Mac.

 Note: *Some games, especially older ones, require that your monitor be set to 256 colors, to minimize the performance hit your Mac takes when redrawing the screen. Action games require a lot of screen redrawing, and low bit depth speeds up that process.*

What is VRAM?

Resolution is displayed on your monitor, but the bit depth of the pixels you see onscreen is determined by your Mac's video circuitry or video card. The video hardware of most Macs is part of the computer's motherboard, and the amount of RAM dedicated to video ranges from a paltry 128K to 1MB in older Macs. Today's Macs generally include 2 or 4MB of VRAM.

Bit Depth	Number of Possible Colors	Macs	Notes
1	2	Early compact Macs; most PowerBook 100 series	Black and white only
4	16	Some older PowerBooks	Grayscale only
8	256	Most non-Power Macs; older PowerBooks; Macs that use RAM to display video	True grayscale, or basic color
16	Thousands	Most early Power Macs; all Macs with 1MB or more video RAM; PowerBook 3400 and newer	General-purpose color
24	Millions	G3 and G4 Power Macs, G3 PowerBooks, AV Macs, and those that come with, or can be expanded to include, video cards	Desktop publishing, graphics
32	Millions (4,295,000)	Systems with graphics accelerators and maximum VRAM installed	Desktop video, computer modeling

Table 8-1 Macintosh Bit-Depth and Color Support

Some Mac II family systems used regular old RAM (the same pot of memory used to run the computer itself) to support video.

The amount of VRAM available to your Mac has a direct relationship with the number of colors your screen can display. With 6–8MB of VRAM available, most Macs support resolutions of 1,280 × 1,024 while displaying millions of colors. Since older PowerBooks and compact Macs can't usually accept VRAM upgrades, their bit depth is limited. Because these systems' built-in displays are not as good as that of an external monitor, there's little point in supplying beefy video circuitry. Apple's current generation of iMacs, iBooks, and PowerBooks do not support VRAM upgrades, but they don't really need them. The newest generation of iMacs, for example, include 8MB of VRAM.

Any Mac with an open slot for an expansion card (NuBus, PDS, or PCI) can be upgraded with a video card that contains 2, 4, or even 8MB of VRAM. Apple has taken to bundling video cards with high-end computers, rather than including lots of VRAM on the motherboard. That's because PCI slots support extremely fast video cards, and because video accelerator vendors like ATI have done a better job of speeding up screen redraw.

How much VRAM should I have?

Given what you already know about resolution and bit depth, deciding how much VRAM you need is just a matter of filling in a formula. First, decide on the highest resolution and bit depth you need. Don't skimp, though. If you underestimate your color and resolution needs, you may have to add more RAM later. For our purposes, let's assume that you want to use a maximum resolution of 1,200 × 1,024—a high number, but not in the resolution stratosphere. Now, assume that you'd like to view millions of colors. To do that, you'll need 32-bit video. Use the formula to determine the amount of VRAM you need:

Resolution width × resolution height × bit depth ÷ 8 = VRAM needed

Dividing the desired resolution and bit depth by 8 converts your result from bits to bytes. With the data in the preceding paragraph, we get the following equation:

$$(1,200 \times 1024 \times 32) \div 8 = 4,915,200 \text{ bytes}$$

That's almost 5MB of VRAM. Since VRAM is typically available in 1, 2, 4, and 8MB increments, you would need 8MB of VRAM to achieve the resolution and bit depth you want. Since current Macs offer 6–8MB of VRAM, you're not likely to need an upgrade. The good news for owners of older Macs is that if you can live without 32-bit color, or if 800 × 600 pixels provides enough resolution, the amount of VRAM that comes with most of even older Macs will do just fine.

I know that VGA and SVGA are PC display standards. How does that affect Mac users?

VGA (Video Graphics Array) and its higher-resolution successor, SVGA, are PC video standards that have come to the Mac. You can't have graphics on a PC without some form of VGA. These days, though the standard is generically referred to as VGA, most people really mean SVGA, which offers support for resolutions of 640 × 480 and above, and supports 16-bit color.

While non-VGA monitors were available to Mac users before Apple got on board the VGA bandwagon, all of today's Macs (all Power Macs and some older ones, in fact) support VGA or SVGA. To get SVGA support on an older Mac, you may have to add a video card. Current PowerBooks also support SVGA, thanks to the built-in VRAM.

CHOOSING A MONITOR

How big should my monitor be?

With monitor prices on a steady decline, you can probably afford much more monitor today than you could have a couple of years ago. Another piece of good news for monitor shoppers

is that most modern Macs can support large monitors. You won't need to buy a video card to use a 17-inch or even a 19-inch monitor.

So, why not get a great big monitor? The only reasons to steer clear of 19-inch and 21-inch displays are desk space and cost. You'll pay $400–$800 for a 19-inch display and $1,000–$1,500 for a 21-inch model. For most folks, a 17-inch monitor strikes a good balance between frugality and big-screen beauty. You'll find 17-inch monitors at $300–$700.

Bob Speaks: Flat-Panel Displays

Also worth considering is the Apple's Studio Display, a 15.1-inch (diagonal viewable image size), thin film transistor (TFT), active-matrix liquid crystal display. In other words, a flat-panel display is a lot like what you find on a PowerBook, except this one sits on your desktop. I was one of the first people I know to get one, and I still love mine and use it as my main monitor all day, every day.

The TFT active-matrix LCD technology enables this puppy to provide outstanding brightness, contrast ratio, and sharpness. It also provides an impressively wide viewing angle, as well as completely eliminating screen flicker, which, according to Apple (and I concur), not only eases eyestrain but also increases productivity.

Another point in its favor is that the Apple Studio Display offers all of this performance in a product that's a fraction of the size and weight of a traditional 17- or 20-inch computer monitor. This is easily one of my favorite things about it. At less than 13 pounds (less than 8 pounds, if you use the supplied "picture-frame" stand instead of the bulkier, heavier, but better-looking desktop stand), you can easily move it around your desk to provide optimal viewing for whatever you're doing. I move it to the back of my desk when I'm editing graphics or playing games and then move it toward the front of my desk to write or surf the Web. I can't do that with my 20-inch glass monitor, which weighs 60+ pounds!

Another nice thing is that it works with almost any existing video card or even built-in Mac video and supports resolutions from 640×480 pixels up to $1,024 \times 768$ pixels, with millions of colors.

The software for adjusting the image is also outstanding. Just install it and hook the monitor up to your ADB port. Once you've done this, your Monitors control panel gains a "flat panel" tab that allows you to adjust your image using onscreen controls rather than the less-accurate hardware controls on the front of the display's case. There's even a one-click "Optimize" button that does a pretty darn good job of adjusting everything—brightness, gamma, image size, focus, and so on—with no user intervention whatsoever.

The image quality is outstanding. This monitor is clear, crisp, and flicker-free, just like Apple promised. And the external design is stunning, with clean lines and a translucent plastic case and stand. Everyone who has seen mine has had the same reaction: "Wow!" They all want one—at least until they hear the price.

For the record, that price is $1,299 as we go to press, which is about two or three times the cost of a traditional 17-inch "glass" monitor and significantly higher than even a 20-inch traditional monitor that can support higher resolutions (the Apple Studio Display maxes out at 1,024 × 768).

Sigh.

Is it worth it? Well, if money is no object and you're the kind of guy or gal who's gotta have the latest, greatest toys or who wants to impress your friends with perhaps the coolest looking display you can put on your desktop, I'd say "absolutely." But, if you're like the majority of folks out there, the availability of quality, 17-inch displays selling for less than $500 makes it still too darned expensive.

Still, I love mine and don't have any plans to replace it.

 ## What is the refresh rate?

Refresh rate refers to the speed at which the monitor redraws its image. Expressed in cycles per second (hertz), a higher refresh rate is better because it's easier on your eyes as you gaze at the monitor. A refresh rate of 75 Hz is very good, while 60 Hz can be harder on the eyes. Monitor specifications state the display's maximum refresh rate. When you change the resolution of your monitor, you may see a number of refresh rate choices, paired with the resolution options in the Monitors

control panel. Choose the highest available refresh rate listed for the resolution you want.

What is dot pitch?

A monitor's dot pitch measures the distance between the pixels displayed onscreen. Lower is better—the closer pixels are together, the easier the monitor is to view. Modern monitors have dot pitches ranging from .25 to .28.

What are multisync monitors? Does the Mac support them?

Monitors communicate with video circuitry in your computer at a certain frequency. In order for them to make the connection and deliver a signal to the screen, the frequencies must be the same. Modern monitors can compensate for frequency differences because they have the ability to adjust themselves to the correct one. That's called *multisynchronization.*

When Macs began supporting monitors, you couldn't get a multisync monitor, and matters were made more complicated by the fact that PCs and Macs used different frequencies to communicate. That meant that PC-compatible monitors wouldn't work with Macs. Vendors produced Mac-only monitors, but that solution limited Mac users' choices.

Today, any Mac can support a multisync monitor.

Can I use a PC-compatible monitor with my Mac?

When Apple started producing computers that could support multisync monitors, there was another problem: PC-compatible monitors and Mac video ports were not compatible. Adapters and special Mac cables solved that problem, but the ultimate solution came about when video card vendors started using VGA ports, making them instantly compatible with any multisync VGA monitor. If you add a video card to your Mac, you should have no trouble hooking up any multisync monitor, without any special Mac equipment.

What are Trinitron and shadow-mask monitors? Is one kind better than the other?

Trinitron and shadow-mask refer to two distinct monitor tube technologies. A Trinitron monitor displays images on your screen by shooting beams of light through a wire mesh, onto red, green, and blue (RGB) phosphors. Sony developed Trinitron technology. Other vendors, including Mitsubishi, offer Trinitron-like monitors. The generic term is *aperture-grille.* Shadow-mask tubes pass light through a denser metal mesh, creating their RGB images based on the angle at which light strikes the painted phosphors on the inside of the monitor's screen.

Aperture-grille monitors are reputed to offer brighter screens than do shadow-mask tubes. Since a bright monitor is usually considered to be a good thing, you might think the more expensive aperture-grille display is always a better choice. Fortunately for price-conscious users, that's not the case. Shadow-mask monitors in general are just as good as Trinitron-style tubes, though individual units can differ quite a bit. Trinitron and (Mitsubishi) Diamondtron monitors still cost more than their shadow-mask counterparts.

Our advice is not to choose a monitor because of the technology inside the picture tube. Look at the monitor for yourself. Your eyes are among the best indicators of how well a monitor will work for you.

 ## Is monitor radiation a potential health risk?

Monitors emit electromagnetic radiation in small amounts. Although the health effects of radiation are not scientifically proven, medical professionals and others worry that computer monitors have the potential to contribute to an increased incidence of cancer. Monitors emit two kinds of radiation: VLF (Very Low Frequency) and ELF (Extremely Low Frequency). The best way to assess monitor emissions is to find out whether or not they are compliant with the MRP II or TCO standards.

Compliance with these Swedish-developed standards is required in some European countries, and monitor vendors that meet them often boast about the fact on their packaging.

What features should I look for in a monitor?

Aside from the specifications we've already described—high resolution, dot pitch, and refresh rate—look for these features:

- **High-quality image**   You'll be looking at your new monitor all day. Choose one that's easy on your eyes and that delivers a clear, sharp picture. Connect the monitor to a Mac before you buy so that you can see how the Finder and your favorite applications look onscreen. If you do graphics work, launch Photoshop, XPress, or another favorite application, and look at high-quality images. If possible, try the monitor with your computer and video card or a comparable system, and view it at the resolution or resolutions you intend to use.

- **Easy-to-use controls**   Most monitors have onscreen menus that control brightness, contrast, and other image parameters. Unfortunately, some of these menus are better than others, and some monitors use menus to the exclusion of the old-fashioned, but more intuitive, mechanical buttons and dials. Look for a monitor whose controls make sense to you without reading a manual.

- **Warranty**   Most monitors have a minimum one-year warranty, while some offer up to five years. The critical warranty component is the picture tube. Some manufacturers offer separate warranties on the tube and the monitor as a whole. The former is much more important, since it's the tube that is the most vulnerable and most expensive component of the monitor.

- **Energy Star rating**   The federal government's Energy Star standard is used to rate computer equipment according to its energy efficiency. Most Energy Star–compliant monitors achieve compliance by including automatic "sleep" modes that kick in when the monitor is not in use.

● **Mac cabling**   If you need to connect your monitor directly to the Mac's video port—rather than to a video card—you'll need a Mac cable or adapter to connect the monitor to the computer.

USING MONITORS

How do I change the resolution, bit depth, or gamma of my screen?

Change monitor settings as follows:

1. Open the Monitors control panel by choosing Apple menu | Control Panels | Monitors. Your monitor type appears in the title bar, and your monitor's current settings appear in the control panel (Figure 8-1).

2. To see all of the resolution options available on your Mac, choose All from the Show pop-up menu. By default, the recommended choices appear in the pane below the menu.

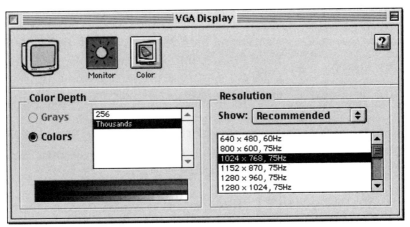

Figure 8-1   Choose the bit depth and resolution you want from the list of available options in the Monitors control panel

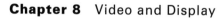

3. Click an option to change screen resolution. The screen will go black for a moment and then return, displaying the new resolution.

4. Click a new bit depth (Color Depth) in the left pane of the window.

 Tip: *You can change monitor resolution from the Control Strip, too. If you use the Control Strip, click the Monitor Resolution button (it looks like a little monitor with a black and white checkerboard on its screen) to see a list of options. The Monitor BitDepth button (it looks like a little monitor with vertical colored stripes on its screen) lets you change the number of colors displayed on the screen.*

What ergonomic issues should I consider when deciding where to locate my monitor?

Whether the discussion of electromagnetic emissions in an earlier question is of concern to you or not, monitor position is an important determinant of healthy computing. Use the following guidelines for positioning a desktop monitor.

- Place your monitor at eye level, so that you look directly into the picture tube without raising or lowering your head. This protects your back, head, and eyes from strain.

- Locate the monitor between 24 and 30 inches from your head (approximately at arm's length). This distance protects you from the effects of monitor emissions, and should avoid eyestrain for most people.

- Use an adjustable monitor stand to fine-tune your monitor's position on the desk. Stands are especially useful if you need to raise the monitor in order to bring it to eye level.

Why can't I change the resolution on my PowerBook? There are no choices in the Monitors control panel.

PowerBooks released prior to the PowerBook 3400 series supported a single resolution setting of 640 × 480. Some early PowerBook G3s offered only a single resolution setting of

Shelly's Scoop: Using Multiple Monitors with Your Mac

My friend Rik Myslewski, former executive editor at *MacUser Magazine*, likes to spread out when he uses his Mac. No, Rik doesn't lounge in a Craftmatic Adjustable Bed when he works, as far as I know, but he does usually have two or even three monitors connected to his Mac.

Rik uses one of his three screens to keep constant tabs on his daily calendar and a second to hold his e-mail. In the center of this setup is a high-quality 21-inch monitor, connected to a fast video card. Rik displays his work documents here. The smaller of the two auxiliary monitors is connected to the Mac's built-in video circuitry, and a third display uses a low-end graphics card. Rik arranges the monitors so that the tops of the three screens are on a horizontal line, creating an even flow from screen to screen.

Because the Mac OS is smart enough to manage multiple screens as if they were a single, really large display, Rik can drag windows horizontally from monitor to monitor as he needs them. RAM permitting, he can also keep lots of applications open, because there's room for them on the desktop. By placing aliases to the applications he uses all the time in the Startup Items folder, as described in Chapter 3, Rik can automate the process of everything running and in place each time he boots his Mac.

Once several screens are connected to the Mac, you can enable multiple-monitor support with the Monitors control panel. When you open it with two or more monitors attached, a new icon labeled Arrange appears. When you click it, you'll see icons for each of your monitors. You can position the monitor windows relative to each other by dragging their icons so that they are arranged left to right, as you want the Mac to see them.

To choose your main monitor, the one that will display the menu bar, drag the image of the menu bar over the icon that represents your main monitor. You can independently set bit depth and resolution for each monitor by clicking the monitor's icon in the control panel. Each display has its own set of options.

1,024 × 768. On these Macs, and any other Mac or monitor that does not support high resolution, you won't see a choice of settings.

MONITOR TROUBLESHOOTING

There's no sign of life on my screen. The monitor is on, but I can't get a picture. What should I do?

Follow these steps to locate the source of the problem:

1. Check the monitor's brightness and contrast controls.

2. Press a key to "wake up" the Mac. If you're using a PowerBook, it may have gone to sleep. If you use the Energy Saver control panel, the software may have powered down the monitor. Some monitors even include their own low-power modes that darken the monitor after a period of inactivity. Pressing a key will wake the monitor.

3. Make sure that the monitor's cable is firmly connected to the Mac's monitor port or video card.

4. Check to see that the Mac itself is turned on by looking for a light on the computer. If the computer does not display a power light, restart it.

How should I troubleshoot my AppleVision monitor?

AppleVision monitors—including the AppleVision 1710, AppleVision 750, and ColorSync displays, all from Apple— are multimedia displays that are plagued with a variety of incompatibilities and problems. After using the troubleshooting techniques above, perform these AppleVision-specific checks. If your AppleVision monitor will not display video at all, you'll need to connect a different monitor to your Mac, or take your Mac and monitor to a dealer or repair shop that will let you test both devices.

● **Software** Be sure that you have installed the AppleVision software. Mac OS 8 and later include the AppleVision extension and install it by default, but

double-check to be sure that yours is up and running before suspecting an AppleVision monitor problem. You can check to see whether the software is both installed and available to the system by opening the Monitors control panel. You should see special AppleVision setting options if you have both an AV monitor and the AppleVision extension. Even if you have AppleVision software installed, it's important that you upgrade to the latest version. Early versions of AppleVision were buggy and didn't support all Macs correctly. The easiest way to update your software is to do a clean install of the most recent version of system software possible—preferably Mac OS 8 or later.

- **ADB cables**   Disconnect ADB devices (mouse, keyboard, and so on) from the AppleVision monitor, and restart the computer to determine whether a problem is related to the monitor or the ADB devices.

- **Recalibrate color**   If you experience color or display-quality problems, try activating the color recalibration option in the Monitors control panel.

- **Replace the internal battery**   If the AppleVision monitor still does not display an image, you may need to replace the internal battery in the Mac.

Chapter 9

Networking Macs

Answer Topics!

Networking Macs @ a Glance

Networking Basics defines networking terms and concepts.

Choosing Network Equipment shows how to choose hardware for a network.

Creating a Network provides information about setting up your network.

AirPort Wireless Networking describes Apple's new wireless networking system.

Using a Network provides tips and tools for working with a network.

Remote Access describes how to connect your remote Mac to a network.

Network Troubleshooting suggests solutions for common network problems.

NETWORKING BASICS

 ## Do I need a network for my home or small business?

It may seem kind of silly, or overly complicated, to create a network for your home, even if you have more than one computer. After all, why does the kids' iMac need to communicate with the Power Mac you use to catch up on office work? If you have a small office, networking Macs may not seem like a high priority, even if you're collaborating on documents or using an e-mail system.

Here are some uses for a network you might not have thought of:

- Share a single printer among two or more computers, whether they're all Macs, or a mixture of Macs and PCs.

- Exchange files too large to be transferred via floppy or removable-media cartridge. Floppy disks don't really hold much data, and even Zip disks have their limits. It's a whole lot easier to drag a file from your Mac to the shared folder on another Mac, over the network.

- Share files with iMacs and other Macs that don't have floppy drives. As cool as those new iMacs and iBooks look, they don't have built-in floppy drives.

- Using a network is often the easiest way to share files with PC users. You can mount PC disks on the Mac, of course, but you can't always pop a Mac disk into a PC. With the right software (we'll talk more about connecting Macs and PCs together in Chapter 10), you can easily transfer files to a Windows-using spouse or coworker.

- Play network games with your family and friends. Of course, we don't suggest you do this at work, but a home network is a great way to get in a little mayhem after dinner.

- Synchronize your desktop and portable Macs. If you work on both a desktop and a portable Mac, chances are you'll want to keep files on the two machines current, without accidentally erasing newer versions of the files.

What is AppleTalk?

AppleTalk is the networking *protocol,* or language, used by the Macintosh. Whether your network is a simple daisy chain, with two computers connected by one wire, or a multiple-building network serving your whole company, the language the computers and printers speak is AppleTalk. Since AppleTalk is a protocol, not an application, your Mac already has it.

What is LocalTalk?

Before we answer the question, you should keep in mind that you won't find LocalTalk on Macs produced in 1999 or later. Apple has abandoned this technology in favor of others that we'll cover in this chapter. If you have an older Mac, read on. If all of your Macs are very new, feel free to skip the next two questions.

As we said in the previous answer, AppleTalk is like a language that Macs and printers use to talk to one another—LocalTalk is like a kind of phone line that carries the conversation.

LocalTalk has been around since the first Macs, and, until recently, every Mac has supported this kind of networking. With it, you can connect computers and printers together using a single cable. LocalTalk networks are not particularly speedy, so they are not usually suitable for business use. Many home users have moved beyond LocalTalk, too, but it has one important advantage: LocalTalk is cheap. Apple used to sell LocalTalk cabling that connected directly to the Mac's printer or modem port, and to a printer's serial port, but it didn't take long for someone to find a better way. In 1985, Farallon invented the PhoneNET connector, a little box with a stubby LocalTalk cable sticking out of it and a pair of what looked like phone jacks on the end of the box. With a PhoneNET connector plugged into each Mac and printer, and twisted-pair phone cable plugged into the PhoneNET's jack, you can set up a daisy-chained network—a continuous connection among all of the Macs on the network.

Today, a number of companies make LocalTalk connectors that work just like Farallon's PhoneNET. You can find them

at Apple dealers and other outlets that sell Mac stuff. Most of them come with the twisted-pair cabling you'll need to create the chain. You'll pay $15–$25 apiece.

Do LocalTalk daisy chains have complicated connection rules, like SCSI chains?

If you've read Chapter 5 of this book, you'll recall that the SCSI connectors used by most Mac storage devices impose a set of rules on the way you connect a series of devices. LocalTalk daisy chains aren't as complex, but there is one important rule: the empty PhoneNET jacks at the end of your daisy chain must each have a terminator plugged into them. These small, wire devices are usually included with LocalTalk connectors.

While you can often make a network work without terminators, the lack of them should be your first concern when something goes wrong with your LocalTalk daisy chain.

What is Ethernet?

Like LocalTalk, Ethernet is a transmission medium—a way for information to move from one computer to another, or to a printer. Ethernet has two advantages over LocalTalk: it's much faster, and it can be used with lots of different kinds of computers and printers, not just Macs.

LocalTalk networks operate at a maximum speed of 230.4 kilobits per second (Kbps). Ethernet, on the other hand, works at a top speed of 10 megabits per second (Mbps), about 40 times the speed of LocalTalk. You probably won't experience all of those 10 Mbps, but an Ethernet network will run considerably faster than any LocalTalk network.

Ethernet is the standard way of connecting most business computers to a network. PCs, Macs, printers, and even file servers and workstations use Ethernet. The hardware for all of these devices includes the same kind of connectors, and the network hardware doesn't care whether you're using a Mac or some other kind of computer.

Most Power Macintoshes and Power PC–based PowerBooks, along with the iMac and iBook, have built-in Ethernet. This

means that you can connect an Ethernet-equipped Mac to a network without buying any equipment for your Mac.

Macs that don't include built-in Ethernet (some 680x0 Macs and the original Power Mac models) either have an AAUI (Apple Attachment Unit Interface) or can be equipped with an Ethernet card or transceiver. A transceiver will cost you $30 or so, while Ethernet cards run $80–$100.

What is 10Base-T?

There are several Ethernet standards, each with its own connectors and cabling. The most common today, though a faster standard (see next question) is quickly gaining ground, is 10Base-T. Using unshielded twisted pair (UTP) cabling and snap-in RJ-45 connectors, 10Base-T networks are easy to set up. Other kinds of Ethernet use coaxial cables that are more expensive and cumbersome to work with. You'll also find many more 10Base-T adapters, hubs, and printers at better prices than the coax kind. Some devices offer both 10Base-T and 10Base-2 (coax, or ThinNet), but that option is becoming less common as 10Base-T grows more entrenched in office networks. Our rule of thumb is if it ain't 10Base-T, don't go near it.

What is Fast Ethernet?

Fast Ethernet looks and acts just like standard Ethernet, but much faster. Fast Ethernet operates at a blazing 100 Mbps. Actually, there are a few differences between the two kinds of Ethernet, but the two work so similarly that the conversion to or addition of Fast Ethernet is a snap.

Fast Ethernet uses the same kind of connectors as standard Ethernet and a high-grade variety of UTP cabling called Category-5 (CAT-5) wiring. The Fast Ethernet standard is called 100Base-T. You can (and should) use CAT-5 cable with standard Ethernet. Fast Ethernet uses the same connectors the standard variety does, too. In fact, a number of Fast Ethernet cards support both kinds of networking, meaning that you can add Fast Ethernet–capable cards to your Mac before you're ready to convert an entire network. The Mac's networking software will work just

fine with Fast Ethernet, though you may need a software driver—provided by the maker of your 100Base-T card—to use Fast Ethernet.

All current Macs include built-in 100Base-T Ethernet ports that support both regular and Fast Ethernet. Since many networks still run on 10Base-T, that speedy port won't do you much good—yet. To implement Fast Ethernet, you need the wiring described earlier and a 100Base-T Ethernet hub.

What is HomePNA?

The latest network standard to gain acceptance among Mac users is HomePNA. The PNA stands for Phoneline Network Alliance. Like LocalTalk and Ethernet, it's a medium for transferring network data from one place to another. With a HomePNA adapter on your Mac, and a connection between the adapter and your telephone wall jack, you can use the phone lines in your home or office (assuming you don't have a PBX-type phone system) to network Macs or PCs.

HomePNA is kind of like modern-day LocalTalk, except that it is designed to share your phone line (you can use the telephone while you work on the network). HomePNA adapters connect to your Mac via USB or a PCI card, and include phone jacks on the back. Just run a cable from the adapter to the wall jack, repeat the process for each computer (Mac or PC) you have, and you've got yourself a network. HomePNA operates at 1 Mbps, about four times the speed of LocalTalk.

HomePNA works best in homes where the computers are spread around the house. Since each computer needs its own connection to a telephone wall jack, HomePNA works less well when all of the networked computers are in the same room—unless you have lots of phone jacks in that room.

What is Open Transport?

Open Transport is Apple's networking architecture. First included as an option with Mac OS 7.5, Open Transport is now a standard part of Mac OS. Open Transport makes it easy for Macs to use a variety of network protocols and types of network media. If a new networking technology becomes available, vendors can write Open Transport components that support it, rather than having to get Apple to add support in Mac OS.

For users, Open Transport is a group of extensions and library files stored in the Extensions folder, and a software interface to networking and telecommunications tools that looks pretty much the same, regardless of the kind of network you're using.

What is TCP/IP?

Like AppleTalk, TCP/IP (Transmission Control Protocol/ Internet Protocol) is a network protocol, or language. Unlike AppleTalk, TCP/IP is used in almost every modern business environment, and by every computer (even your home-based Mac) that connects to the Internet. In fact, it's the Internet that has made TCP/IP a near-household word.

TCP/IP can be used like any network protocol in an office environment to transfer files, send e-mail, and even print. On the Internet, it does all of those things and also makes it possible to connect to the World Wide Web and other Internet services. One of the greatest benefits of Open Transport is the improved support it provides for TCP/IP on the Mac.

What is a router?

Routers are used to connect two or more networks; they convert information delivered by one kind of network so that it can be used by another network. Typically, a router is a box with network ports on the sides, but sometimes it is a software package that runs on a network server. In Mac-only networks, routers are often used to connect LocalTalk and Ethernet networks, or a local AppleTalk network to TCP/IP, for Internet access. You'll also need a router to bridge an AppleTalk network to networks that use other protocols, like Novell's IPX.

When you connect to the Internet, the Internet service provider (ISP) or your corporate network uses a router to deliver TCP/IP-based information to your Mac, either via a network or via phone lines.

Is an Internet gateway the same as a router?

Internet gateway software performs a function very similar to that of a router. Usually, Internet gateways are used to provide access to the Internet for multiple computers on a network that

are not themselves connected to the Net. You can set up a gateway on a single Mac that is networked both to the other computers on your network, and to the Internet via a dial-up or high-speed connection. When configured properly, users whose computers are connected to the gateway simply open a browser, check mail, or otherwise make an Internet connection. The request is passed to the gateway computer, which connects to the Internet and relays the request. Finally, data is forwarded from the Internet to the gateway and then to the requesting computer. It doesn't take as long as it sounds.

What are AppleShare and Personal File Sharing?

AppleShare and Personal File Sharing make it possible to transfer files between Macs using LocalTalk or Ethernet to connect your Mac to a network and AppleTalk or TCP/IP to deliver data. AppleShare is both file-server software and an extension that makes it possible for your Mac to connect to or mount another Mac's shared information. An AppleShare IP server can support many users who all need to share the same information. AppleShare IP server software can also deliver e-mail and serve Web pages on the Internet.

Personal File Sharing, just like the name says, lets you share the files and folders on your Mac with another user who's connected to your network, and who uses the AppleShare extension to log onto the shared part of your computer. Personal File Sharing and the AppleShare extension (*client*, to use the networking lingo) are both included in all modern versions of Mac OS. Apple sells AppleShare IP server software separately, and includes a copy with its Workgroup Servers—souped-up Macs that support an office full of file sharers.

Are Mac networks different from other kinds of networks?

As we discussed earlier, Mac networks typically use AppleTalk, while PC networks don't. PCs usually do use Ethernet though, with the same kind of cables and adapters that Macs use to communicate. PC users in large organizations often use a protocol like Novell's IPX, though the trend is toward TCP/IP. That's good news for Mac users

who have been doing everything possible to add AppleTalk to PC-only networks. Macs and PCs on TCP/IP networks are on an equal footing from the start.

Is AppleTalk going to disappear?

Mac® OS 9

You'll find AppleTalk in every Mac OS version Apple sells, and the company has announced no plans to discontinue it. However, Mac OS 9 has taken a giant step toward making AppleTalk unnecessary, at least in medium to large organizations, where every computer is connected to a TCP/IP network.

You see, prior to Mac OS 9, Mac users could connect to servers or other Macs via TCP/IP using Internet applications, or with AppleShare. But to mount a remote Mac volume, view its files and folders, and drag icons to and from the remote system, you had to use AppleTalk. In Mac OS 9, Apple has bundled something called ShareWay IP, a little goodie that allows you to cut out the AppleTalk middleman and mount remote resources via TCP/IP. Hence, many organizations that use AppleTalk primarily for file sharing don't really need it anymore, as long as everyone's upgraded to Mac OS 9 or gotten a copy of ShareWay IP from the nice people who developed it, Open Door Networks.

Now, don't panic if yours is not a TCP/IP network. AppleTalk may have been rendered superfluous in some places, but it's not likely that Apple will take it out of Mac OS just yet. One big reason is printing. Unless you print on a mixed network to a print server that's connected to a TCP/IP printer, you need AppleTalk, and we think you'll still be able to use it for a good while yet.

If you're already on a TCP/IP network, though, and you and a friend have Mac OS 9 installed, try using TCP/IP to transfer some files. You may find that it's faster than AppleTalk, especially on large transfers.

CHOOSING NETWORK EQUIPMENT

What do I need to buy to create a network?

Once you've decided that you need a network, and whether to go with LocalTalk or Ethernet, the next decision you'll need to

make is what network *topology* you will use. Topology simply means the physical shape of the network, and the way machines are connected to it. Topology determines the kinds of connectors and network-specific equipment that you'll use. You have two basic topology choices: daisy chain or active star.

As we discussed earlier, LocalTalk networks, in which one Mac connects to a second, and then a third, and so on, via a single wire, are daisy chains. A star topology connects all of the devices on your network to a central point, much like the points of a star, converging at the center. In the case of a star network, the center is a device called a *hub*. To create a star network, each computer and printer connects to the hub, which serves as traffic cop, directing network information as it moves to and from devices in the star. Hubs contain 4, 5, 8, or 16 ports, each of which connects to a single device. If you have more devices, you can usually connect a second hub to the first via a special port.

Hubs operate the same way whether the network uses LocalTalk, Ethernet, or Fast Ethernet. The hub, though, can only support one of those protocols, unless it's a 10/100 hub—one that supports both Ethernet and Fast Ethernet.

Tip: *Though LocalTalk hubs are still available, we strongly recommend that if you choose a hub topology, you skip LocalTalk and invest in Ethernet. It's not that expensive, and it's much faster. If you're willing to go to the trouble of wiring your network for a star topology, you will almost certainly benefit from Ethernet or Fast Ethernet.*

If your network is large, you may also need to buy repeaters and routers to amplify and organize network traffic, respectively.

What should I look for in a hub?

Your first task is to find a hub with enough ports to support your network. Each computer and printer on the network needs a port. Most home users will do fine with a four- or five-port hub, and these little boxes, sometimes called hublets, are usually available for under $100. If you're adding a hub to a business network, don't scrimp on ports. Make sure you plan for the PowerBooks that connect to the network and for the new employees or temps you'll be hiring next year. Even if you buy a relatively small hub today, make sure it comes from a well-established vendor that offers a wide selection of networking equipment. Hubs work best together when they come from the same company. Some companies, like Asanté Technologies, offer software that helps you manage multiple hubs.

If your network currently includes standard Ethernet, consider buying a hub that includes a Fast Ethernet bridge. When you're ready to add Fast Ethernet to the office, you can connect some or all of the folks in the office to 100Base-T, as long as you have a bridge to standard Ethernet.

 ## Can I add LocalTalk devices to an Ethernet network?

It's not as simple as connecting the device to the network, but it can be done. As we discussed in Chapter 6, you can add a LocalTalk Mac or printer to your Ethernet network using Apple's LocalTalk/LaserWriter bridge software and one networked Mac as a host for the LocalTalk device. The host Mac must be connected to both the Ethernet and to the LocalTalk device you want to add to the network. If that device is a Mac, you may notice that network tasks for both the host and the LocalTalk computer are pretty slow. A software bridge is most useful for printing and shouldn't be relied upon as an alternative to upgrading your Macs to Ethernet.

Can I create an Ethernet network without a hub?

Yes, you can. Farallon, inventor of the PhoneNET connector, created EtherWave devices that do essentially the same thing on an Ethernet. Using a 10Base-T transceiver or adapter, you can daisy chain up to eight devices together using built-in Ethernet, or by adding Ethernet via the LocalTalk port.

EtherWave is not ideal for everyone. You will have to buy an EtherWave device for each Mac, printer, and PC on the network, even those with built-in Ethernet. For machines (printers and older Macs) that don't have built-in Ethernet, an EtherWave adapter is about twice the price of an expansion card.

Because basic Ethernet hubs are pretty cheap, you should do the math before setting up an EtherWave network. Add up the cost of Ethernet cards and transceivers (for Macs and printers that do not have built-in Ethernet) and the hub you'll need in order to give each device on the network a port of its own. Compare the cost to buying an EtherWave device for each Mac and printer.

I have just two Macs. Is it possible to connect them without getting a hub or hublet?

Indeed it is. If all you want to do is hook up a pair of Ethernet-equipped Macs for file sharing, you just need a crossover cable. You're looking for a UTP Level 5/Category 5 crossover cable. Belkin and others manufacture them, and any decent computer store or mail-order house will have one for about $10 or $15.

A crossover cable will also allow two Ethernet-equipped Macs to play network games at high speeds.

What kind of users would benefit from EtherWave?

If you have a single Mac and a LocalTalk printer, EtherWave may be the cheapest way to speed up printing. If your network consists of a desktop Mac and an older PowerBook (a PowerBook without built-in Ethernet), or a PC with no Ethernet on board, get an EtherWave PowerBook adapter and a parallel-port adapter and start networking.

When should I consider a HomePNA network?

As we described in the "What is HomePNA?" question, HomePNA looks a lot like LocalTalk, and acts a lot like Ethernet. If you need to network several computers in your home, particularly if they are located in different rooms, you can add HomePNA adapters to each, and use your existing phone wiring by plugging them into wall jacks. Because HomePNA adapters come bundled with Internet gateway software, they add one feature not available in most Ethernet or LocalTalk home networks: you can share an Internet account among the computers networked with HomePNA.

To use HomePNA, you'll need to purchase an adapter for each (around $70 as we write this), and make sure that there's a wall jack near each computer. To share Internet access, you'll need one machine that's connected to the Internet by modem, ADSL, cable modem, or Ethernet. Diamond Multimedia and Farallon are two vendors who offer HomePNA products for USB and PCI Macs, respectively.

CREATING A NETWORK

 ### What kind of cabling do I need?

LocalTalk and Ethernet each use a version of unshielded twisted-pair (UTP) cabling. The differences in cabling are the number of wires within each cable and the type of connectors used to hook the wire to your Mac or other network device.

Many LocalTalk networks operate on common phone cable. To be used with LocalTalk, the cable must include two pairs of wire, which almost all phone cabling does. If you want to improve the performance of your network, buy high-quality cable. The saying "you get what you pay for" definitely applies when choosing network cabling. The connectors at the end of a LocalTalk cable are RJ-11s, just like the ones used in phone cabling.

Quality is even more important when cabling an Ethernet. Don't scrimp when you buy cable. One indicator of cable quality is the number of twists in the wire inside the cable. Cable is twisted in order to lessen the impact of radio interference and other noise. 10Base-T Ethernet uses RJ-45 connectors. They look like RJ-11s but are a bit larger.

 ### I've heard that there are limits to the length of cables I can use with my network. What are they?

Cable carries signals between network devices, and the longer the cable, the weaker the signal becomes. Both LocalTalk and Ethernet impose maximum cable-length limits. These limits vary based on what kind of network (LocalTalk or Ethernet) and topology (daisy chain or star) you use. The following table gives cable-length maximums for a selection of network types and topologies. These

cable-length limits apply to a network connected by one hub
or a network using a single daisy chain.

Network Type	Daisy Chain	Active Star
LocalTalk	100 feet	2,000 feet
Ethernet	606 feet	328 feet*

*Ethernet networks allow up to 1,024 users to connect to a single network with cable
lengths of up to 328 feet between each user.

Should I hire a professional installer to wire my network?

Large companies (and even middle-sized ones) usually hire
wiring contractors to run wire for new or upgraded networks.
Cabling is a big job—usually bigger than you think—and
a professional has the tools and experience to deal with
difficult wiring problems, like dropping cable between walls
and assessing the maximum cable length allowed on the
network. Professionals can also help you plan the network
for expandability and best performance. Because they test
network connections as they go, you should have fewer
surprises after the job is done than you would with a
do-it-yourself operation. Of course, cable installers don't
come cheap. It may not be cost-effective to hire someone to
create a small network for you, especially if you don't need
new network wall connections created, or if everyone in your
company is physically close together.

AIRPORT WIRELESS NETWORKING

What is AirPort wireless networking?

AirPort makes it possible to network up to ten Macs wirelessly,
via radio signals. Each Mac must have an AirPort card
installed, and the network must include an AirPort Base
Station, which looks something like a flying saucer. With the
base unit installed somewhere in your home or office, Macs
with AirPort cards interact with the network just as they would

when connected by Ethernet. They can exchange files and even share Internet access if the base unit is connected to the Net. An AirPort network can operate at up to 11 Mbps.

AirPort-using Macs must be less than 150 feet from the base unit. Since AirPort uses radio waves, not infrared beams, to make a connection, your Mac can be on the opposite side of a wall, downstairs, outside, or otherwise out of "sight" of the base unit.

Which Macs support AirPort?

Only in iBook™

iMac™

As we write this, you can add an AirPort card to an iBook, a Power Mac G4 (450 or 500 MHz), and to the iMacs released in October 1999 (iMac 350 MHz, iMac DV and DV Special Edition). You can add AirPort as a $99 option when you order an iBook, Power Mac, or iMac from Apple, or buy one to install yourself. Apple says that you can add a PowerBook G3 series to a wireless network with a third-party PC card. We don't know of a PC AirPort card that's available now, but chance are you'll be able to find one by the time you read this.

How does AirPort Internet sharing work?

The AirPort base unit includes an Ethernet port and a 56 Kbps internal modem. You can use either port to connect to the Internet. Once that's done, Macs on your AirPort network can share Internet access just by launching a browser.

How do I print from an AirPort network?

You can't print directly from a wireless Mac unless the network also includes computers and printers that are connected to Ethernet. Since the base unit has an Ethernet port, you can connect it, just as you would a printer or computer, to an Ethernet network by cabling the base unit to an Ethernet hub. Then you can print to a printer that is also on the Ethernet network.

If you don't have an existing Ethernet, but you do have a printer that supports Ethernet, just connect the AirPort base unit to the printer with a crossover cable.

Finally, if you have a USB printer connected to a Mac on the AirPort network, and you want to print from a wireless Mac, you'll have to transfer the file to the connected Mac and ask its owner to print for you. If your wireless Mac is portable, it might be easier to bring it to the printer and plug it in while you print.

USING A NETWORK

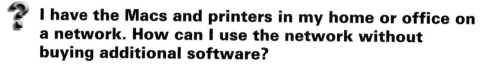 **I have the Macs and printers in my home or office on a network. How can I use the network without buying additional software?**

As we mentioned earlier, in the question, "Do I need a network for my home or small business?", networks are useful for sharing files and printing. You can do either of these things with the tools included in Mac OS. If your network is connected to the Internet, you can also surf the Web or read e-mail using a Web browser or e-mail program that's included with your Mac.

You'll also find shareware and freeware tools on the Net that let you "chat" or send e-mail on the local network.

How can I set up my Mac for file sharing?

Every version of Mac OS since version 7 has included Personal File Sharing software. With it, you can exchange files with other Mac users on your network just by dragging a file onto a shared folder icon, or onto your own hard drive from that same icon. You can share your whole hard disk or a single folder, either with a single user or with everyone on the network. To get started with Personal File Sharing, you need to give your Mac an identity and set it up to share. To set up your Mac for file sharing, follow these steps:

1. Choose Apple menu | Control Panels | File Sharing.

2. In the File Sharing control panel, type your name (or whatever identity you want others on the network to know you by). Press TAB.

3. Type a password for your Mac. The password protects your Mac from unauthorized access on the network. As the owner of a shared Mac, you have access to all folders and files. You may never need to log into your own Mac from another computer, but a password prevents others from getting access to your stuff. When you press TAB, the password you typed changes into bullets. From now on, when you type the password, you'll see bullets—not the password itself.

4. Give your Mac a name. The name will identify your computer on the network, so pick one that is descriptive and unique. Bob's Bucket of Bits is a good choice, as is Marketing Mac. You're certainly free to name your Mac Rocket J. Squirrel, but if you work in a large office, Rocket may mean little to those who need to share files with you. Our advice is to have as much fun with naming as you can, but not so much that you confuse people.

5. Click the File Sharing Start button. After a few moments, Start will change to Cancel, indicating that File Sharing is starting up. When File Sharing has finished the startup process, the button reads Stop. Figure 9-1 shows the completed File Sharing window.

Mac® OS 9

6. If you're using Mac OS 9, click the Enable File Sharing Clients To Connect Over TCP/IP check box to give TCP/IP users access to your Mac. If you click the check box, you'll see a URL in the File Sharing window. TCP/IP users can use it, or your IP address (also visible in the window), to connect to your Mac from their Chooser or Network Browser. Those you share with don't need Mac OS 9. Mac OS 8 or later supports TCP/IP access through the Chooser.

With this process complete, your Mac is ready to share files; it's on the network as a shared computer. Now, you need to give specific people access to it. To do that, follow these steps:

1. In the File Sharing control panel, click the Users & Groups tab. You should see an icon with your name on

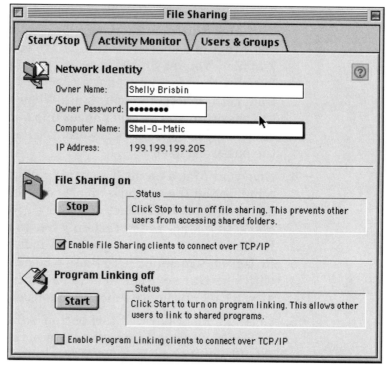

Figure 9-1 When File Sharing is activated, the Start button changes to read Stop, and a network connection is displayed next to the folder icon. If you've enabled TCP/IP access, you'll also see a URL along with your Mac's IP address

it (the name you entered in File Sharing, that is) and one that is labeled Guest.

2. Create a new user by clicking the New User button.

3. Give the user a name and password, just as you did in the File Sharing window.

4. Leave the Allow User To Change Password box checked if you want to give the user that option. You can give the user a simple password and ask that he or she change it on first connecting to your Mac. If you uncheck this option, only you can change the password.

5. Close the user's sharing window.

6. Click New Group. A group consists of several users who all share the same file-access privileges. The group's window opens.

7. Give your new group a name, and close the window.

8. To add users to your group, drag their icons from the Users & Groups window onto the group's icon in the Users & Groups window. Note that the user icon does not disappear from the window. You can verify that the user has been added to the group by double-clicking the group's icon. You'll see a list of users in the group's window.

9. Close the File Sharing control panel when you have finished adding users.

The next step in sharing files is to tell the Mac what to share. To do that, follow these steps:

1. In the Finder, locate a folder you want to share, or create a new one. Sharing an existing folder will make its contents available to people you authorize to see or work with it.

2. Click the folder's icon to select it, and choose Get Info | Sharing from the File menu (or hold down the CONTROL key, and choose Get Info | Sharing from the contextual menu). The sharing section of the folder's Get Info window appears.

3. To prevent anyone from changing the shared folder, click the Can't Move, Rename, or Delete This Item check box.

4. Share the folder by checking the Share This Item and Its Contents check box. More options light up in the window.

5. Choose an Owner for the folder. You, as the owner of the Mac, can own the folder or give ownership to someone else. A folder's owner has more rights than other users, and you, as owner of the Mac, can reserve rights for yourself that even the owner of the folder doesn't have.

Click the Privilege pop-up menu to the right of the Owner's name. Figure 9-2 shows your options. The owner has Read & Write privileges, meaning that there's no restriction on what

the owner can do with the folder. Confirm that the owner has Read & Write privileges in the pop-up menu.

6. Click the User/Group pop-up menu and select the group you created earlier.

7. Choose Write Only (Drop Box) from the Privilege pop-up menu. Just like it says, Write Only privileges mean that a user can add to a folder, but cannot read files that are already there.

8. The final user option for this folder is Everyone. Since the folder's owner already has read and write privileges, and the group has drop box privileges, there isn't much left for Everyone. You must give privileges in descending order, from the top of the folder's sharing window to the bottom. If you leave the Privilege for Everyone set to

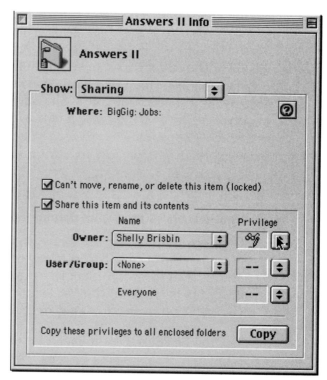

Figure 9-2 Choose privileges for the owner of a shared folder

None, people who are not in the group assigned to this folder won't even see it on the network. If you choose Read Only, Everyone will see, but not be able to change, the folder being shared. That's useful if you want to distribute information to your entire company without allowing readers to change it.

9. If you want all folders within your shared folder to have the same set of privileges as the current folder does, click Copy at the bottom of the folder's sharing window.

What tips or rules of thumb apply to setting up shared folders?

First and foremost, be careful. Share only what you want others to be able to see and use. Don't share an entire hard disk if you don't need to. This is not only a security issue, but a way to keep your Mac from slowing down unnecessarily.

One easy way to share just what you want to is to organize your folders for sharing. If you collaborate on documents with a coworker, keep files you both use in their own folder, and share that folder only. For extra security, copy files from one part of your hard drive to a shared folder so that if a shared file is accidentally altered or deleted, there's always a fresh copy in a protected location on your drive.

Drop boxes are a great idea. Anyone you give access to can leave you a file, but won't be able to see files that others have left there unless you want them to. A drop box is also a great way to limit the number of folders you have to share, because everyone who needs to send files to you can drop them in the same shared folder.

What is guest access?

File-sharing guests are users who can log onto your Mac without entering their names or passwords. You can enable guest access on the Users & Groups tab of the File Sharing control panel. If you haven't enabled it, the Guest radio button won't be illuminated in the logon box a user sees when connecting to your Mac.

Are there limits to the number of folders I can share with Personal File Sharing?

You can share up to ten folders. Each shared folder has a small effect on your Mac's performance. It's the number of shared folders, not their size, that can make your Mac sluggish, so use sharing carefully and cut back on shared folders if you notice that your Mac is slower, even when users are not connected. File-sharing usage is limited to a maximum of ten users connected to a shared Mac at any particular time. You can create as many users as you like, however.

How do I use file sharing to view or copy someone else's stuff?

To use shared items, follow these steps:

1. Select Apple menu | Chooser.

2. Click the AppleShare icon. A list of computers with shared items appears on the right side of the window.

3. Double-click a server's name.

4. In the dialog box that appears, shown here, type your name (if it isn't already entered for you) and your password for the shared Mac or file server. If you are not a user of this Mac (the owner hasn't set up an account for you in his or her Users & Groups window), click the Guest button. If Guest is not illuminated, the Mac's owner has not enabled it, and you're out of luck.

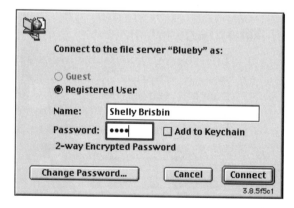

5. Click OK.

6. If your user name and password passed muster, a dialog box shows you the shared folders available, as shown in the following illustration. Click one, and then click OK. An icon for the folder appears on your Mac's desktop.

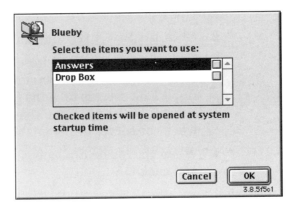

7. Double-click the icon to see the folder's contents. If you have Read & Write access, you can use the folder just as you would a local folder. If you have Write Only (Drop Box) access, you can copy files to the shared folder, only.

8. When you've finished working with a shared item, drag it to the Trash to remove the icon from your desktop. Don't worry, you're not actually trashing the disk or folder that was shared. You've just logged off the other user's Mac and given up access to the shared folder.

Tip: *Next to each of the volumes listed in the dialog box shown in the preceding illustration is a check box. Clicking it will cause your Mac to attempt to mount this volume or folder each time you boot the Mac. If you have an assigned folder on a file server, this is a great way to be sure that it's available each time you start the Mac. Of course, the remote server or shared Mac must be on and sharing. A dialog box will tell you that the server can't be found if it isn't available when you boot your Mac.*

How do I connect to a server via TCP/IP?

You can use the Chooser to connect to servers that support AppleTalk over TCP/IP. These include Macs where file

sharing via TCP/IP is enabled, and AppleShare servers that use it. To connect to a TCP/IP server, you must know its IP address or, if it has one, its URL.

To connect to a TCP/IP server with the Chooser, follow these steps:

1. Open the Chooser and click the AppleShare icon.

2. Click the Select IP Address button.

3. Type the server's IP address in the dialog box that appears, or use the shared computer's URL. URLs for TCP/IP-based AppleTalk servers take the form afp://*server.com*/. Each server's URL appears in the File Sharing control panel when the server owner enables TCP/IP access.

4. When the log on dialog box appears, enter your password and click OK.

Tip: *You can log on to a TCP/IP server with the Network Browser by clicking the server menu, and then choosing Connect to Server.*

 I use file sharing a lot, but there are so many steps involved in getting and opening a shared item. Is there any way to save steps and avoid using the Chooser?

There are a couple of easy ways to get quick access to shared resources you use all the time. Just like on your Mac, with your own folders and files, aliases are a great tool to use with file sharing and servers. You can create an alias to any remote item and store it on your desktop or in a folder. We explained earlier how to mount a shared item at startup by clicking the check box as you log on to a server or remote Mac. Another version of this technique is to put an alias to your favorite shared resource in the Startup Items folder. It will launch and log you on at startup time. Cool, huh?

If you like the idea of saving time by using aliases, open the Recent Servers folder from your Apple menu. You'll see the ten (more or less, if you've altered your Apple Menu Options) most recent remote volumes to which you've connected. Drag these aliases out of the Recent Servers folder

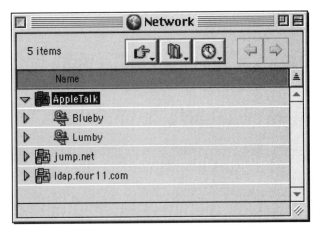

Figure 9-3 The Network Browser shows you a list of available network servers

and find them a convenient place on your desktop or in a relatively permanent folder—the oldest item in Recent Servers is replaced when you log on to a new remote volume.

It seems that each version of Mac OS brings us closer to getting rid of the Chooser, but not close enough for those who hate it. We don't really dislike the Chooser, but we're glad to tell you that Mac OS 8.5 and later include an easier way to get to file servers. The Network Browser lets you connect to file servers and shared folders, and even lets you choose and save your favorite shared items with ease. The Network Browser, shown in Figure 9-3, shows AppleTalk servers and lets you enter an IP address for TCP/IP servers. Either way, when you add the chosen server to your Favorites list, it becomes available from the Apple menu, under Favorites. When you choose the item, the Network Browser appears, with the icon of the selected server.

I want to share a folder, but I get an error message that says I can't because a folder inside it is already being shared. What does that mean, and how can I figure out which folder it is?

You can't share a folder if a folder inside it is already shared. You can share folders within other folders, but you have to start from the top and work your way down.

Here's the quickest way to find out which folders are already shared.

1. Choose Apple menu | Control Panels | File Sharing.

2. Click the Activity Monitor tab. A list of shared folders appears in the Shared Items portion of the window, as shown in Figure 9-4.

3. To change sharing privileges or stop sharing an item, click it and then click the Privileges button. The item's Privileges window appears.

4. Uncheck the Share This Item and Its Contents check box, and close the window.

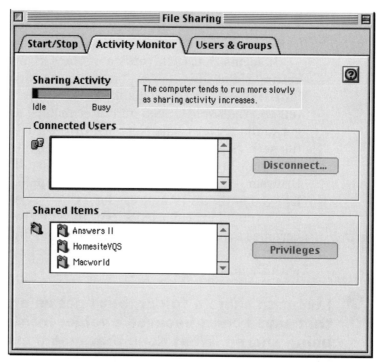

Figure 9-4 Use the Activity Monitor to view a list of connected users and shared folders on your Mac. You can change the status of a shared item by clicking on it, and then on Privileges

Shelly's Scoop: Managing Networks with Aliases

I used to spend my days taking care of the Macs in a large office. My job title was Mac Guru, and I loved it! My users would call to say that their systems weren't working, network printers weren't showing up, or some such thing. Mostly they just hollered "Help!" into the phone, and waited.

My routine was always the same: I'd grab my pouch full of floppy disks and head down the hall to save the day. Upon arriving at my destination, I would displace the user at the keyboard and assess the situation. With floppies splayed out on the desk, I would update printer drivers, defragment hard disks, and even reinstall system software. (Of course, this story takes place in the days when a fistful of 1.4MB disks would do that job nicely.)

One day, my boss brought me a present: a shiny new file server. The fact that I saw the new computer as a gift should give you an idea just what sort of geeky gal I am. But I knew that the server was not just a toy; it was an opportunity to be more productive on my rounds.

First, I created a server volume called Software, and gave myself full access. Next, I copied system software, our suite of site-licensed applications, Norton Utilities, TechTool, my favorite virus checker, and some shareware fix-it tools I'm fond of, all into my Software folder. Then, I went back to my desk and mounted the server volume on my desktop using the steps I showed you earlier in this chapter. I found the Software folder and made an alias, which I left on the desktop. Last, but not least, I reached for a floppy disk and copied the new alias onto it.

The next time my phone rang, I left the fistful of floppies in the desk drawer and took a single disk with me to see what was the matter. I inserted it into the user's drive, double-clicked the alias, logged on to the server, and grabbed all the software I needed to reinstall an ailing printer driver.

When I went to work at *MacUser Magazine*, I expanded my use of aliases to remote Macs; the floppy I carried with me into the lab included an alias to my own desktop Mac, and to several file servers we used to store data files and software.

Aliases: don't leave home without 'em.

How do I know when my network has outgrown Personal File Sharing and needs a dedicated file server?

As we've already discussed, Personal File Sharing has its limits; you can't share a single folder with more than ten users, for example. If your organization shares a lot of information and needs to get at it quickly, you should consider adding a file server to your network. A file server usually includes a very large, high-speed hard drive (or two), lots of memory, and a fast processor; all the better to give lots of people access to the files stored there. Server software allows an administrator to set up user accounts (just like the Users & Groups accounts in Personal File Sharing) for each person in the office. Folders on the server can be shared with everyone, or with individuals and departments. Because a file server's only job is to provide access to shared files, and because the server software is designed for that purpose, file servers are much faster than Personal File Sharing.

Apple sells a line of server Macs called Workgroup Servers. These server machines are based on high-end Mac models, with extra memory, fast hard drives, and AppleShare IP server software. A Workgroup Server is the easiest way to add a file server to a network of Macs. Because AppleShare IP supports both AppleTalk and TCP/IP, you can even give server access to PC users, if you have TCP/IP running on your network.

AppleShare IP can do much more than serve files on a local network, though. The package also includes a World Wide Web server, and an FTP server that you can use to mount your own Web site or share files via the Internet.

Which other file servers support Mac users?

The two leading file-server software packages for PC networks, Windows NT Server from Microsoft and NetWare from Novell, each support Mac clients. That means that Mac users can log on to an NT or NetWare server just as if they were using AppleShare or Personal File Sharing. This support is possible because both kinds of servers support AppleTalk and Apple's AFP (AppleTalk Filing Protocol).

Can I share CD-ROM drives and other removable media over a network?

Well, you could do that, but…

Personal File Sharing allows you to share any volume on your local Mac. The trouble is that removable media like CD-ROMs, Zip cartridges, and floppy disks operate much more slowly than hard drives, and that slowness is multiplied when you provide access over a network.

The good news for determined sharers is that you can add a CD-ROM jukebox, with room for six or more CD-ROM players, and a high-speed SCSI interface or Ethernet connection that allows you to share the discs over the network. The software is designed to manage the task of serving multiple volumes and squeeze every bit of speed out of inherently slow CD-ROM drives.

Can I launch applications on other Macs when their volumes are mounted on my desktop?

Once again, you could, but…

Launching an application on someone else's Mac requires tremendous resources from both your machine and the computer where the application is stored. If you need to launch programs that live on another machine, get a file server.

Can I control another computer over a network?

Running someone else's computer (Mac or PC) is not just for control freaks. It's useful for training new users, for calling in to the office from the road, or for diagnosing computer problems from a distance.

Netopia's Timbuktu Pro software lets you view and/or control the desktop of another computer from your networked Mac. You can do everything in a Timbuktu window that you can while sitting in front of a Mac. Since the software is also available for Windows 95/98 and NT, you can also log on to Windows machines. Timbuktu includes a copy of Apple Remote Access client software, which is integrated into the Timbuktu interface, so you can log in remotely, too. Finally, Timbuktu has a TCP/IP option: you can control Macs or PCs with IP addresses, whether they are in your office or across the country.

 How can I speed up my network?

As networks grow, the amount of data transferred across them tends to increase. Your network may seem slower to you because you have to wait while others print or move files back and forth. As networks grow larger, users also tend to want more from them. A two-person office probably doesn't need a local e-mail server or lots of printers. Twenty people, on the other hand, are likely to need network backup, three or four printers, and more. That means more competition for network bandwidth.

Here are three strategies for speeding up your network:

● **The Band-Aid approach** Try speeding up certain parts of your network with an accelerator. Not an accelerator for the computer, but a software accelerator that increases the speed at which Macs on the network transfer files. Asanté Technology's NetDoubler speeds up file copying when it is installed on both Macs involved in the copy. It does this by using TCP/IP, not AppleTalk, to move the files. NetDoubler often lives up to its name, especially when transferring very large files. If you need to speed up transfers to and from a file server, you can use the server version of NetDoubler, or Run Technologies' RunShare. Each is designed to work with AppleShare to copy files to and from a file server.

● **Subdivide and conquer** Take some of the pressure off a growing network by splitting it into two or more pieces. With a hub for each subnetwork, and a router or switch connecting them to each other, you can isolate traffic to a single department or workgroup, for example. For subdivision to work, folks on the same network segment should share files most often with each other, and have a printer or printers of their own. If you have a subdivided network, but only one file server that's shared by everyone, consider using a network switch and giving the server its own port on it.

● **Upgrade** Move all or part of your network to Fast Ethernet. You'll find more details about how Fast Ethernet works earlier in this chapter. If you're not ready to upgrade

the whole network, you can put a department (say, creative services, graphic design, or desktop publishing, all of which make heavy use of printers and tend to move lots of very large files around) on 100Base-T. You'll need Fast Ethernet cards for each computer, CAT-5 cabling, a Fast Ethernet hub, and a bridge between the fast portion of the network and everyone else.

REMOTE ACCESS

Can I log on to a file server with a PowerBook, or from home?

Apple Remote Access (ARA) is software that lets you dial directly into an AppleTalk network. Once connected, your Chooser displays the servers, printers, and other resources on the network. To connect via ARA, your office network must include an ARA-compatible server—usually a box with modems connected to it—and an Ethernet connection to the rest of the network. If your company uses a TCP/IP-based network, you may be able to connect to office servers when you're connected to the Internet.

As we've described earlier in this chapter, Mac OS 9 allows you to enable TCP/IP file sharing so that you can log in from anywhere on the Internet. Your company may, however, have restrictions on logging in from outside the office, including firewalls that make your office Mac inaccessible. Ask your network administrator if it's possible to use TCP/IP to mount file servers or other network resources on your remote Mac.

Mac OS 8.5 and later include ARA client software. Actually, it's just called Remote Access now, and it includes both software that connects to an ARA server, and to the Internet via PPP (Point-to-Point Protocol). Mac OS 9 also includes the server component, so that an individual with a modem connected can set up the Mac to accept dial-in ARA connections. You can use this feature to log into the home or office Mac while on the road.

How do I set up a remote access server of my own?

As we mentioned in the previous question, a remote access server usually consists of a networked device that administers connections, and several modems to handle calls from remote users. A number of vendors, including Sonic Systems and Shiva, make remote access servers that support Macs (via AppleTalk) and PCs (via Novell NetWare's IPX protocol), and can also use PPP and TCP/IP to connect either a Mac or PC to the office network. Apple has its own remote-access server, a PCI expansion card that you can install in a Mac. The card has serial modem connectors. Finally, you can use Mac OS 9 to provide dial-up access to a single Mac with Mac OS 9 installed. Most remote-access servers require that you add your own modems.

Mac® OS 9

Remote-access servers check to see that users dialing in have access privileges for the network. They can be set up to give each user a time limit, or even to call the user back at a predetermined phone number, for further security. Since the remote access server is connected to your Ethernet network, making a remote-access connection puts your Mac directly on the network, as if it, too, were connected by Ethernet. You have access to networked servers, e-mail systems, and any other network service you would be able to use from your desktop Mac. Since most modern remote-access servers support TCP/IP, too, you can usually connect to TCP/IP-based network services while connected to the server.

How do I set up Remote Access client in Mac OS?

To set up Remote Access for a connection to an ARA server, follow these steps:

1. Choose Apple menu | Control Panels | Remote Access.

2. Type your name (it may be filled in for you), password, and the phone number of your ARA server in the boxes provided.

3. Click Options.

4. Click the Protocol tab.

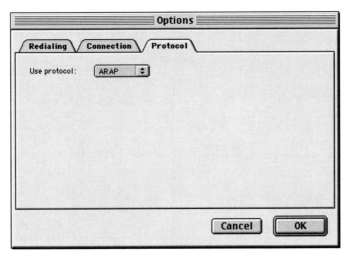

Figure 9-5   Choose a protocol to use with Remote Access

5. Choose the ARAP option from the menu. Figure 9-5 shows the Protocol tab.

6. Click OK.

7. Close the Remote Access window, and click Yes when asked if you want to save the changes you've made to your connection settings.

8. Click Connect to initiate a session with the server.

9. When you are connected, open the Chooser to locate a file server or shared Mac you want to work with, and mount it as described earlier in this chapter.

How do I set up Remote Access to accept calls with Mac OS 9?

Mac® OS 9

With Mac OS 9 installed, you can set up your Mac to accept calls from remote computers using PPP or ARAP. To do so, follow these steps:

1. Choose Apple menu I Control Panels I Remote Access.

2. Choose Remote Access I Answering.

3. Click the Answer Calls check box, as shown in Figure 9-6.

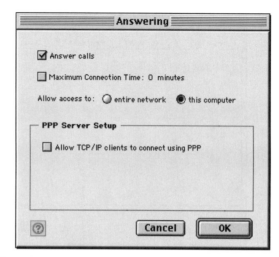

Figure 9-6 Enabling call answering in the Remote Access control panel allows other users to dial into your Mac

4. Click the Maximum Connection Time check box if you want to limit users to a certain amount of connection time.

5. If you plan to use the Apple Remote Access protocol, you're done. If you're using PPP, click Allow TCP/IP Clients To Connect Using PPP, and set the IP address to use.

NETWORK TROUBLESHOOTING

 No network devices appear in the Chooser. What's wrong?

The Chooser normally displays file servers and printers available on the network when you click the LaserWriter or AppleShare icon. If no devices appear when you click the icon, there is a problem with the network itself, or with your connection to it. Well, that sounds pretty obvious, but the first rule of network troubleshooting is to understand the possible causes of network problems.

To locate the cause of your missing network devices, follow these steps:

1. If you discovered missing network devices while looking for a specific printer or file server, click the other icon(s)

in the Chooser to see if your problem is with one device or all of them. If other devices appear, the problem is with the remote device. Contact the network administrator, or check the missing device yourself to determine what's wrong.

2. With the Chooser open, check to see that the Active radio button is selected. If AppleTalk is not active, your Mac is not connected to the network, even though cabling and other software may be in place. If AppleTalk is active, the next step is to see whether you're on the right AppleTalk network.

3. Choose Apple menu | Control Panels | AppleTalk.

4. Check to see that the pop-up menu displays the right network. If you're using Ethernet, the menu should display Ethernet. If you're using LocalTalk, the menu should read Printer Port or Modem Port, depending on which your Mac is using to make a network connection. The menu may also display Remote Only, in which case you're either connected to nothing or to a remote network via Apple Remote Access.

5. Change the pop-up menu if necessary. If the network software is all OK, the next step is to check your cabling.

6. Examine your network connection. If you are using Ethernet, check for a green light on the network card or transceiver. If the light is yellow, blinks, or does not appear at all, the problem is with your network or with the connector. Try disconnecting and reconnecting the cable and/or transceiver. If you're using an Ethernet card, open your Macintosh and reseat the card in its expansion slot.

Caution: If you're using LocalTalk, don't disconnect and reconnect cabling from your Mac while it's turned on. Plugging cables into the Mac's DB-9 port with the Mac turned on risks damage to the motherboard. Instead, shut down your Mac, unplug the LocalTalk cable, and restart. Open the Chooser and see if your network access has returned.

7. If everything on your network checks out, the problem is related to the network itself. If there is only one remote device available under normal circumstances, the problem might be with the printer or server you're trying to reach. Either way, contact your network administrator, or hike over to the recalcitrant device to check its vital signs.

How do I diagnose a problem with missing devices that originates on my network?

Once you have assured yourself that your Mac, its software, and its cabling are all okay, take a look at the network. If you manage your own network, begin at the Ethernet hub. Check to see that the light associated with each device plugged into the hub is on. Some hubs have only one status light per port, while others have both a send and receive light for each, indicating that traffic is coming to and from the device. If lights associated with a particular port are blinking, or are otherwise indicating a problem, try moving the cable to a different port. Watch the lights to see if the problem recurs.

If the hub still indicates a problem with a specific device, check it out. If it's a Mac, use the same troubleshooting procedure outlined in the previous question: checking software and cabling. Printer problems could be caused by faulty cabling or by a printer-related error. Printers with paper jams can sometimes go offline, causing them to disappear from the network. Reset the printer and check the Chooser to see whether the printer has returned to the network.

My network seems much slower than normal, but nothing has changed. What's wrong?

Heavy traffic, slow computers, or unrealistic expectations can bog down networks. We've already discussed major fixes that can alleviate real network problems caused by increased usage, but there are a few things you can do to get your current network humming again.

First, assess the source of network slowness. Is it most noticeable when you print, when you transfer files, when you send e-mail? If one function seems more affected than others,

concentrate your efforts on the way your organization uses the service. For instance, if you use Personal File Sharing extensively, make sure that you are sharing only the folders and volumes you need to, and that you log off from shared Macs when you're not using them. Make sure that no shared Macs on the network have the Calculate Folder Sizes option selected for shared folders. Calculating folder sizes slows down both the Mac and the network, because a Mac with this option turned on searches shared volumes for their folder sizes. You can check for this option by selecting a folder in the Finder and choosing View | View Options.

You may also be able to speed up a network by doing some preventive maintenance on individual Macs, especially if they're used for file sharing. Defragment your hard drive, rebuild your desktop, and try some of the other housekeeping suggestions we offered in Chapter 4.

Believe it or not, a faulty network can actually cause network slowness. Determine whether your network is cabled as efficiently as possible. Both LocalTalk and Ethernet impose cable length limits (see the cabling questions, earlier in this chapter), which should be followed. If you're using LocalTalk, make sure the network is properly terminated. We discussed termination earlier in this chapter, in the question "Do LocalTalk daisy chains have complicated connection rules, like SCSI chains?"

Chapter 10

Bridging the Gap Between Macs and PCs: Networking, Sharing, and Translating

Answer Topics!

Bridging the Gap Between Macs and PCs @ a Glance

Networking Macs and PCs explains how PCs are connected to, and use, networks.

Sharing Networked Resources shows how PCs and Macs can use and share the same files, applications, and printers.

Sharing Disks and Files describes how Macs and PCs exchange files and disks.

Electronic File Transfer and Compression explains how to exchange and compress files via e-mail and other electronic means.

PC Emulators describes options for running PC software on a Macintosh.

NETWORKING MACS AND PCS

 How do PCs connect to networks?

Like most modern Macs, the current generation of PCs typically has built-in 10Base-T Ethernet, for a direct connection to a network. If a PC does not include built-in Ethernet, you can buy a PCI expansion card that will add 10Base-T. PC printers, too, are often connected to the network via Ethernet, though personal ink-jet printers usually connect directly to a PC, via its parallel port.

Windows 95-, 98-, and Windows NT–based PCs gain access to file servers and other PCs in much the same way Macs do, through a metaphor called the Network Neighborhood—a Chooser-like window that shows the available printers and shared computers on the network. PC users can choose to share folders or volumes on their hard drives, just as Mac users can. It's a pretty safe bet, though, that most shared computers on a PC network are servers—dedicated computers running Windows NT Server, Novell's NetWare, or some other server application. Indeed, before Windows 95, a server was the only way to share information between PCs over a network, and the only way to network a printer. Most networked PC printers are still controlled by a print server—software on a server computer that intercepts print jobs from users and doles them out to a networked printer.

 How can I create a home, or small-office, network including a Mac, a PC, and a printer?

Using Netopia's EtherWave connectors (including an adapter that hooks up to a PC's parallel or USB port), you can create an Ethernet network without a hub that includes one or more PCs, Macs, and a printer. You can connect a maximum of eight devices this way, and it's often cheaper to get an Ethernet hub. For more info about creating networks with and without hubs, see Chapter 9.

You can also network PCs and Macs together with products that use the HomePNA networking standard. HomePNA devices use ordinary phone lines to make a connection between your computers, and usually allow you to share files locally and use a single Internet connection with all of your networked computers. Again, check out Chapter 9 for more details about HomePNA.

SHARING NETWORKED RESOURCES

 How can I share my Mac files with PC users over the network?

To use or copy Mac files over a network, a PC must be able to see the Mac's shared folders, or you must transfer and store Mac files on a PC. For this to work, the PC must normally support AppleTalk; you'll need to add AppleTalk support to the PC, since it's not built in, as it is on the Mac. Miramar Systems' PC MACLAN and Cooperative Printing Solutions' COPStalk do this. We like MACLAN's implementation. With MACLAN installed on a Windows 95, 98, or Windows NT PC, shared Mac volumes become visible in the PC's Network Neighborhood window. You'll need to install the software on each PC that needs access to Mac resources.

There are a couple of non-AppleTalk ways to achieve the same goal. If your network uses TCP/IP (it does if you have network access to the Internet), you can install Thursby Systems' DAVE on any Mac whose folders or disks you want to share with PC users. To share folders on the Mac, you must use DAVE's Sharing control panel, shown in Figure 10-1, to share Mac items via TCP/IP. That's in addition to any AppleTalk sharing privileges you set for Mac users. Just like an AppleTalk server, PC users see your shared folders in Network Neighborhood. By the way, Mac users with AppleShare client software 3.7 or later, shown in Figure 10-2, can connect to folders or volumes you've shared via DAVE and TCP/IP, too.

We'll have more to say about configuring and using both PC MACLAN and DAVE in subsequent questions, so follow along.

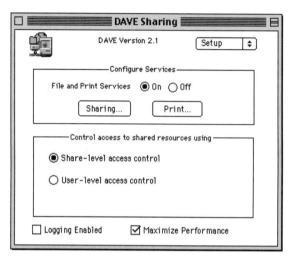

Figure 10-1 Enable sharing in the DAVE Sharing control panel, and then click a folder to share it with PC users, using DAVE

What's the difference between TCP/IP-based file sharing and FTP?

Both FTP (File Transfer Protocol) and TCP/IP-based file sharing use the same TCP/IP protocols to move data from place to place, and your network should be configured the same way to use each. Traditionally, FTP has been used to make software available over the Internet, and that's still its main job. But if you don't have a TCP/IP-based file server, like AppleShare IP or Windows NT Server, FTP is one way to use TCP/IP to share files with everyone on the network, whether they use a Mac or a PC. FTP also allows you to give remote users (or customers) access to your files via the Internet. Using NetPresenz on any networked Mac, you can set up access privileges under FTP just as you can with networked file sharing.

On the user side of things, most FTP client software is free, meaning that you won't need to buy software to bridge the gap between Macs and PCs.

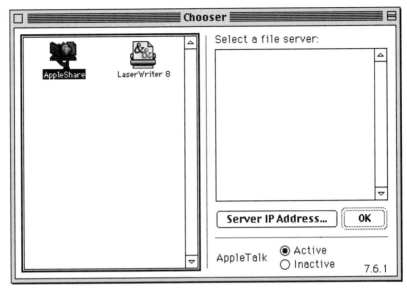

Figure 10-2 You can connect to a TCP/IP-based server if your Mac is connected to a TCP/IP network and if the Chooser shows the Server IP Address button when you click the AppleShare icon

How can PC users share their files with Mac users over the network?

Both PC MACLAN and DAVE display shared PC folders in the Chooser. You will only be able to see folders from PCs that have PC MACLAN installed and AppleTalk Sharing enabled, or that have file server software installed (see the earlier question, "How do PCs connect to networks?"). DAVE will show you any PC resources that are networked with TCP/IP, including both workstations and file servers.

How can Mac users share PC printers?

Macs support printing via AppleTalk or TCP/IP—for TCP/IP printing, you'll need the latest version of the LaserWriter software. PCs use either a straight TCP/IP connection to a printer or a print server setup that routes print jobs through

IPX or NetBEUI protocols. PC users can use Windows' printer sharing software to share printers connected directly to their computers. Printer sharing creates a print server on the host computer.

Shelly's Scoop: Transferring Files Between Macs and PCs

When I was doing research for this book, I got copies of all of the tools I write about in this chapter from the nice folks who make them. Because I am both a Mac user and an e-mail freak, I communicated with and downloaded software from the vendors electronically. When it came time to work with Miramar Systems' PC MACLAN, I found that I had an interesting problem. I'd downloaded the latest version of MACLAN from the Miramar Web site to my Mac. MACLAN, as you've read, is PC software. Now, I had to get it over to my PC. What to do?

First, I switched my TCP/IP settings from Internet dial-up to local network, so that I would be able to communicate with my PC via the Ethernet network in my home office. Next, I loaded up the Conflict Catcher extension set that includes Thursby System's DAVE software. After a restart, I shared my Downloads folder and walked over to the PC. In Network Neighborhood, I located my Mac, mounted the Downloads folder, and copied the PC MACLAN software from the Mac to the PC.

Now, I had a choice. I could use DAVE to share Mac and PC files (but I'd have to switch my TCP/IP settings on the Mac each time), or I could use the AppleTalk-based PC MACLAN to trade files and print to my LaserWriter. Cool, huh?

I know what you're thinking: you don't want to buy two pieces of software that do the same thing. You want one tool that lets you move files from computer to computer without a hassle. If you decide on PC MACLAN, be sure to get the package, including PC disks, from Miramar or, if you buy online, download the software to your PC. If you decide to trust your computer-sharing to DAVE, consider creating an AppleScript that switches your TCP/IP settings and maybe even enables DAVE's extensions for you, since you won't need them while TCP/IP is set for dial-up.

Since Macs and PCs print so differently, connecting to a PC printer from a Mac requires extra software, unless you both are using a TCP/IP network to connect the computers in your office, and have printers that use TCP/IP. In many networks, especially those with lots of Macs, the printers are the last non-TCP/IP devices around, because older printers don't support this protocol.

There are four ways to give Macs access to a PC printer, as follows:

● *Use an existing print server.*   If your network includes one, you can usually connect to it through the Chooser. If you can't, and the print server communicates with TCP/IP, you can use DAVE to get at the server from your Chooser.

● *Add AppleTalk to a Windows machine, and connect a printer to it.*   With PC MACLAN or COPStalk installed on a PC that has a printer connected, you can access the printer over the network by enabling printer sharing on the PC.

● *Print directly via TCP/IP.*   Printers with IP addresses will appear on the network and be available to you when DAVE is installed on your Mac. You'll have to configure the printer within the Chooser using DAVE (the process is similar to setting up desktop printing for the first time), or you can use DAVE's own print client application.

● *Use a printer with multiple ports.*   It's not a networking solution, but many printers have both a serial port and a parallel port on the back. You can switch connections to use the printer with Macs and PCs that are in close proximity.

How can PC users share Mac printers?

Printers on an AppleTalk network can be reached by any AppleTalk device, including a Windows machine with PC MACLAN installed. From there, you can use printer sharing to connect to a networked AppleTalk printer from an AppleTalk-using PC. If you're using TCP/IP, PCs won't know whether your printer is a "Mac printer" or not, and can simply find and configure access to the printer individually.

DAVE also allows you to set up a print server on your Mac, which a networked PC can use to print to an AppleTalk printer. In this case, the network uses TCP/IP to transfer PC documents to the Mac, and then to the AppleTalk printer.

Can I use AppleShare IP's print server module to give PC users access to Mac printers via TCP/IP?

Yes. AppleShare IP 6 improves on the print server software by adding support for TCP/IP printing, as well as the AppleTalk kind. Older versions of AppleShare include AppleTalk-only print server software.

Can I connect to a Mac network remotely from a PC?

To connect to any network remotely, you need dial-up access to it. That usually means that the network must include a remote access server that supports PPP and/or Apple Remote Access (ARA). (For more about remote access, see Chapter 9.)

If the network includes an ARA server, you can use PC MACLAN Remote to dial in from a mobile PC. If the network includes TCP/IP-based servers (AppleShare IP, for instance) and you can connect to them from the Internet, you can use a PPP connection to first dial into the Internet, then log onto TCP/IP resources via the Network Neighborhood.

Can I connect to a PC network remotely from a Mac?

There are no Mac clients for PC remote access servers, but there are workarounds. Most PC remote access servers use PPP as a dial-in method, making it easy to get connected. To reach PC resources, you will either need software like DAVE, which can connect you to TCP/IP-based servers in the Chooser, or client software for the network's file server, usually NetWare. While you can't dial into a server-based PC network from your Mac, you can connect to individual PCs and control the PC long distance.

How can I control a PC remotely from my Mac?

We included this question so that we could plug another one of our favorite tools, Farallon's Timbuktu. With it, you can

observe, control, or exchange files with another networked computer. Best of all, there are versions for Macs and PCs.

Think of Timbuktu as a window into another computer. When you control another machine, you can move around the screen, open and manipulate files, and even open applications. Opening items uses the processing power of the remote computer, not yours, and creates minimal strain on the network.

Timbuktu is a great way to connect to your office or home computer while traveling with a PowerBook. Using PPP or ARA, you can dial in to your network, or directly to your Mac, using Timbuktu's dial-direct capability. Once again, it doesn't matter whether one or both of the machines connected via Timbuktu is a PC or a Mac.

SHARING DISKS AND FILES

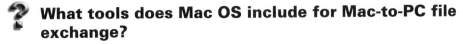

What tools does Mac OS include for Mac-to-PC file exchange?

The most important Mac tool for exchanging files with PCs is File Exchange. The Exchange control panel makes it possible for the Mac to mount PC disks on a Mac desktop and read their files. Exchange can mount floppies or removable media cartridges—Zip, Jaz, SyQuest—that are formatted for use with DOS or Windows PCs. File Exchange also launches the files via a Mac application, even though they're on a PC disk. For this to work, you must first configure File Exchange to map the PC file's extension to a Mac equivalent.

How do I set up File Exchange?

File Exchange combines what were PC Exchange and Mac OS Easy Open in earlier versions of Mac OS. The combination of these tools pretty much covers your file translation and mapping needs in Mac OS. To add a new PC extension to the PC Exchange map, follow these steps:

1. Choose Control Panels | File Exchange. Note that File Exchange includes a large number of PC suffixes, and

matching Mac applications. The list is not drawn from your hard drive, so many of the choices may need to be updated with applications you have.

2. Click Add. Figure 10-3 shows the Add Mapping window. The first time you open this window, File Exchange builds a list of applications on your Mac.

3. Type a PC extension.

4. Choose an application from the list and click Add.

 Note: *Once you have added a new suffix, and thus built a list of the applications on your Mac, the File Exchange window places icons next to items for which there are matching applications on your system. Items with no icons need to be mapped in order to open with File Exchange (see Figure 10-4).*

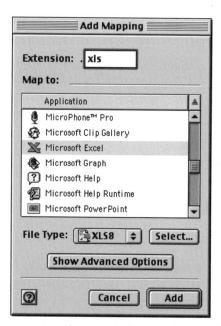

Figure 10-3 Type an extension, and choose the application you want to use to open PC files with that extension

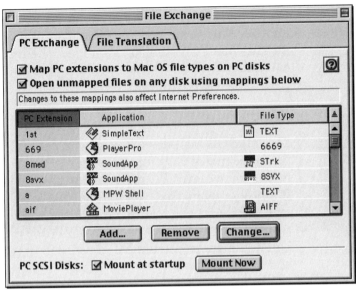

Figure 10-4   File Exchange items with icons are properly mapped to Mac applications

I've just installed a new application, and now I get an error when I open File Exchange, telling me to install Internet Config 2.0. I thought Mac OS included Internet Config. What's going on?

Mac OS 8.5 includes Internet Config version 2.02, and Mac OS 9 includes Internet Config 2.05. File Exchange requires version 2.02 or later. This file may be overwritten with an earlier version of the extension if you install software that includes Internet Config, such as a Web browser, e-mail program, or another Net-aware application. Before installing, drag the 2.02 or later extension out of your System Folder, install the software, and replace the extension by dragging it over your System Folder.

I have a lot of File Exchange extensions mapped on my Mac. Someone else in the office would like to use them, rather than creating a set from scratch. Can I share my File Exchange map?

Yes. File Exchange mapping information is stored in the File Exchange Preferences file, stored in the System Folder's

Preferences folder. Just copy that file to the same location on another Mac to share your extension map. If the other Mac already has PC extensions mapped, the information for those extensions will be lost when you replace their existing file with the copy of yours.

Can Macs read PC CD-ROMs?

Yes. Mac OS includes an extension called Foreign File Access that recognizes CDs formatted for Windows. That doesn't mean you can run PC games, or other CD-based applications. It simply means that you will be able to see the files stored on the PC and use a translation program to open them. (To run PC programs, you need an emulator program, such as SoftWindows or Virtual PC, discussed in more detail near the end of the chapter.)

✳   *Note:*   *Many CD-ROMs containing software or data are hybrids. They include applications in both Mac and PC formats, but share common data files. For example, a hybrid CD might contain installers for both Mac and PC versions of a game. The online documentation and the game's QuickTime tutorial can be read on either Mac or PC, so there's only one copy on the CD.*

Can I format a disk in my Mac for use with a PC?

File Exchange adds a DOS option to the initialization options available under the Special menu's Erase Disk command. That works for floppies, but you will need to buy software to format removable media for use with a PC; it is beyond the capabilities of File Exchange. DOS Mounter, from Software Architects, is a spiffy replacement for File Exchange that includes the ability to initialize disks in PC format and even format hard drives and removable media with partitions for both platforms.

Can PCs read and format Mac disks?

Windows does not include the ability to read Mac disks. To do this, you'll need third-party software. An inexpensive solution

is MacOpener, from DataViz. MacOpener is especially cool because it works with Windows 3.1, 95, 98, and NT.

Like File Exchange, MacOpener mounts foreign disks, maps their file extensions, and can format media for use with Macs. Several other tools can do this work, too, including MacDrive 98 from Media4 Productions.

I can mount PC disks, but File Exchange doesn't recognize the files on them. I don't know what application created them; all I know is that they are word processing files. What should I do?

If you have a recent copy of Microsoft Word, open it, and then try to open the file through Word's File | Open menu option. If you can't open it, consider getting a utility like MacLinkPlus. MacLinkPlus is a set of translators that can convert a file into something that's readable by your Mac. If you have a really old file that Word can't open by itself, MacLinkPlus applies a translator when you double-click the file, and tries to open it in Microsoft Word.

ELECTRONIC FILE TRANSFER AND COMPRESSION

Can I send a Mac file to a PC user via e-mail?

We provide a primer on file encoding and compression for Mac users in Chapter 13, but the issues are a little more complicated when you're sending or receiving files with PC users.

There are three aspects to sharing files electronically with another user, especially if that person has a different kind of computer. They include transferring, compressing, and translating the files:

- **Transfer** When you transfer a file by modem, the file is broken down into its most basic binary form. But even binary files use formats. Mac files are almost always encoded in the BinHex format, while PC and Unix files are often transferred using uuencode or Base64 formats. The main thing to remember when transferring files is

that the format you use to send the file must be understood on the other end. Transfer formats are usually set in the e-mail program or other applications used to send or receive the file.

● **Compression** Using a utility to compress a file or files for transfer can save lots of transfer time, and allow you to send a group of files together. The standard compression format on the Mac is Aladdin Systems' StuffIt, while PC users typically compress files with Zip format.

● **Translation** While files created with many common applications don't need translation, others do because there is no direct match between Mac and PC formats. In that case, you'll need to translate the file so that it can be recognized by an appropriate Mac or PC application, depending upon which direction you're transferring.

What do I need to know about transferring files to and from PC users?

Almost all Mac file transfers (e-mail and otherwise) are done with BinHex. Mac and PC mail programs support it, and automatically encode it into files you attach to messages. If the recipient of your file also uses BinHex, your file will arrive safely and need only be decompressed and translated (see the next two questions). If files you send arrive garbled, it may be because a PC user on the other end is not using BinHex, but uuencode or Base64. You can save files in these formats for transfer, or ask your recipient if he or she is able to decode BinHex files. If it's up to you to make files you send readable in uuencode or Base64 (also called MIME) format, first check to see if your e-mail program supports these options. It probably does. If not, try a freeware tool like Bernie Wieser's UUTool, or Aladdin's commercial StuffIt Deluxe.

On the receiving side, there's a lot you can do to make sure that files transfer okay. First, make sure you have StuffIt Expander at the ready. It can decode BinHex files (automatically if you use Internet Config and set StuffIt Expander as your BinHex helper). Expander Enhancer,

which is part of Aladdin's DropStuff, can decode uuencode or Base64 files. There are also free tools, such as Jeff Strobel's UULite, that will do the same thing.

What do I need to know about compressing files I exchange with PC users?

As we mentioned in a previous question, StuffIt is the standard compression format on the Mac, and Zip fulfills that role in the PC world. There are free tools available for each platform that can decompress files compressed in either format.

You can choose whether to use StuffIt or a Zip utility, depending upon which option is more convenient for you and the recipient of your files. If you know that the receiver does not have a StuffIt-compatible utility, you can use Tom Brown's ZipIt (shareware) to compress files in Zip format. To decompress a StuffIt file, your PC-using friend needs a copy of Aladdin Expander for Windows. It's free and available on the Internet. Our favorite PC download site, if there can be such a thing, is http://www.tucows.com.

On the receiving side of the equation, Mac users can decompress Zip files sent by PC users with StuffIt Expander. That's right. You can decompress both StuffIt and Zip files with a free utility that's already on your Mac. Such a deal!

What do I need to know about translating files I exchange with PC users?

Once you have decompressed PC files on your Mac, File Exchange should take care of the extension mapping chores required to make the file readable by an application on your Mac. If, for example, you have transferred and decompressed a Microsoft Word document that was created on a PC, it will open when you double-click its icon on your Mac. If you're opening a file that does not have a Mac equivalent, try launching an application you think should be able to open the file, and then open the file from within the application. If you anticipate receiving more files with this extension, use File Exchange to map the file's extension to a Mac application.

How do I transfer files in standard graphic and sound formats to a PC?

The important word in this question is "standard." Graphics are created with lots of different applications, and each has its own format. Even if you do use one of the several common graphic file formats, it's not always guaranteed that your computer's opposite number will be able to read it. The first thing to do is agree on a format that both parties can work with. For publishers and others who want to use graphics on a printed page, the standards include TIFF and EPS, with TIFF being more common. If your goal is to send a graphic for viewing onscreen or for inclusion on a Web page, save your graphic files as GIF or JPEG.

The nice thing about the GIF and JPEG formats is that they are readable by lots and lots of applications, including Web browsers.

PC users that I exchange files with get frustrated because I use a Mac. I've done everything I can to make file transfers easy, but they still blame the Mac when things go wrong. What should I do?

As Mac users, we must practice tolerance and patience with our PC-using brethren, many of whom think that we use inferior technology. We know it's not true, but it won't do any good to get into an argument. More to the point, the better informed you are, the better your file transfers will go. We suggest that you take a deep breath and follow these suggestions.

We've described how PC users can run a Windows version of StuffIt Expander to decompress files you send and how you can Zip files on your Mac, but, sometimes, more hands-on measures are called for. If file transfers to PC users consistently don't work, try these strategies:

● Ask the PC user to check his or her e-mail program to see whether it transfers attachments as BinHex, uuencode, or Base64 (MIME). If he or she uses Eudora, Microsoft Outlook, or Netscape Navigator/Communicator

to read e-mail, you're in luck, because they—and you—are talking the language of BinHex. If you discover that your recipient is not using BinHex, you can follow the suggestions we made previously in the question, "What do I need to know about transferring files to and from PC users?", about using another transfer format to deliver your files.

- Even if you have agreed to compress files with StuffIt or a Zip utility, try sending some files without compression. This works more often than you might think for reasons we're not entirely sure of.

- If you are sending graphics files, try saving them in a different format before sending them. The problem may be that your PC-using colleague simply can't open the file type you've sent.

- Suggest that the folks you exchange files with get a copy of DataViz's ConversionsPlus. This package of utilities, from the folks who bring you MacLinkPlus, includes not only MacOpener, a tool that mounts Mac disks and maps Mac file types, but also a cool tool called Attachment Opener. This is not simply a tool for opening Mac files, but will come in handy when your file exchanging fan receives documents from any platform. Attachment Opener can convert and open a wide variety of e-mail attachments, and recognizes the tell-tale signs of the formats we've discussed in this chapter.

PC EMULATORS

 ### How can I run PC software on my Mac?

To use a PC application on your Mac, you need a PC emulator. Software- and hardware-based emulators are available. When in use, each "takes over" your Mac, making the screen look like a Windows display. You can also run most emulators in a separate window on your Mac, allowing you to switch between Windows and Mac easily. Emulators essentially convert a portion of your hard disk into a PC drive and, since they run Windows instead of the Mac OS, allow you

to manipulate files, launch applications, and work as if you were using a PC.

How do hardware emulators work?

A hardware emulator is a PCI or NuBus expansion card containing a PC-friendly processor, usually an Intel Pentium or AMD processor. The card also contains RAM for the PC and ports on the back that support PC peripherals, usually game hardware. Install supporting software on your Mac, configure it, reboot, and your Mac takes on a Windows interface.

Orange Micro makes PC emulator cards. Apple has also made the cards available on a few Mac models, including the Power Mac 7200. As we write this, there are no current PC compatibility cards available from Apple.

How do software emulators work?

Software tools like Virtual PC from Connectix or SoftWindows from Insignia Solutions use the Mac's processor to emulate a PC. Like hardware emulators, these tools reserve a large portion (at least 100MB) of your hard disk for the PC files and operating system. The PC screen appears in a window, just like any Mac application.

What are the pros and cons of PC emulation cards versus software emulators?

The difference between hardware and software emulation comes down to speed. Because hardware emulators actually include a processor of their own, they're much faster than the software variety. Hardware also allows you to connect PC peripherals, like joysticks, to your Mac, via the card.

On the other hand, software emulators are much less expensive than cards. For a little more than the price of a hardware emulator with last year's Pentium chip, you can buy a new, consumer PC. And if you've read this chapter, you know how to share its files and folders with your Mac.

What should I do to prepare my Mac to use an emulator?

As we mentioned earlier, emulators work by reserving a portion of your hard disk for the PC emulation partition. For that reason, it's a good idea to defragment your hard disk before you install a PC emulator. That way, the PC partition created by the emulator will be in a single, contiguous part of the disk.

And when you install the emulator, give it a generous disk partition. It's easier to do it now than it will be later when you're running out of disk space.

Chapter 11

Taking Your Mac on the Road

Taking Your Mac on the Road @ a Glance

PowerBook Basics answers questions about Mac OS support for PowerBooks.

Using a PowerBook provides suggestions for getting more from your portable.

iBook Issues describes iBook-specific problems and solutions.

PowerBook Battery Issues explains the care and use of batteries.

PowerBook Displays, Pointers, and Peripherals describes storage and display options for portables.

PowerBook PC Cards describes expansion cards for your PowerBook.

Traveling with Your PowerBook or Other Mac includes information about how to prepare for, and travel with your computer.

POWERBOOK BASICS

? What's the difference between a PowerBook G3 and a G3 Series PowerBook?

There's a big difference. When Apple upgraded its PowerBook 3400 by replacing a PowerPC 603e CPU with a G3 processor, they simply changed the name of the computer to the PowerBook G3. When the next generation of PowerBooks was released a few months later, Apple decided to name them, collectively, the G3 Series.

The original G3 and the G3 Series PowerBooks look quite different from one another, and they feature different processors, ports, and other options, too. Original PowerBook G3 systems have a small, six-color Apple logo on the top near the latch, while G3 Series systems have a large white logo in the center of the top panel.

But wait, there's more. Apple's 1999 PowerBooks are sometimes referred to as "Lombard" (a reference to their pre-release Apple code name) or "bronze" (referring to the color of the keyboard). Apple just calls them PowerBook G3 Series, since they have replaced the previous G3. Oh, by the way, the 1998 G3 Series systems went by the code name "Wall Street."

! *Caution:*   *When you shop for batteries, memory upgrades, and expansion bay peripherals, be sure that the stuff you buy is actually intended for the G3 or G3 Series PowerBook you have. If the packaging, salesperson, or online store does not list the specific PowerBook models supported, double-check and/or make sure that there is a money-back guarantee available if you receive an incompatible part.*

? What tools does Mac OS include to help me use my PowerBook better?

When you install Mac OS on a PowerBook (or boot your PowerBook with its original version of Mac OS), you'll find several control panels designed just for PowerBooks. In Mac OS 8 and later, they are as follows:

- **File Synchronization**   Compares two folders and synchronizes their contents.

- **Location Manager** Allows you to set up multiple locations from which to dial an ARA or Internet account. While Location Manager ships with desktop Macs, it's most useful for portable owners.

- **Password Security** Allows you to set a password for your PowerBook.

- **PowerBook SCSI Setup** Allows you to choose a SCSI ID for your PowerBook when using it in SCSI Disk Mode or HD Target mode. For more details on these options, see questions later in this chapter.

- **Trackpad** Includes the same options you'll find in the Mouse control panel on a desktop Mac.

The control strip also includes several PowerBook tools, most of them for showing the status of your battery:

Why can't I find the PowerBook Setup control panel in Mac OS 8.5 and later?

Mac OS 8.5 and later add the battery conservation features formerly found in the PowerBook Setup control panel to the Energy Saver control panel. Figure 11-1 shows the Energy Saver control panel, with PowerBook features visible. You won't see them if you're using a desktop Mac.

USING A POWERBOOK

Why do PowerBooks run more slowly than desktop Macs that use the same processor?

Until the G3 generation of PowerBooks, most PowerPC portables came equipped with a PowerPC 603e chip—a lower-power processor than the 604 and 604e CPUs included in most desktop Macs. But when PowerBook processors are comparable to desktop Macs, they do often run much more slowly and receive poorer scores on benchmark tests. Video, too, is slower in portables, which don't include the same high-speed video circuitry found in most of today's desktop Macs.

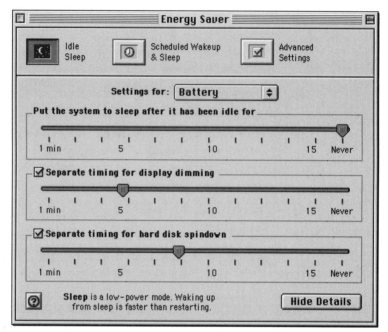

Figure 11-1 The Energy Saver control panel contains options formerly found in PowerBook Setup. Click the buttons in Energy Saver, and choose Battery from the pop-up menu to make changes

An important contributor to the speed of a computer is the bus—the data highway on which the CPU, storage devices, video, and other circuitry communicate within the system. PowerBook buses are not as speedy as those in desktop machines, partially because every attempt is made to conserve power when designing a portable. That need for a battery-friendly environment also leads Apple to create power supplies, peripherals, and other components that are not power-hungry. That's great for battery life, but not so good for speed-seekers.

The good news is that each successive generation of PowerBooks Apple produces seems to do a better job of balancing power-consumption and speed issues than the previous one did.

How can I synchronize my PowerBook with my desktop Mac?

When you travel with a PowerBook, chances are that you work with a number of files. In some cases, you work with

lots of them, and it becomes difficult to remember which files need to be copied to the desktop Mac when you return from a trip or return to the office after working at home in the evening. The problem becomes more pronounced if you check e-mail and/or receive files by modem on the PowerBook.

You could synchronize files by copying them to your desktop Mac over a network, or using floppies or removable media cartridges as a go-between. But why do that when Mac OS provides a perfectly good utility to help?

Before you can effectively use the File Synchronization control panel, or any of the several third-party utilities that can synchronize your systems, you'll need to be sure that you store your files logically on both the desktop Mac and your PowerBook. Use folders for each project you work on, or a single folder for all documents you need to synchronize. Be sure to use the same folder structure on each machine. Next, identify the folder your e-mail is delivered to, and the folder that accepts files you download from the Internet, and plan either to synchronize them or to move their contents in some other way. For example, you can avoid synchronizing e-mail by choosing the "leave mail on server" option when you check mail on your PowerBook. When you return to your desktop Mac, all of the mail you received on your trip will be delivered as usual. To include messages you send in this setup, send yourself a CC copy of each message you send from the PowerBook.

To synchronize folders on two different Macs, follow these steps:

1. Connect your PowerBook to the same network your desktop Mac is on.

2. With Personal File Sharing enabled on the desktop Mac, open the PowerBook's Chooser and locate your desktop Mac.

3. Log on and mount the volume that contains the folder you want to synchronize with your PowerBook.

4. Choose Apple menu | Control Panels | File Synchronization.

5. Double-click the folder icon on the left, and choose your PowerBook documents folder.

6. Double-click the folder icon on the right, and locate the same folder on your desktop Mac.

7. Click Scan to compare the contents of the two folders.

8. Click Synchronize to copy the latest versions of files in each, creating identical folders on both Macs.

Once you have synchronized a folder pair, File Synchronization saves your settings, allowing you to resynchronize the folder pair the next time your files have changed. You can also add folder pairs to your synchronization list. All of the pairs you create will appear when you next open the control panel.

Why is using a RAM disk with a PowerBook an especially good idea?

A RAM disk is a chunk of RAM that is mounted on your desktop as a disk, and that can then be filled with applications or Mac OS items to speed up your PowerBook. RAM disks are fast because RAM is accessed much faster than your hard drive or CD-ROM drive is. You can create RAM disks of any size, as long as you have enough memory installed. To create a RAM disk, follow these steps:

1. Choose Apple menu | Control Panels | Memory.

2. In the RAM Disk section of the control panel, click the On button.

3. Use the slider (see Figure 11-2) to decide how large your RAM disk should be, as a percentage of memory. The RAM disk's size will adjust as you use and free up RAM while working with the PowerBook.

How can I conserve battery power when using my PowerBook?

Batteries are both an essential ingredient in PowerBooks and the bane of many a user's existence. Batteries are expensive. Batteries stop working. Batteries even get old and useless. But that's the next section. Here, we'll concentrate on how you can keep a battery running as long as possible. Here are some suggestions:

● Put the PowerBook to sleep when you're not using it.

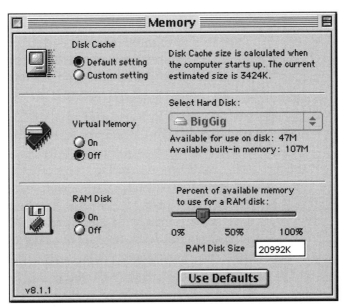

Figure 11-2 Create a RAM disk using the Memory control panel. You can use the Save on Shut Down check box to preserve your RAM disk after a reboot

- Use the battery conservation settings in the Energy Saver control panel. Decrease the amount of time your PowerBook remains awake when it's idle. That way, you won't have to put the computer to sleep manually if you don't use it for 5, 10, 20 minutes, or more. You can also adjust the intervals at which your hard disk spins down and the brightness of the display. If you don't want the computer to sleep after 5 minutes of inactivity, consider allowing the display to dim, and then allow the computer to sleep when it has been idle for 10 minutes or so.

- Even while you're working, keep the screen as dim as you can; lighting the screen uses precious battery power.

- Turn off virtual memory, AppleTalk, and File Sharing, all of which require battery power, and two of which you won't need unless you're connected to a network. Though you can use virtual memory with a PowerBook, the fact that it is slower than RAM, and that accessing your hard disk will consume power, make it a good idea to do without it while using your battery.

● Put your System Folder on a diet. Booting a PowerBook with lots of extensions and control panels takes time, and that wastes battery power. And you probably have a large number of extensions installed that you won't need while flying or when checking e-mail from a hotel room.

● Avoid power-hungry applications. The software you use on your desktop Mac may work on your PowerBook, but launching and using it can take a toll on your battery. Try installing a minimal version of the application you use or substitute a simpler tool. For example, you can use a text editor like Bare Bones Software's BBEdit to type that report, and then format it in Microsoft Word when you get back to your desktop Mac.

● Try installing and running that simpler application from a RAM disk, as mentioned previously.

● Don't use the floppy, Zip, or CD-ROM drive, or remove the disks from it when you have finished. The PowerBook will try to access the drive even when you aren't opening or moving files stored there. If your PowerBook's drive is housed in an expansion bay, consider removing it before you boot up with the battery. Similarly, keeping the PowerBook's ports free of external devices will conserve some battery power.

● Plan your work. If you are moving directly from an area with AC power to one where you will only be able to use the battery, boot the PowerBook while connected to AC, put it to sleep, and wake it up when you're ready to use the battery. You can even launch applications while plugged in (but don't open documents, which could be lost if your PowerBook crashes) and use them when you're dependent on the battery.

Shelly's Scoop: Conserving Battery Life by Managing Settings

I used to travel with a PowerBook Duo 230. I loved it, because it was my first PowerBook. I typed on planes, faxed from hotels, read e-mail on public transit conveyances. It was cool!

But the little Duo's battery power left a lot to be desired. To keep the juice flowing, I harnessed the power of Extensions Manager. You see, the Duo was not only my traveling companion, but also my desktop Mac. When working at the office, I used it to connect to the Internet, work with CD-ROMs, and even play the odd game. But on the road, with no network connection or even a CD-ROM drive, I didn't need Open Transport, QuickTime, the Microsoft extensions that work with Internet Explorer, and so on. So I created a set of extensions just for those times when I used the Duo on a plane, undocked.

But I had a problem. When I reached a hotel, I needed to check e-mail and use the Web. I plugged in my mini-dock and created a second set of extensions that gave me access to the built-in modem, Apple Remote Access, e-mail, and the like.

Finally, I saved a set of extensions that made it possible for me to dial into my e-mail account, but very little else, while using the battery. This came in handy when I found myself stuck near an airport phone, but without easy access to a power outlet.

One last thing: I did all this before Apple kindly created Location Manager, which not only gives you a way to save phone numbers for dial-up access, but can control the behavior of AppleTalk, File Sharing, and even system extensions, using Extensions Manager. See the next question for some fun with Location Manager.

+ *Tip:* *You can follow our advice about disabling unneeded extensions and turning off tools you don't need by using the Location Manager. Besides disabling things you don't want, Location Manager lets you turn file sharing and AppleTalk on and off (turning them off saves battery power) and provides a set of Internet and dial-up options.*

 ## How can I use Location Manager to customize my PowerBook for the traveling life?

Location Manager brings together several other sets of pickable preferences. In addition to Extensions Manager sets, you can create multiple Remote Access TCP/IP, AppleTalk, and other configurations within those control panels. To use Location Manager, you should set up these other preferences first, and then join them in one Location Manager set.

To create a location, follow these steps:

1. Choose Apple menu | Control Panels | Location Manager.

2. Click the Edit Locations triangle to view more of the window.

3. Choose File | New Location.

4. Name the new location in the dialog box. Editable options appear in the Location Manager window, shown in Figure 11-3.

5. Click Auto-Open Items. A dialog box appears, allowing you to choose items that will open automatically when you invoke this Location Manager set.

6. Click Apply when you've added all the items you want to use.

7. If you have set up multiple Internet accounts in the Remote Access control panel, click Remote Access.

8. Click Edit to view a list of accounts available.

9. Choose one and click Apply.

10. Continue creating Location Manager items until you're satisfied with your set.

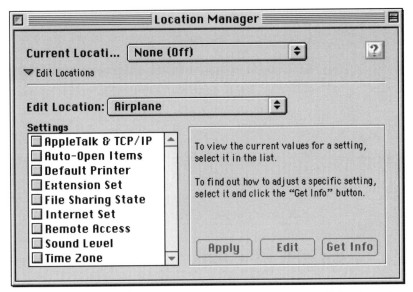

Figure 11-3 Choose an item to edit and save as part of the Location Manager set

How can I choose a location at startup?

In the Location Manager, choose Edit | Preferences, and then choose Always under Startup Switching Preferences. Each time you boot the PowerBook, Location Manager will ask you to choose a location to use.

Lately, I've noticed a lot of hardware problems with my PowerBook 5300, but it's no longer under warranty. What is Apple's policy on 5300 repairs?

Apple's PowerBook 5300 series computers were plagued by problems during their year or so on the market. After a well-publicized problem with the 5300's lithium batteries was solved, Apple was forced to contend with a variety of persistent defects in plastics and circuitry. The end result is that PowerBook 5300s and 190s qualify for Apple's Repair Extension Program (REA). Apple will repair or replace defective units that meet the program's criteria. Problems covered by the program, on PowerBook 5300 and 190 systems, are as follows:

- Loose or inoperative AC power connectors.
- Cracked plastics: this problem can affect the display housing or bezel, at the hinge, as well as the lower case plastics, including the trackpad button.
- Problems accessing PC cards with high power draws.

REA also covers PowerBook 5300s that take an excessive amount of time to reboot when plugged into AC power and that unexpectedly "drop off" of large LocalTalk networks.

iBOOK ISSUES

Is an iBook really just a more portable iMac?

Only in iBook™

As we write this, the answer to that question is a bit complicated. The iBook, released in September 1999, duplicates many features of the original iMac, including its USB ports, 32MB of memory, modem, CD-ROM drive, and lack of a floppy drive. The iBook's 300 MHz processor is a bit slower than the generation of iMacs that was available when the iBook was released. It is unlike the original iMac in that it offers support for Apple's AirPort wireless networking technology.

Shortly after the iBook came to market, Apple announced a new, more powerful batch of iMacs, all of which include faster processors than the iBook has, as well as more memory. iMac disk drives are bigger, and two of the three newest models include DVD drives, rather than CD-ROMs.

The long and short of it is that the iBook is a lot like an iMac, but not as powerful or as cheap. The good news is that any peripherals you use with an iMac will work with an iBook, and you can easily add either to a network or connect to the Internet, using tools you know well.

How do I reset the iBook?

Only in iBook™

The iBook's reset button is located inside a pinhole on the keyboard. To reset the iBook in the event of a crash, locate the pinhole just above the Power button on the keyboard. Put the end of a paper clip into the hole, and gently push the button. The iBook will restart.

Why does my iBook display not appear to be as sharp when the resolution is set to 640 × 480 pixels?

Only in iBook™

The iBook's LCD display and video provide a default resolution of 800 × 600 pixels. To achieve a different resolution, the iBook interpolates pixels, making them larger, to achieve the lower resolution. Remapping the image in this way makes the display appear less sharp. This is called *scalable resolution*.

POWERBOOK BATTERY ISSUES

What types of batteries do PowerBooks use, and what rules should I follow when recharging them?

All PowerBooks use one of four different types of batteries. Each type of battery has different recharging rules. Table 11-1 lists the battery types, the PowerBooks that use them, and how to properly recharge each.

The best way to completely drain a PowerBook battery is to use the computer until it runs out of power. Be sure to save your work often once warning messages begin to appear on your screen.

You can recharge a battery while you are using your plugged-in PowerBook, but the battery will recharge more quickly if the computer is not in use.

Why does my battery not last as long as it used to?

First, we would like to refer you to a pair of earlier questions. Be sure that you're using some or all of the battery conservation tips we provided earlier in the "How can I conserve battery power when using my PowerBook?"

Battery Type	PowerBook Model(s)	Recharging Method
Sealed Lead Acid (SLA)	PowerBook 100	Store fully charged, and recharge whenever they are depleted. Do not fully discharge.
Nickel Cadmium (NiCad)	PowerBook 140, 145, 160, 165c, 170, 180, and 180c	Fully discharge before recharging. Recharging a partially charged battery causes the battery to lose capacity.
Nickel Metal Hydride (NiMH)	PowerBook Duo 210, 230, 250, 270c, 280, 280c, 2300, PowerBook 190, 520, 520c, 540, 540c, 1400, and 5300	Fully discharge before recharging. Recharging a partially charged battery causes the battery to lose capacity.
Lithium-ion (LiIon)	PowerBook 2400, 3400, G3, and G3 Series, iBook	Fully discharge before recharging.

Table 11-1   All PowerBooks Use One of These Four Battery Types

question, especially those that involve power-saving settings in the PowerBook's control panels. Next, check Table 11-1 to see if your battery is one that is subject to the "memory effect." If you don't fully discharge a Nickel Cadmium or Nickel Metal Hydride battery before recharging it, you won't get the battery's full capacity. Use your PowerBook until the battery is completely dead, and then recharge it overnight. This is called reconditioning the battery. You can use Apple's Battery Reconditioning application included with several Duo models, and the PowerBook 190 and 5300. It's on the Battery Tools disk, or on your PowerBook's hard drive. PowerBook 500 series users can recondition a battery with the Intelligent Battery Update. Both applications are available from Apple's Software Updates Web site, under Battery Tools.

 Tip: *If you upgrade your older PowerBook to Mac OS 8.5 or later, you'll find the latest version of Battery Reconditioning in Apple menu | Apple Extras | Portables on your hard drive, after you install the system software.*

 How can I determine that my battery actually is bad or dead?

Rechargeable batteries should last up to 500 charges, according to Apple's Tech Info Library. Under normal conditions, that's about two years of use. New batteries sometimes arrive dead, too.

Here are a couple of ways to make sure yours is really dead before replacing it:

● Recharge and/or recondition the battery, as described in the preceding question.

● Boot the PowerBook using AC power, and with the fully charged suspect battery installed. When the desktop appears, and with no applications running, unplug the power adapter. Repeat the procedure with a battery you know to be good. If the first battery doesn't maintain a charge, while the second operates the PowerBook correctly, chances are that the battery is dead.

 How do I dispose of a dead PowerBook battery?

All batteries contain hazardous chemicals and metals, and should never be thrown away with regular trash. Undamaged batteries can be returned to Apple or to an authorized Apple service provider who can send them back for you. Apple recycles nickel metal hydride and lithium batteries. Other types are disposed of according to federal environmental regulations.

If you need to dispose of a damaged battery, don't return it to Apple, but use your community's hazardous waste disposal program. Whatever you do, please don't throw batteries into the trash. They are very dangerous to the ground-water system.

 How can I get batteries for outdated PowerBooks?

Apple, and a few third parties, including Absolute Battery, BTI, and VST, sell replacement PowerBook batteries. Check

with mail-order and online resellers for these items, and be sure to let them know which PowerBook you have before making a purchase.

Tip: *If your local Apple dealer tells you that he or she doesn't carry batteries for old PowerBooks, ask the dealer to check the Apple price list. You can look this information up yourself on the Apple Web site. Armed with a part number for the battery you need, you should be able to have your dealer order a replacement unit for you. And while you're there, please dispose of your old battery as described in an earlier question.*

I've heard that I can solve some battery problems by resetting the power manager. How do I reset it?

Resetting the power manager chip on the PowerBook's motherboard is a last resort measure. Doing so will remove and erase RAM disks you have created.

Apple's Tech Info Library provides detailed instructions for purging the power manager for each PowerBook series. There's also an option that works with all models, and that will simultaneously zap your parameter RAM (PRAM). For details on the effects of zapping PRAM, see Chapter 14.

To reset the power manager and zap the PowerBook's PRAM, follow these steps:

1. Shut down the PowerBook. Make sure that the CAPS LOCK key is not turned on.

2. Restart the PowerBook.

3. When you hear the startup bong, hold the COMMAND+OPTION+P and R keys for 10 or 15 seconds—until you hear the startup bong again.

4. If the computer shuts down, press the Reset button, and let it complete the startup process.

POWERBOOK DISPLAYS, POINTERS, AND PERIPHERALS

What do I need to connect an external display to my PowerBook?

All but a few of the 100 series PowerBooks support external video. To add it to a Duo, you'll need a dock or mini-dock with a video port. iBooks don't support external video.

Other PowerBooks' video ports can support an external monitor directly or indirectly, depending on the model. Most PowerBooks use an adapter that converts the video port for use with standard video cables. More recent PowerBooks include an SVGA port that directly supports a video cable. You can buy video adapters from Apple and from online and mail-order companies. As always, make sure that the adapter you buy is designed for the specific PowerBook you have.

I've been to meetings at which a presenter used a PowerBook to display slides on a screen or overhead projector. What equipment is used to do this?

To display a PowerBook image on a screen or overhead, you'll need an LCD projector or an LCD display panel. Both kinds of devices connect to your PowerBook just like an external monitor does and display an enlarged image on a screen or wall. Projectors include their own lighting, and can usually support sound, too. A less expensive way to project a PowerBook image is to connect an LCD panel to your PowerBook, and place it on top of an overhead projector. The image is transmitted to the overhead and onto the screen.

One or more pixels on my PowerBook screen is always on, even on a black background. What's wrong?

We're going to turn to Apple to answer this one, because it is Apple that determines what is acceptable in terms of dead

pixels on a PowerBook display. We suggest that if you are shopping for a new PowerBook, you check it out before you buy it to make sure that the number of dead pixels (if any) is acceptable to you. Here's the text of Apple's technical note on the subject of pixel anomalies in color active-matrix displays.

"A color active matrix display contains three sub-pixels (Red, Green, Blue) to generate one pixel on the display, therefore there can be over 2.3 million sub-pixels on the higher resolution LCD panels.

Due to current manufacturing methods of active matrix display panels, a certain number of sub-pixel anomalies are acceptable. The yield of perfect active matrix panels is very low, so to keep prices of these Apple products at a reasonable level, displays may have some sub-pixels that are either always on or always off.

If you suspect your display contains an abnormal number of anomalies, call Apple Technical Support or take the unit to an Authorized dealer for examination. Please note that a dealer may charge you for sending your PowerBook into the repair center for this evaluation."

When I got my new PowerBook, I was horrified to find that it had no trackball or mouse, but used a trackpad. Is there a way around the trackpad?

We sympathize with you, but would like to suggest that a trackpad can grow on you. Shelly's first PowerBook (the Duo 230) included a perfectly lovely trackball. But the Duo's replacement—like all modern PowerBooks—has a trackpad.

First, open the Trackpad control panel, shown in Figure 11-4, and adjust the settings so that the pad tracks more slowly. Now, spend some time practicing basic mousing techniques with the trackpad, and adjust the Trackpad settings again when you're more comfortable with it. Even if it takes a few weeks to get the hang of it, we promise that the trackpad is not as bad as it seems at first.

In some instances, though, nothing works like a real mouse. You can use any ADB mouse with PowerBooks that

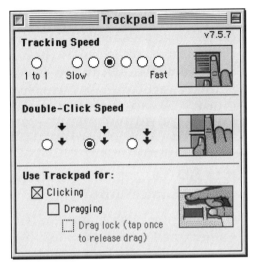

Figure 11-4   Use the Trackpad control panel to make your pointing
device a bit easier to use, especially when you're learning
the ropes

include ADB ports. Just shut down the computer, plug the
mouse into the ADB port, and restart. If yours is a USB
portable, get a USB mouse and plug it in. You don't need to
change any settings; just start mousing. If you do opt for a
mouse, at least part of the time, we suggest you don't use it
when you are operating on battery power. Like other external
peripherals, mice drain batteries.

   Tip: *You can also substitute a desktop-sized keyboard for
your PowerBook's Chiclet-like built-in one.*

How do I set up my PowerBook to operate in SCSI Disk Mode?

SCSI Disk Mode allows you to connect a PowerBook to another
Mac as if it were a hard disk. The PowerBook's disk drive
mounts on the host Mac's desktop. SCSI Disk Mode or its
cousin, HD Target Mode (explained in the next question), is
available on most PowerBooks. The exceptions are several
PowerBook 100 series systems. Duos require a dock containing
a SCSI port in order to use SCSI Disk Mode.

To work in SCSI Disk Mode, you need a compatible cable. Apple sells the HD-30 SCSI Disk Adapter Cable, which connects the PowerBook to the host Mac. There's a separate Apple cable that allows you to connect external SCSI devices to the PowerBook. APS Technologies sells a nifty device called SCSI DOC, an adapter with a little switch on it that lets you use the PowerBook in SCSI Disk Mode or regular mode with external SCSI devices connected to it.

What is HD Target Mode, and how is it different from SCSI Disk Mode?

On PowerBooks with internal IDE drives, the ability to connect the PowerBook to another Mac as if it were a disk drive is called HD Target Mode. Though the name is different, the PowerBook does connect to the SCSI chain of the host Mac in the same way it does when using SCSI Disk Mode with other PowerBooks.

POWERBOOK PC CARDS

What's the difference between a PC card and a PCMCIA card?

There isn't any. The use of the term "PC" card is a bit confusing, but it's just a shortened version of PCMCIA (Personal Computer Memory Card International Association).

Can I use a Newton PC card with my PowerBook?

No. Newton cards use a different PCMCIA implementation and won't fit into most PowerBook PC card slots.

Can I use a DOS-formatted PC storage card with a PowerBook?

Like floppies and Zip cartridges, a Mac can support DOS/Windows-formatted PC cards if you're using a current version of PC Exchange (at least 2.0.2) or File Exchange under Mac OS 8.5. For more information about using files on a DOS/Windows disk, see Chapter 10.

TRAVELING WITH YOUR POWERBOOK OR OTHER MAC

 I'm taking my PowerBook overseas. Will I need a special power adapter, and if so, where can I get one?

Apple's PowerBook AC adapters come in two parts: the power cord and the "brick" and adapter that plug into the PowerBook. To use a PowerBook in a country where AC power is delivered at a voltage that differs from the U.S. standard, you need only purchase a power cord that supports the new voltage. The PowerBook can handle them. If your AC adapter is not an Apple product, make sure that it has these words on it:

AUTO RANGING INPUT: 100-120V-1.5A 200-240V-0/75A

You should be able to find a power cord to support non-U.S. voltage at Radio Shack or other electronics retailers.

 PowerBooks are too expensive, but I need to travel with a Mac sometimes. Can you give me some tips for traveling with a non-portable?

Only in iBook™

Have you priced an iBook? While a new PowerBook will still cost you almost $2,500, the iBook is priced at $1,599, a bit more than an iMac, but less than a Power Mac. If you really need to travel with a Mac, and can live with a little less power, go for the iBook.

If an iBook doesn't work for you, try these ideas. First, try to avoid taking a non-PowerBook with you. If there are Macs available at your destination, you could take an external hard drive or removable-media drive with you, and connect it to a Mac when you arrive.

If taking a disk won't work, lighten the load by not taking a monitor with you. Monitors are heavy and bulky, and are best carried in the box they were shipped in. If you're headed for a remote office, just take the Mac and your monitor cable along with you, and plug into a display when you arrive.

When carrying Macs or peripherals on a plane or by car, make sure that they are well protected by a box and some

sort of padding. The ideal, but bulky, solution is to use the Mac's original packaging.

If you must take a desktop Mac with you, try an iMac. Its all-in-one design and built-in handle make it a bona fide luggable. We don't know of any vendor who currently produces an iMac carrying case, but we suspect that someone has just such a tote in the works.

 ### Can airport x-ray machines harm a PowerBook?

It's not the x-rays, it's the metal detector. PowerBooks don't suffer when passed under x-rays in the usual airport security check. The metal parts of the conveyor belt may have magnetic fields that can disrupt your hard disk, but neither we nor Apple know of a case where that has happened. You should either pack the PowerBook securely in a bag with adequate padding before sending it through the x-ray machine or ask that the security guards check it by hand. In either case, you may be asked to demonstrate that the PowerBook works. It's best to have the computer turned on and in sleep mode, to expedite this process.

Shelly's Scoop: PowerBook Travel

I carry my PowerBook onto airplanes in a wonderful computer bag, along with way too much other stuff. I often pack my AC adapter and other items I won't need on the plane in a suitcase, which gets checked as baggage. On one particular flight out of San Jose, I was carrying an external modem because my PowerBook didn't have an internal one. For some reason, I packed the modem with my PowerBook and its power cord in the suitcase. Bad plan.

When I walked up to the security checkpoint, the guard asked me to turn on the PowerBook and modem. Since my PowerBook—like me, on that early morning—was sleeping, I complied with no trouble. Of course, I couldn't turn on the modem, and it was only the guard's good nature that got me out of San Jose that day.

The moral of this story is this: keep your PowerBook charged and your peripherals with their power cords.

What items should I bring along with my PowerBook when I travel?

We assume two things: that you want to use your PowerBook to dial into your e-mail account or to the office, and that you would like it if the PowerBook didn't become unusable on your trip. You may not need all of the items we are going to list here, but we've used most of them at one time or another.

- **One or more long telephone cables** You don't know how far your PowerBook will have to be from a hotel telephone. Bring two long cords and a cord extender (available at any electronics store) so that you can double the length of your phone cord.

- **A digital line converter** Digital phone systems in hotels can fry your modem, so it's best to have a converter like SystemSoft's Inside Line to disable the digital signals to your modem.

- **Extra batteries and/or a battery charger** Even if you think your battery will last, bring along a spare for those long airport layovers.

- **Diagnostic software** Bring along a copy of your favorite diagnostic tool and/or a bootable disk, just in case the PowerBook gives trouble.

- **Some kind of removable-media drive and some disks** This applies to PowerBooks with no floppy drive or CD-ROM drive. If your PowerBook stops working, or has problems that lead you to believe that you need to reinstall software or run a diagnostic application, you won't be able to do much unless you have a way to add software. Carry backup copies of your documents, e-mail folder, and other important files that you will want to recover if your PowerBook goes south. If you can't bring a floppy drive or Zip drive, carry a SCSI adapter and cable so that you can connect to an external drive while you travel. That way, you can buy or borrow a drive and install the software you need.

Part Three

Getting Online with Your Mac

Chapter 12

Setting Up for the Internet: Hardware and Service Providers

Answer Topics!

Setting Up for the Internet @ a Glance

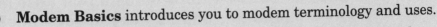

- **Modem Basics** introduces you to modem terminology and uses.

- **Modem Troubleshooting** describes common problems and solutions for modem users.

- **High-Speed Telecommunications** describes cable modems, ISDN, DSL, and other hardware options for Internet access.

- **Internet Service Providers** describes your options for choosing and using Internet access.

- **Connecting Your Office to the Internet** describes the tools you'll need to put your business online.

MODEM BASICS

Why is it called a modem?

Modem is actually shorthand for MOdulator-DEModulator. Modems work by converting digital signals into analog ones, so that they can be transferred over telephone lines. At the receiving end, another modem converts (demodulates) the signal back to digital, so that it can be used by another computer.

I have an old 14.4 Kbps modem that I use mainly to surf the Internet. Should I buy a faster one?

Modems are cheap, today. You can get a 56 Kbps modem for around $100. If you're using a modem to download e-mail, or look at primarily text-based Web sites, 14.4 will work just fine. But Web publishers are adding graphics and multimedia content to their sites rapidly, as the number of folks using slow modems declines. Stick with your old standby as long as it works for you, but don't be afraid to upgrade the next time you finish a cup of coffee before your favorite Web page finishes loading.

Should I replace my 28.8 Kbps modem with a 56 Kbps one?

Sounds great, doesn't it? Buying a 56 Kbps modem will double the speed of your Internet connection, right? We're afraid not.

The truth is that a 56 Kbps modem will not move data back and forth from the Internet at the stated speed. Instead, you'll get a theoretical maximum 56 Kbps on the receiving end—when you're downloading files from the Internet—only. Information you send to the Internet (e-mail files you upload, and so on) can only move at a maximum of 33.6 Kbps. Even that 56 Kbps maximum is a misnomer. Modem vendors have limited the speed of their equipment to 53 Kbps, citing FCC regulations that prohibit faster speeds because they can cause phone line crosstalk.

Modems can send data to you more quickly because they are able to take advantage of the digital phone lines that the phone

company has installed at its central office facilities. Data can be moved faster over digital lines, all the way to your modem, at which point it is converted back to analog. Since the lines that go to your house can't initiate a digital signal, they can't deliver data at 56 Kbps. When Internet service providers (ISPs) offer 56 Kbps service, they need digital lines and special modems that can transmit at the higher rate. But even the ISPs' higher rates don't provide a full 56 Kbps. Although the modems themselves are capable of delivering data at that speed, FCC regulations limit them to a top speed of 53 Kbps.

The real question for 28.8 Kbps or 33.6 Kbps modem owners is whether to make the fairly inexpensive, and incremental, move to 56 Kbps, or to step up to a cable modem or other high-speed option. We'll have more to say about high-speed Internet connections later in this chapter.

What are Flex, x.2, and V.90?

When a modem chip vendor like Rockwell or AT&T comes up with a way to create a faster modem, that company proposes a standard for all modems of that type. In the case of 28.8 Kbps modems, the standard is called V.34. The developer of the technology submits the set of specifications associated with the proposed standard to the ITU, which accepts it, rejects it, or modifies it. Once a specification gets the ITU stamp of approval, vendors begin producing modems that meet the standard. Adhering to a standard is important, because modems from different manufacturers must negotiate and agree on the signals they use during a call. The process we've just described is how it's supposed to work. In fact, modem vendors sometimes don't wait until they have the ITU's blessing to produce and sell products. There's nothing illegal about that; it just makes it risky for consumers to buy modems that may be useless when and if the ITU blesses a standard for that modem speed.

In the case of 56 Kbps, two potential standards were offered: x.2 and Flex. It took the ITU the better part of a year to agree on a standard, and most modem vendors couldn't wait that long. Some chose up sides, offering products for one or the other of the two 56 Kbps offerings, while a few offered products for each. To get the most from one of these fast modems, you had to

use an Internet service provider that supported the same standard (x.2 or Flex) that your modem did.

Notice the past tense? In August 1998, the ITU adopted a standard called V.90. Most 56 Kbps modem vendors have announced or shipped V.90 upgrades to their products. If you're using a 28.8 Kbps or 33.6 Kbps modem, don't replace it with any 56 Kbps modem that isn't compliant with the V.90 standard—assuming you can find one.

Do I need to buy a Mac-specific modem?

A modem is a modem is a modem, but not so the cables that connect them to your computer. PC-compatible modems include a cable with a long flat connector on each end that matches the serial port on most PCs. Mac serial ports are different; they are small and nearly round DB-9 connectors. In most cases, you'll want to stick to a Mac-specific modem. If you get a really good deal on a PC-only modem, you could buy a Mac cable for it (RS-232-to-DB-9), but there's another problem. Most modems include fax software and other programs that help you use the modem better. You'll miss out if you don't choose a Mac modem, and may also end up with a device that isn't supported by Mac OS. While most modems don't require driver software specific to the modem (Global Village modems are an exception), Mac OS does look for an Open Transport CCL script that matches your modem in the Modem Scripts folder of the Extensions folder. Scripts for most popular modems are installed with Mac OS, but you should check the folder for a script before you buy a PC-centric modem, and ask the makers of so-called Mac-friendly modems whether the appropriate script is included with their hardware.

What makes some modems better, and usually more expensive, than others?

Modem prices have declined significantly in the past couple of years; you can get a 56 Kbps modem for $100–$150. Although modems are very similar internally, they differ in a few ways that are important to some people and not so important to others.

- Software bundles are the biggest modem variable. Each modem vendor creates or buys software to bundle with the modem. The bundle usually includes fax software and Internet connection software. Global Village offers the most distinctive software bundle—a spiffy fax application with a well-designed interface. Other Mac modem software bundles usually include a version of STF Technologies' FaxSTF, or MacComCenter from Smith Micro. Internet access software packages included with modems are typically promotional offerings from service providers who hope you'll sign up for Internet access when you've got your modem up and running.

- Mac cabling, as we discussed earlier, can differentiate modems. Unfortunately, a few vendors charge a small premium for Mac-specific modem packages, which include the cable and software you need. Steer clear of these models, and let their manufacturers know you've chosen a modem package that does not cost extra just because it supports Macs.

- Flash-upgradable ROMs (sometimes called EPROMs) make it possible to upgrade your modem when speed improves or standards evolve. Flash upgrades consist either of software or a new ROM chip that can be installed by the modem's manufacturer. As valuable as flash upgrades are in the fast-moving world of modem standards, they can also offer a false sense of security. If you have a flash-upgradable 28.8 Kbps modem, for example, you won't be able to add a chip that will take you to 56 Kbps. Flash upgradable x.2 or Flex modems can, however, be boosted to the V.90 standard, in most cases. A rule of thumb is that a flash upgrade will move your modem up by one performance step. Don't count on it to take you further than that.

- Almost all modern modems support sending and receiving faxes. Many now support voice calls and caller identification. Modems with these bells and whistles can be used as answering machines and call management systems.

● Modem construction and design vary, too. If you need to carry an external modem with you when you travel, you'll find some offerings as small as a pack of cigarettes. Others are about the size of a clock radio, while some manufacturers build units that fit nicely on top of a monitor, but don't exactly fit easily in a briefcase. Look for easy to see and read indicator lights on the front of the modem, too.

MODEM TROUBLESHOOTING

 ### Why doesn't my modem connect at full speed?

Like most numbers that have something to do with computing, the speeds associated with modems are maximums, not the actual speed you should expect when you log onto the Internet. With that said, it is possible to achieve the modem's stated speed, but everything has to be working just right. Here are a few things that can conspire to keep your modem from reaching top speed.

● The modem at the other end of the connection (usually the one belonging to your Internet service provider) must be able to communicate at least as fast as your modem can.

● Telephone connections are often a source of trouble; they are susceptible to line noise that slows down communication between modems. A modem's response to a noisy phone line is to retry its connection at a more leisurely pace.

● Misconfigured software can affect modem speed. If you don't have the correct modem script selected in the Modem control panel, your modem may not function correctly. That means either that the modem won't work at all, or that the two modems negotiate a lower-than-maximum speed. If you're connecting to AOL, you may have chosen a low connection speed. Fortunately, the Modem control panel is smart enough to connect at the highest speed that both modems involved in the transaction support, and there's no need to choose a connection speed.

 What do the lights on my modem mean?

Most external modems have four to eight lights on the front, which can be useful in determining the status of your connection. Here's a list of the eight possible lights:

Light	Description
RI	Receiving ring signal
HS	Modem is operating at its maximum speed
M	Auto-answer mode on
CD	Carrier detect signal
OH	Phone off the hook
RD	Receiving data
TD	Transmitting data
MR	Modem ready

 How can I disable call waiting before I make a modem call?

If your phone line has call waiting, a modem call will be disconnected when you receive a second call. That's because, unlike your telephone, the modem can't negotiate the call-waiting signal, and so it disconnects. You can prevent this from happening by disabling call waiting for the period of time you're connected via modem.

To disable call waiting, you need to enter a code along with the phone number your modem dials. These codes vary, and you should ask your phone company what the correct sequence (*1170 is a common one) should be. Follow these steps to disable call waiting:

1. Open the PPP or Remote Access control panel.

2. Place your cursor at the beginning of the Phone Number field.

3. Type the call-waiting code (*1170, for example) and a comma, before the phone number you wish to dial. Don't leave any space between the comma and the phone number.

4. If you use an alternate phone number in the PPP or Remote Access control panel, make the above changes to those dialing strings, too.

5. Close the control panel.

When you dial a phone number with a call-waiting code entered, the phone line first disables call waiting and then pauses for three seconds (that's what the comma is for) and dials the phone number normally. When you disconnect, call waiting returns.

? My modem won't make a connection. What should I do?

Going online with a modem, like most things you do on your Mac, involves several variables. Any one of them can contribute to problems making connections. To determine why your modem won't connect, do the following:

1. Make sure that the modem is turned on and plugged in, and that cables fit securely to the Mac and modem.

2. Check the cable and phone, too, by plugging a phone into the cable you're using with the modem.

3. Try dialing a different phone number.

4. It's possible that you've plugged your RJ-11 jack into the wrong port on the back of the modem. Try switching ports.

5. If your modem has an on/off switch, turn it off and on to reset the modem

Open the Modem control panel, and check to see that the port and modem model are correct. Figure 12-1 shows the correct configuration for a US Robotics Sportster modem. If you have a Global Village modem, open the TelePort or PowerPort control panel, and click the Modem Reset button.

6. Turn off the modem and restart the Mac; then try to make the modem connection again.

7. Finally, reinstall the modem software from the Mac OS disk and the driver software (if any) that came with your

Figure 12-1 Choose the correct port and the type for your modem, all in the Modem control panel

modem. Read your modem's documentation to find out which software affects the ability of your modem to connect. There's no need to reinstall Internet browser software, for example, because it does not actually dial your modem.

If none of these steps solves your problem, you may have a hardware failure. Contact your modem vendor's technical support department.

Since I installed Mac OS 9, my GeoPort modem no longer works. What's wrong?

Mac® OS 9 For some reason, Apple chose not to include Apple Telecom, the software that drives GeoPort modems and provides voice mail and other goodies, in its Mac OS 8.5 and later installations. You'll need to reinstall the software from your Apple Telecom disk after you upgrade to a new version of Mac OS. You'll find Apple Telecom on the Mac OS 8 and 8.1 CDs, and on the Apple Software Updates Web site. If you are going to download it from the Web site, remember to do so *before* you install the new Mac OS, because your modem won't work after the installation.

HIGH-SPEED TELECOMMUNICATIONS

How can I get faster access to the Internet?

Unless you had your very own leased telephone line in your home or office, modems were the only way to get onto the Internet a few years ago. It's probably not a coincidence that faster ways of getting online became available to consumers at just about the same time the World Wide Web became popular, and its content made a speedy connection necessary to get anything out of the Internet. Home users have four choices when it comes to high-speed access:

● *Dual-modem devices* combine the data streams of two modems to double the speed of your connection. You'll need two phone lines, and so will the Internet service provider (ISP) on the other end. Dual-modem equipment is available, but it's unclear whether it will become popular, given the cost-to-speed ratio. ISPs are likely to charge hefty fees for tying up two phone lines for a single connection, and by the time you pay for your own pair of lines, you will be well on your way to affording one of several faster alternatives.

● *ISDN (Integrated Services Digital Network)* is a lot like the phone line you're used to using. In fact, ISDN is a digital version of traditional analog lines and is sold by the telephone company in your community. To use it, you'll need a device that's often called an ISDN modem or router. Actually, it's not a modem at all. ISDN does not convert analog signals to digital, but conducts the whole data transaction in digital mode. You'll also need to buy ISDN service from the phone company. It's like adding a phone line, but a bit more complicated to install and configure. When you get an ISDN line, you're actually getting two 64 Kbps data channels that can be used separately or together, for a top speed of 128 Kbps, a little more than twice the (theoretical) speed of the fastest modem.

- *Cable modems*, which do modulate digital and analog signals, transmit data over cable television lines and usually require that you use the local cable company as your ISP. Unlike an analog or ISDN phone line that serves only your home, cable modems share the data channel (the cable) that connects your computer to the Internet. For that reason, it's hard to say exactly how fast your connection will be. Cable modems can move data at a maximum of 27 Mbps. It is estimated that individuals on a cable data network could see data rates of 1–1.5 Mbps, which is still much faster than modems or ISDN.

- *DSL (Digital Subscriber Line)* is, like ISDN, a phone company service. Actually, it's a group of services, sometimes called xDSL because there are several flavors. The most popular at the moment is ADSL— the A stands for Asynchronous. Like a 56 Kbps modem, ADSL modems move files at different speeds, depending on whether you're uploading or downloading. Maximum ADSL download speed is around 1.5 Mbps, while upload speed is 384 Kbps. ISPs often sell several ADSL packages, charging more for greater maximum speed. Either way, it's much faster than ISDN, and you don't share an ADSL line as you must with a cable modem. DSL service is not universally available, and service at the highest speeds is pretty pricey, but DSL is fast and is gaining in acceptance from ISPs and business users—the surest road to cheap access for all.

If you're seeking Internet access for a business, you have another option—using part or all of a high-speed, dedicated phone connection. With a frame relay connection, you get your Internet access from another company or organization that has purchased a leased line from the phone company. This kind of piggyback arrangement is a great way for a mid-sized business to get fast access without the expense of a leased line. To use frame relay, you'll need a router that supports frame relay, as well as the AppleTalk and TCP/IP protocols you use on your own network.

 ## How can I get ISDN connected in my home?

First, you'll need to make a couple of phone calls—the analog kind—to your Internet service provider (ISP) and the telephone company. If you already have an ISP that you're happy with, you'll need to find out whether that provider supports ISDN and what it costs. It's probably a good idea to shop around a bit, since ISDN Internet access costs vary widely and are almost always higher than simple analog access.

Your next call should be to the local phone company, which will need to install your new ISDN line. The telephone company will schedule installation of the line. (It's not like analog service, with which phone company installation is optional.)

You'll need to choose ISDN equipment. Ask both your ISP and the phone company what equipment they recommend, and be sure to mention that you're using a Mac. While one or both companies may have a vested interest in selling you a particular ISDN adapter, it's often wise to heed their advice because not all ISDN devices work with all phone systems. If you're interested in using a particular ISDN product, ask about it when you call.

 ## What is a bonded ISDN connection?

ISDN lines include two 64 Kbps data channels. You can use them separately, downloading files on one channel, while you read e-mail via the other channel, for example. You can also combine, or *bond* the two channels for a maximum speed of 128 Kbps. In order to bond ISDN channels, your ISDN adapter must support it, and so must the software you use to make a connection (included with Mac-specific ISDN products). To bond channels, the software uses what's called Multi-Link PPP, a version of the familiar PPP (Point-to-Point Protocol) that can do the bonding.

Can I make voice phone calls with an ISDN line?

Most ISDN equipment includes a POTS (plain old telephone service) port where you can plug in a phone or fax machine. From there, you can use the phone or fax normally. The only drawback is that, since ISDN requires access to electricity to operate, you'll lose analog phone access if your power goes out. It's best to keep your old phone line for the bulk of your voice and/or fax phoning needs, and use the ISDN equipment's POTS port as a second voice line.

 ## What kind of equipment do I need to use ISDN?

To use ISDN, you'll need an ISDN adapter or router. What we call adapters are often called ISDN modems, but that's not technically accurate, because ISDN doesn't modulate analog signals. ISDN devices do look conveniently like modems, though, and usually plug into a Mac's serial port. For that reason, you'll need a Mac-specific unit. Some ISDN adapters, including Big Island Communication's BoogieBoard, are expansion cards that can be installed in your PCI Power Mac.

ISDN routers are a great option, especially if you're adding the service to a small office or home network. A router makes it possible to share ISDN access among several computers, and will also route TCP/IP over AppleTalk so that you can give Mac users access over the network. Routers provide speedy access, too. They communicate with your network via Ethernet, which is quite a bit faster than a serial port.

If you don't yet have a network, or would like to expand an existing one, consider an ISDN router that's also an Ethernet hub. This device is the only network hardware you'll need to give everyone access to both the local network and the Internet.

 ## What are the pros and cons of ISDN?

We would like to be able to recommend ISDN; it's a faster alternative to modems and is widely available. But what began as a promising alternative for consumers has lost much of its luster as other technologies have overtaken it.

ISDN has never been a piece of cake to install or maintain. The phone company will charge you a few hundred dollars for installation, and may have to return to your home or office several times before the connection is stable. Like other kinds of phone connections, ISDN is subject to line noise and, even where the service is available, results and speed will vary accordingly. Some users report that their single-channel connection speeds are not much faster than those of 33.6 Kbps modems.

Price is also an issue for potential ISDN users. After a short period during which phone companies charged $20–$50 a month, prices have been creeping up. Beyond the monthly access charge, most phone companies are metering their service or charging on a per-connection basis.

 ### Are cable modems available everywhere?

Cable operators have brought Internet access to a number of large markets. Most of the companies that have done so are large outfits, like Time-Warner, TCI, and Cox Cable, who have the money to upgrade their physical plants to the fiber-optic cable needed for cable-based Internet access. To

Bob Speaks: ISDN vs. Cable

I used to have ISDN. Between the phone company and my Internet service provider (OuterNet, here in Austin), I paid about $100 a month. In return, I got a 128 Kbps full-time Internet connection that was stable and fast in its day—at least three or four times faster than 56 Kbps analog modems, regardless of what the theoretical specifications might imply.

Then I got a cable modem, which I consider an order of magnitude better than ISDN. No more phone bill. No more separate ISP bill. The whole shebang costs me $44 a month, which appears on my cable TV bill. It's significantly faster than ISDN, and it's given me no trouble whatsoever since the day I installed it. It just works and it works great. So I'm sold on cable.

Which brings me to the biggest problem with all of the higher-speed Internet connection options—they may not be available where you live or work. For example, for several years, ISDN was the only option available to me where I live. I had no choice for "faster-than-56 K" access. Cable modems became available recently, thank goodness, but I still can't get any form of DSL.

find out whether your cable company has plans to deploy cable-based Internet access, give them a call.

What are the pros and cons of cable modems?

As we mentioned in an earlier question, cable modems use a shared channel. That means that you and your neighbors all compete for access to the same data pipe. To implement cable-based Internet access, the cable company will create nodes around its service area, each with several thousand subscribers connected and sharing access to the network. If the cable company in your town manages demand effectively, you won't have a problem, but you are at the mercy of the cable provider's ability to make sure that you don't have to share with too many others. Since Internet access has usage peaks and valleys, it's likely that your connection will be slower in the evening and on weekends, when lots of people go online.

Cable modem access costs $40–$60 per month in most places, which is substantially more than a modem-based connection, but remember that you can disconnect that second phone line if you own a cable modem. If, like one of your authors, you choose not to purchase cable television, a cable modem makes no sense—the cost of cable modem–based Internet access usually does not include cable service itself, which is usually required before you can use a cable modem.

When will DSL be available in my area?

Like ISDN, DSL comes from the phone company. Unlike ISDN, there's no need for enhanced phone lines, although you and the phone company each need equipment that supports it. DSL uses the phone companies' existing copper cable to make a connection.

Unfortunately, DSL is also limited by distance. The technology only works within a mile or two of the phone company's central office facility, and it's prohibitively expensive to add large numbers of phone switching stations in areas that aren't densely populated. With that said, DSL (especially ADSL) is spreading. A number of phone companies are offering ADSL in many metropolitan markets, where their physical plant can handle it. You may find that though it's available in your area, you still can't get it, because you're too far away from the central office. Even if the phone company offers DSL in your area, you'll still need an ISP. Baby Bells have gotten into the ISP business, though their services may not be as complete as those of independent ISPs. Once you know you can get DSL, shop around for an ISP that will help you get it installed and offers the services you want.

Can I make voice calls on a DSL line?

You bet. ADSL happily coexists with your voice telephone service, because the data travels through a different pair of wires than do your voice calls.

What kind of equipment do I need with DSL?

First, your Mac must have an Ethernet port. Fortunately, most do. If your Mac has no Ethernet port, you can buy a PCI card. When DSL is installed, you'll get a DSL modem (around $200) from the phone company. The package may even include the PCI Ethernet card. If your older Mac uses NuBus, you'll probably have to purchase your own network card.

If your home or office already includes an Ethernet network, simply plug the DSL modem into your Ethernet hub. If not, you'll connect the modem directly to your Mac, using a special Ethernet cable called a *crossover cable*. For more details about networking devices, see Chapter 9.

What are the pros and cons of DSL?

If you can get it and can afford it, DSL offers very fast access to the Internet. Users don't report the kind of problems that plague most ISDN users (slowness, failed connections, complicated configuration routines).

With DSL, like ISDN, you can usually choose your ISP. Cable modem users are stuck with the cable company, in most cases. You'll pay a fee to both the phone company and the ISP, but the total, for the slowest flavor of DSL, is usually not much more than cable.

On the downside, keep in mind that DSL, or any high-speed connection, is most useful when performing intense tasks, like downloading files or playing multimedia files. If you have an older Mac, you may not experience the full benefit of a fast connection, because the computer may not be able to draw Web pages as fast as the zippy connection can deliver them.

Shelly's Scoop: DSL Rocks!

I bit the bullet and got an ADSL connection in my home office in August, 1999. I logged on to a local Internet service provider's Web site and filled out a form called a Loop Qualification. Soon, I received the happy news that I was "in the zone" and eligible for an ADSL connection.

After shopping around (at least two local ISPs and the phone company, itself, offer ADSL to individuals in Austin, Texas) I ordered Personal ADSL, which offers a maximum download speed of 384 Kbps, with a maximum upload speed of 128 Kbps. Business plans provide ADSL with download speeds of up to 1.5 Mbps.

After a demand-related delay of a couple of weeks, a representative from Southwestern Bell came to my house. After climbing the pole in 100+ degree heat, the friendly phone man set to work inside, connecting the ADSL modem to an existing phone jack. Next, he tested the connection and gave me an IP address and other configuration information I needed to fill out the TCP/IP control panel on my Mac. Since I have an Ethernet hub on my desk, I plugged the ADSL modem into an open port. My Mac has built-in Ethernet, which connects it to the hub. With its TCP/IP control panel properly configured, it can communicate with the ADSL modem. After a couple of false starts and an unaccountably slow connection, my very helpful phone technician had everything running smoothly, gave me his pager number, and went on his way.

For me, the ability to share an Internet connection over a local network is an important benefit of ADSL. You can share any Internet connection by purchasing a network device called a *router*, but ADSL equipment is the cheapest way to do this. Since I have five computers in my office, I elected to purchase a block of static IP addresses from my ISP ($10 a month), so that each machine could have its own. Your networked computers can share DSL without static addresses, and if

you only need to connect one computer to DSL, or don't intend to use your Mac as an Internet server, you will probably use a dynamic IP connection. Either way, your phone company or ISP should provide the configuration information you will need.

Oh, how do I like ADSL? Didn't you read the title of this box? It's fast, fast, fast!

INTERNET SERVICE PROVIDERS

 ### What is an Internet service provider?

An Internet service provider (ISP) sells you a connection with, and access to, the Internet. ISPs maintain very fast connections to the Internet and beefy servers that process mail, store Web pages, and route your requests for Web pages and other services from their system to the Internet at large. When you buy an account with an ISP, you're getting access to their servers and an identity (through an e-mail address, and a Web page, if you like). ISPs usually have a bank of modems and/or ISDN connections to handle dial-up accounts, and sell faster access to businesses.

Telephone companies, cable operators, and even Microsoft are in the ISP business. Some national names, like Netcom and Earthlink, do nothing but provide Internet access. Many ISPs offer connections to a city, state, or region.

 ### How can I find an Internet service provider?

There are lots of ways to get information about ISPs that serve your area. Here are a few:

● **Friends** Ask people you know about their ISPs. Many problems with Internet service have to do with poor customer service or overloading of phone lines. Your friends can tell you about their experiences.

● **The phone book** Though the ISP listings may not be comprehensive, the yellow pages are a place to start.

- **Books and magazines**   It's amazing how much printed material has been generated about the Internet. You'll find ISP guides and directories in lots of computer magazines, and a slew of Internet books with similar lists.

- **The Internet**   If you have access to the Internet, point your browser to one of these sites. You'll find extensive lists of ISPs and the areas they serve.

Here are some Web sites that feature lists of ISPs:

http://thelist.internet.com/
http://www.isps.com/
http://www.barkers.org/online/index.html

Newsgroups can also be a good source of real-world feedback from ISP customers. Look for a newsgroup that covers your geographic area or one that focuses on Internet access issues.

How do I choose an Internet service provider?

Finding an ISP is a lot easier than choosing one. You will find lots of ISPs to choose from in your town; but, to make your final decision, you should figure out what features and services are most important to you. Here are some criteria for choosing an ISP:

Criteria	Description
Price	Monthly access charges hover around $20, but the unlimited access of a year or two ago has given way to more complex pricing. Some ISPs have hourly charges if you stay online more than the prescribed number of hours, and some charge extra for high-speed access or for Web page hosting. Discounts for long-term commitments are also popular. If you sign up for a quarter, a year, or even for life, you get a big discount over the normal monthly rate; at least, you should. Do the math.
Hidden catches	Some ISPs offer extremely low prices, or even a free account or free computer. The price of such a deal is often a lot of advertising, both on Web pages and in e-mail. You may have to supply marketing information about yourself, which can then be sold to marketers who want to tell you about their products.

Criteria	Description
Mac support	Though much about Internet access is platform-independent—the Internet doesn't care whether you have a Mac or PC—you might choose a Mac-savvy ISP if you think you'll need help setting up your connection. Fortunately, Mac OS includes all of the software you'll need to go online, so the issue for most Mac users is configuring the dial-up connection. If you read Chapter 13 of this book, you won't need much help from a service provider unless something goes wrong—in which case it would be helpful if your chosen ISP has some idea of what Open Transport and its tools are and how they work.
Speed	Your access to the Internet will be no faster than your ISP's. Most ISPs have a frame-relay or T-1 connection—a high-speed link that provides plenty of speed for dial-up users. Be wary of an ISP whose own connection is supplied by a larger service provider, or who relies on ISDN. There is a flavor of ISDN called a PRI that offers much more speed than the kind you can buy for your home, but even a PRI is dependent on access from an upstream ISP.
Connection options	If you want to use a 56 Kbps modem, ISDN, or DSL, your ISP must support those kinds of connections. If you think you might want to upgrade in the future, find out whether the ISP you are considering will let you move up without a new setup fee, and/or what the ISP's plans are to upgrade its own equipment.
Ease of connection	Get the modem phone number for an ISP you're considering, and dial it at times you're likely to use the Internet. If you get lots of busy signals, look elsewhere.
Local/ remote access	You should always choose an ISP whose access phone number is a local call. If you travel a lot and want access to your account, check out ISPs that do business nationally. That way you can use a local phone number in the city you're visiting to log on without paying long distance charges.
Customer support	What kind of support does the ISP provide? Can you call during evening or weekend hours? Do the support folks know anything about Macs?

 ### Should I choose a local or national Internet service provider?

For some people (one of your authors, included), choosing a hometown ISP is a great way to support businesses in the community. Personal experience has shown that the little guys often offer customer service and technical support that's just as good or better than a national ISP. But that's our experience. For other folks, a national provider with its CD-ROM full of software, toll-free tech support, and massive network is just the ticket. That's particularly true if you want access to your account as you travel around the country, without having to make a long distance call. In short, our answer is that choosing an ISP is a very individual decision. And we think that's the way it should be; there's still a lot of choice in the ISP market, and that's good for consumers.

Is AOL a good choice for my Internet service provider?

America Online is the largest provider of Internet access around. It began as a service that built its own content and provided a doorway onto the Internet. Now, lots of people use it as an Internet service provider. Though AOL requires less configuration than any other Internet access method and is reasonably priced, we can't recommend it to people who are mainly interested in Internet access, rather than AOL's own extensive content. For one thing, the Web browser that comes with AOL is inferior to Netscape Communicator or Microsoft's Internet Explorer, although you can now use either one as your browser of choice, if you like. For another, AOL is subject to slowdowns and even outages. AOL users also must contend with massive amounts of unsolicited e-mail (spam) and the service's annoying advertisements that pop up on your screen while you are online. Finally, having an "AOL-dot-com" e-mail address is considered déclassé by veteran computer geeks like us.

If you like AOL's own content—chat rooms, games, and special interest sections—or if simplicity of configuration is absolutely essential to you, choose AOL. For most folks, though, it's not the best option.

Tip: *As we write this, many local and national ISPs have taken direct aim at AOL. Many offer lower prices, multiple e-mail accounts (AOL calls them screen names), and space for a personal Web page. Be sure to shop around before you slip that AOL disk into your CD-ROM drive. You may be surprised at what you find.*

Shelly's Scoop: Choosing an Internet Service Provider

I've been buying Internet access since 1990. My first account gave me command-line access to a Unix machine, enabling me to read e-mail and newsgroups. Since then, I've used large and small ISPs in different parts of the country, and I have had accounts on AOL, Genie, and CompuServe, too. When picking a provider, I've always tried to make my choice by logically writing down the prices and features each company offers, and picking the best. But when it comes down to filling out the form, or handing over my credit card number, the choice isn't always completely scientific.

On a couple of occasions, I've opted for one company over another based on a gut feeling that the service I could expect would be attentive, and that upgrade and pricing options were fair and flexible. The best way to get a gut feeling about an ISP is to talk to the folks who run the place. Though many ISPs allow you to sign up for an account online, with no need for human contact at all, I always make the phone calls. I like to figure out how my future ISP feels about its individual customers—whether the tech support or customer service people seem stressed out or willing to help me understand their services, and so on. I can also ask informally when the ISP will offer things like faster access, Web hosting, or other services I might like to buy in the future. If the provider seems surprised that I'm interested in ADSL access, I can guess that it will be a while before the ISP offers it.

I also use these phone calls as a way to get a sense of how knowledgeable the staff is about things Macintosh, and whether it's likely that many of my fellow customers are Mac users. (You can also find this out by connecting to ISP-specific newsgroups, where users help one another and where the better companies' tech support staffs maintain a presence). You and I know that the Mac isn't dead, and an ISP who thinks so is not likely to take good care of you when you need tech support.

CONNECTING YOUR OFFICE TO THE INTERNET

 ## What do I need to get my small office online?

To get a group of people Internet access, you can either give each one a modem and a single-user account with an Internet service provider (ISP) or you can buy equipment and services that make it possible for everyone in the office to share access. The advantages of shared access are that a single person can set it up for all, and that sharing, especially if you have four or more people in your office, is usually cheaper than giving everyone a modem of their own. To set up shared access for the office, you'll need these tools:

- **Hardware that connects to the Internet**   Choose a modem, ISDN adapter, DSL, or high-speed WAN connection, depending on how many people need access, and how you plan to use it.

- **A router**   As we discussed in the ISDN section of this chapter, a router is a great way to give several people access to ISDN using the same connection. Whether you use ISDN or some other technology to make the Internet connection, you must add a router to your network if that connection is to be shared. Choose a router that supports AppleTalk, TCP/IP, and any other protocols you use in the office. The router should either include its own hub or should have an Ethernet port, so that you can add it to your existing network. If you opt for a frame-relay connection, at least one hub must support frame relay.

- **A business Internet account**   You can buy Internet accounts that support several users. Your ISP will sell you IP addresses for each computer you want to connect simultaneously. That means that if you have ten Macs in the office, but never think more than five will be connected at once, you can get by with five IP addresses. But don't be

tempted to cut corners; the difference between the cost of five and ten addresses is not very great. The account will also include e-mail addresses for everyone and should not be metered (that is, priced according to how much time you spend online). Those costs can mount quickly and are hard to manage.

● **A domain of your own**   Your company can be known as smallwidgets.com for a fee. Your ISP can sell you a vanity domain (in the format *yourcompany.isp*.com) or a full-fledged, Network Solutions–approved domain (without the ISP name in the middle). Real domains require registration with Network Solutions, the organization in charge of managing domains, to make sure that no two people or organizations use the same one. Your ISP can register your chosen domain name with Network Solutions for you, and will probably charge a service fee in addition to the fee Network Solutions charges for the domain itself. Altogether, this should cost you about $150 a year.

● **A server computer**   Not every company needs its own Internet server, especially if you rely on an ISP to host your Web site. But many organizations choose to use a server to distribute e-mail within their office and to manage IP addresses. Using your own e-mail server makes sense if you have lots of users or if you run your own Internet mailing lists. One organization we know uses lots of contract employees and gives each an e-mail address so that they can work from home. You can only do this if you manage your own e-mail and don't rely on the ISP to create and delete accounts as employees move into and out of your organization. Eudora Internet Mail Server from Qualcomm and CE Software's QuickMail Office are among your mail server software choices. There's also a mail server component in AppleShare IP, Apple's file and Web server application.

 Tip: *ADSL is very well-suited to small office Internet access. A single ADSL modem, connected to your existing Ethernet, can handle lots of traffic and requires no more configuration than a dial-up connection. You can start with a low-speed DSL connection and then upgrade as your needs grow, without adding more equipment.*

 I want to start a Web site for my business. What's the best way to go about it?

Internet service providers (ISPs) will rent you space on their servers for your Web pages. Many personal Web accounts come with 10MB or so, while business accounts can include 25MB or more of free space. You can usually buy additional space for $50–$100 a month, if you need it. To maintain your site, just create the pages and upload them to the ISP's server using FTP.

Things get more complicated if you want your Web site to include fill-in forms, e-commerce, or some other feature that requires programming. When you fill in a form on the Web, the data you enter onscreen is processed by an application that runs in conjunction with the Web server. To create your own server applications, called CGIs (common gateway interfaces), you need to create or buy the software and upload it to the ISP's server. Many ISPs charge extra for sites with CGIs, because they require more processing power and network resources than plain old HTML pages and graphics. Many ISPs can also help you with CGIs by directing you to programs that have already been written to do the job you want or by suggesting consultants who can write CGIs for you.

 I'd like to cut out the middleman and run my own Web server, on a Mac! How can I do this?

We described the equipment you need to get your office online in the question "What do I need to get my small office online?" earlier in this section. To run your own Web server, you'll need all that and one more thing—a Web server. You can use a Mac as a Web server, or a Windows NT or Unix system, if you're so inclined.

AppleShare IP server software from Apple includes a Web server module; setting up a site is a simple matter of dragging files into a folder and enabling Web access. You can also run Mac CGIs on the server. For a more robust Mac Web server solution, try StarNine's WebSTAR. You can run it on any Power Mac, though it's probably a good idea to pick a fast one with lots of memory. Once again, WebSTAR supports a variety of commercial CGIs that let you provide forms, database access, and much more, right on a Mac. In fact,

good Mac CGIs, or plug-ins, to use StarNine's term, are said to be WebSTAR API-compliant.

To operate a Web server in your office, you need a full-time, relatively speedy (at least one 64 Kbps ISDN channel) connection, an Ethernet network, and a static IP address for the server computer.

I've heard about all-in-one Internet access solutions that include both hardware and ISP accounts. Are these combos a good way to provide Internet access for a small business?

Many Internet service providers (ISPs) offer a combination of Internet access and the hardware to make it possible. In most cases, the provider will recommend or sell a specific brand of router, modem, or other equipment. ISPs do this for two reasons: compatibility and profit. It's a lot easier for an ISP to provide tech support to its customers if it understands the hardware setup. Providers can also make extra money by reselling hardware vendors' equipment to their customers. If you really don't like the equipment your ISP wants you to buy, look elsewhere for Internet access.

Several companies have tried to tie Internet access and hardware even more closely together. One, Whistle Communications, supports the Mac, while several others have come and gone in the past couple of years.

Here's how it works. You contact Netcom, PSINet, or another ISP that provides Whistle's InterJet all-in-one Internet access device. The ISP sells you the hardware and provides the access your company needs. Whistle's InterJet, a box that's a little bigger than a toaster, is a combination Internet server, router, and ISDN- or modem-based connection to the Internet. Unlike most Internet "appliances," the InterJet actually includes a computer and hard disk that you manage with a Web-based administrative interface. Your ISP communicates with the server over the Internet, providing all of the configuration information your network needs. Since the InterJet's internal server supports AFP (AppleTalk Filing Protocol), users in your office can log onto the InterJet and download Internet software from, and upload HTML pages and graphics to, the built-in Web server.

The InterJet is not for everyone—you must use an ISP that supports it, and you can't use Macintosh Web server tools to enhance your Web site—but its simplicity makes it worth considering if having something that "just works" is an important consideration for your company.

Chapter 13

Setting Up for the Internet: Configuring and Using Software

Answer Topics!

Setting Up for the Internet @ a Glance

Using Mac OS Internet Tools discusses working with the Internet software that is part of Mac OS.

E-mail describes the e-mail tools included with your Mac, how to use them, and how you can use e-mail more effectively.

Web Browsing shows which browsers are available in Mac OS and how to configure some of their features.

Web Sharing describes how to use the personal Web Sharing features of Mac OS.

File Transfer describes FTP and how you can use it to download files via the Internet.

Other Internet Tools discusses several other Internet tools and how to use them.

USING MAC OS INTERNET TOOLS

Do I need to buy software to connect to the Internet with my Mac?

No. Mac OS versions since 7.5 include all of the software you need to go online. You can substitute your own Internet-access applications if you like, but you won't need to buy anything other than an account with an Internet service provider (ISP) to get online.

What Internet tools does Mac OS include?

Here is a breakdown of the Internet tools included in Mac OS. We also indicate where a tool is included only in certain versions.

- **Internet Setup Assistant** An application that walks you through the process of setting up your Internet software and configures TCP/IP, Remote Access, and other tools automatically. You can also use the assistant to set up a new Internet account with Earthlink, a service provider that has partnered with Apple. Find it in the Internet folder at the root level of your hard drive.

- **TCP/IP** Software that gives your Mac an identity on a TCP/IP network. TCP/IP is part of Open Transport, the Mac's networking architecture. Find it in the Control Panels folder.

- **PPP/Remote Access** Tools you use to dial in to your Internet service provider's network. PPP is included with Mac OS 7.5 through Mac OS 8.1. You may need to install it from the Mac OS CD-ROM if you're still using pre-Mac OS 8 software. In Mac OS 8.5 and later, PPP has been replaced by Remote Access—a combination of PPP and what was Apple Remote Access (ARA), a software package used to dial into Mac networks. Find it in the Control Panels folder.

- **Internet Config extension/Internet control panel** A central location for entering Internet account information, including your e-mail address, server address, preferred browser and e-mail software, and preferred helper applications. The Internet control panel is a part of Mac OS 8.5 and later; it replaces the Internet Config application that previous versions used to enter the same settings. Recent versions of Mac OS include the Internet Config extension, the engine behind the Internet control panel or the Internet Config application, depending on which version of Mac OS you use.

- **Web browsers**   Microsoft Internet Explorer and Netscape Navigator are installed as part of Mac OS 9, and Navigator is available in Mac OS 8.5. Internet Explorer is set as the default browser, but you can change that—we'll show you how later in this chapter.

- **E-mail**   Mac OS 8 and 8.1 included Emailer Lite, a pared-down version of Claris's spiffy (but now discontinued) e-mail application. Mac OS 8.5 and later include Microsoft Outlook Express for e-mail. You can also use Netscape Messenger, which is installed as part of Netscape Communicator, and comes with Mac OS 9.

- **Compression tools**   DropStuff and StuffIt Expander are compression utilities from Aladdin Systems. StuffIt Expander is a freeware utility that can expand Stuffit files as well as several other formats, including the ubiquitous PC compression standard, Zip. DropStuff is a shareware tool for compressing files.

- **Web Sharing**   Like Personal File Sharing, Web Sharing allows you to make files on your Mac available to others, via a Web browser.

How do I use Internet Setup Assistant?

Apple's Internet Setup Assistant gets you ready to surf by asking you a series of questions. Using your answers, it sets up all the software your Mac uses to get and keep you connected. You can also use the assistant to choose a new ISP, though your choice is limited to a provider Apple has partnered with to bring you the marketing pitch. To open a

new Internet account with Internet Setup Assistant, follow these steps:

1. Open the Internet Setup Assistant either by double-clicking the Browse the Internet icon on your desktop or by locating and opening the Internet Assistant alias, in the Internet folder.

2. When asked if your Mac is set up for the Internet, click Assist Me.

3. Answer the assistant's questions, filling in your name and phone number. The phone number is important, because Internet Assistant uses it to locate an ISP that serves your area.

4. Tell Internet Assistant what kind of modem you have, and what port it's connected to, when asked. The software will dial a toll-free number, log in to the registration server, and launch Internet Explorer (IE). IE displays buttons representing several ISPs in your area. At this writing, there was only one ISP available through this system—Earthlink/Sprint.

5. If you like the deal offered, fill out the information asked for on the Web site and complete the ISP registration process. If you do, the system will configure your Mac for you.

If you're not ready to sign up for an ISP account, or don't like the service offered, quit Internet Explorer and click Cancel in Internet Assistant. For more information about choosing an ISP, see Chapter 12.

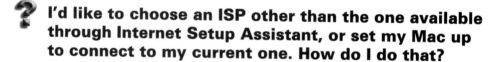 **I'd like to choose an ISP other than the one available through Internet Setup Assistant, or set my Mac up to connect to my current one. How do I do that?**

You can use the Internet Setup Assistant to configure your Mac for online access, or you can fill in the blanks in each of several control panels and applications that are part of Mac OS. Since the Internet Setup Assistant includes step-by-step help, in the next few questions we're going to walk you through setting up an Internet connection the hard way.

Our goal is to help you understand how the pieces of Mac OS work together to get you connected. Before you get started with the Internet Setup Assistant or our step-by-step guide, read the next question to learn what information you'll need to get started.

What information should I have before I set my Mac up for the Internet?

When you sign up for Internet access, your Internet service provider (ISP) should provide some basic information that you can use to set up your account:

- **A phone number**   Your ISP should provide one or more phone numbers to use when you connect to the service. If you upgrade a standard Internet account to ISDN, you should be given a new number.

- **IP address**   This numeric address identifies your Mac to the rest of the Internet. Some ISPs assign each customer a *static* IP address—one that only you use, every time you connect. Some ISPs assign you an address each time you dial in. In that case, you won't receive an IP address for your Mac when you sign up with the ISP, though you will probably receive the rest of the items listed in this question.

- **Addressing method**   The ISP should let you know whether or not you will be connecting to a PPP or DHCP server (which assigns you an IP address), or whether you will be using a static address.

- **Server address**   If you are dialing into an IP server that supports dynamic addressing, you should have an IP address for it. This server dispenses IP addresses to customers as they dial into the ISP's network.

- **Domain name server address**   Sounds a lot like the previous item, but you'll need a name-server address, whether you have a static IP address or not. Name servers match server IP addresses with domain names (for example, mycompany.com). You may be given two or more name-server addresses.

- **User name and password** Your provider will probably ask you to choose a user name, and may give you a password to use until you are connected and can change it yourself. Once you are online, you should change the password as soon as possible, for security reasons.

- **Special logon instructions** Some providers require you to use a prefix or suffix. For example, you might enter P (for PPP) before your user name when dialing your ISP. Other ISPs use a suffix—something like username.ppp.

- **E-mail address, POP account, and SMTP host name** Besides the e-mail address you will use to send mail and that you will give to those who send you mail, you'll need to know the name of the computer—called an SMTP server—your ISP uses to manage mail. In many cases, the POP account (in the format, *user*@mail.*isp*.com) points to the SMTP host (mail.*isp*.com), but sometimes POP and SMTP are on different machines.

- **News server name** To read Internet newsgroups, you must have access to a news server. ISPs usually include news-server access with your account. Most news servers are named using the format news.*isp*.com, but make sure that's the correct name.

How do I configure my Mac for the Internet?

We're going to show you how to set up TCP/IP and PPP (Remote Access, in Mac OS 9). These tools make it possible to connect to the Internet for a dial-up connection. If you have a cable modem or DSL connection, you will need to configure TCP/IP, but not Remote Access. To configure TCP/IP for the Internet, follow these steps:

1. Choose Apple menu | Control Panels | TCP/IP.

2. Choose a connection method from the Connect Via pop-up menu. If you're dialing your way onto the Internet, choose PPP. If you are connecting from an office network, cable modem, or DSL, you will probably choose Ethernet, but be sure to check with your network

administrator or ISP before you make a choice, or before you complete the TCP/IP control panel.

3. From the Configure menu, choose the address method your ISP has assigned you. If you have been assigned a static IP address, choose Manually.

4. If you have been assigned a static IP address, fill in the IP Address field. If you've chosen a server-address method, this field is not visible.

5. Enter a subnet mask and/or router address if you're using a BootP or DHCP server to connect. These addresses help the Mac locate the router and server used to connect you to the Internet.

6. Enter the name server address(es) in the field on the bottom left side of the TCP/IP control panel, and the domain name your ISP gave you—in the format *server.isp*.com—on the right. Figure 13-1 shows a typical TCP/IP setup for dial-up access.

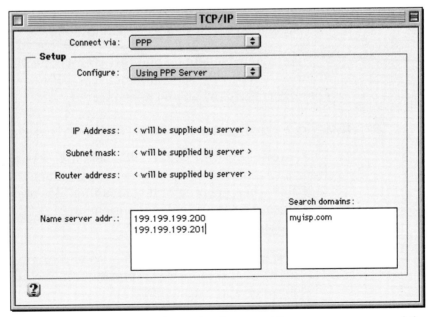

Figure 13-1 Choose PPP from the Connect Via pop-up menu, and then choose the kind of server your ISP uses. When you use these options, fields that you don't need will be dimmed

7. Close the TCP/IP control panel. Save your changes when asked.

To configure Internet dial-up access:

1. Choose Apple menu | Control Panels | Modem to verify that your Mac is set up to work with the modem you have connected. If not, choose the correct port and modem type from the pop-up menus. Close the Modem control panel.

2. Choose Apple menu | Control Panels | PPP (or Remote Access, if you have Mac OS 8.5 or later).

3. Type your user name and any prefixes or suffixes provided by your ISP in the Name field.

4. Enter your password. Click the Save Password button if you want PPP to dial without asking you for a password each time you connect.

5. Enter the ISP's phone number in the Number field. If you want to disable call waiting when you connect to the Internet, enter the proper code here too. For details on disabling call waiting, see Chapter 12.

Turn your modem on and test your connection by clicking Connect in the PPP control panel. The PPP window will look like Figure 13-2 when you're connected.

 How do I configure the Internet control panel?

The Internet control panel holds personal settings, as well as information that allows Internet applications to work together when opening or downloading files and reading messages. To set up Internet options in Mac OS 8.5 or later, follow these steps:

1. Use TCP/IP and Remote Access to configure your IP address and connection information, including phone number and user name.

2. Choose Apple menu | Control Panels | Internet.

Remote Access (Default)

▽ **Setup**

           ● Registered User   ○ Guest

Name : Shelly

Password : •••••

☐ Save password

Number : 555-1212

Status

Connected at :   31200 bps.

Connected to :   209.198.128.3

Time connected : 0:02:47

Time remaining : Unlimited   Send   Receive

[Options...] [**Disconnect**]

Figure 13-2   With information correctly entered in the Modem, TCP/IP, and Remote Access control panels, a successful dial-up connection looks something like this

3. Type your name and e-mail address in the Personal tab. Figure 13-3 shows a sample configuration.

4. Click the E-mail tab, and enter your e-mail account information.

5. Click the Web tab to enter a default home page and a search page. The home page appears each time you launch your Web browser.

6. Under the News tab, enter the address of your news server.

The Internet control panel provides a place for you to choose your default e-mail program, Web browser, and news reader. When you install Mac OS 8.5 or later, Internet Config chooses Outlook Express (mail and news) and Internet Explorer (Web browser), and displays these options in the Internet control panel.

Internet

Active Set: | untitled | ⇕ |

▽ Edit Sets

Edit Set: | untitled | ⇕ | [**Duplicate Set...**]

/ **Personal** \ / **E-mail** \ / **Web** \ / **News** \

Identity: _____   **Examples:** ___

Name: | Shelly Brisbin | Pat Smith

E-mail Address: | sbrisbin@brisbin.net | psmith@apple.com

Organization: | | Apple Computer, Inc.

Other Information:

Signature:

Figure 13-3   Enter your name and e-mail address in the Internet control panel's Personal tab

I have several Internet accounts. How can I set up my Mac to work with them?

It's easy to set up your Mac to dial multiple Internet accounts and check mail for each. With one account set up in Remote Access or PPP, follow these steps:

1. Choose Apple menu | Control Panels | TCP/IP.

2. Choose File | Configurations, or press COMMAND+K.

3. Click Default or the name of your existing Internet account, and click Duplicate.

4. Click Rename, to give the new configuration a name.

5. Click Make Active to work with the new configuration. Replace the information in the active configuration with the details of your second Internet account.

6. If you want to use your new account, close TCP/IP and save changes when asked. To return to your original account, press COMMAND+K and choose the account from the dialog box.

7. Repeat this procedure with the PPP or Remote Access control panel. The options and command shortcuts are the same as for TCP/IP.

The Internet control panel also supports multiple configurations. To create a new set of preferences, open the control panel, click Duplicate Set (or choose New Set from the File menu), and enter your alternate e-mail address and other information.

To use your alternate configuration, open the Internet control panel and choose it from the Active Set pop-up menu.

E-MAIL

What e-mail software is included with Mac OS?

Mac OS 8.5 and later include two e-mail applications, Microsoft Outlook Express and Netscape Messenger. Outlook and Messenger are flexible and easy to use. Because both are widely in use, we'll use both in the examples for this section of the chapter.

How do I configure Outlook Express to send and receive e-mail?

To configure Outlook Express to read e-mail, follow these steps:

1. Double-click the Mail icon on your desktop or Microsoft Outlook Express in the Internet folder.

2. When the New Account window appears, name it anything you like. Leave the POP button selected.

3. Type your user name, password, and other e-mail information provided by your ISP in the Preferences window, if it's not already entered (see Figure 13-4). It will be there already if you've used the Internet control panel to set mail preferences. You can set preferences for sending

Figure 13-4 Configure your e-mail account in the Outlook Express Preferences window. You can add more e-mail accounts by clicking New Account

and receiving mail, as well as other Outlook Express options, in other panes of the Preferences window.

How do I configure Netscape Messenger to send and receive e-mail?

Mac OS 9 users will find Netscape Communicator in the Internet Applications folder, inside the Internet folder on their hard disk. Communicator is also available for download at Netscape's Web site (http://www.netscape.com).

To set up Netscape Messenger to read e-mail, follow these steps:

1. Open the Netscape Communicator folder and launch Communicator.

2. If you haven't used Communicator before, you will be asked to create a user profile. Netscape forces you to do this whether or not you want Communicator to be your default e-mail application.

3. Fill in your profile by entering your name, e-mail account, and server information, as provided by your ISP and directed by the Profile application. When you've finished, the Netscape Navigator browser appears.

4. Click the Inbox button in the application launch pad window, as shown here.

5. Enter your password when prompted. The Messenger application opens, and the Inbox appears.

Can I use a different e-mail program if I'm not satisfied with Outlook Express or Netscape Messenger?

You certainly can. Eudora Light and Eudora Pro from Qualcomm are popular choices.

If you pick an e-mail program that's not included with Mac OS, choose one that uses Internet Config to pass settings between programs. If you do, you can probably get away without having to fiddle with e-mail options. When you

install a new program, just update the Internet control panel
(Mac OS 8.5 and later) or Internet Config to recognize the
new program.

Can I retrieve e-mail from multiple accounts using a single application and mailbox?

Outlook Express allows you to log in to multiple e-mail
accounts at the same time. Netscape Messenger does not.
Like Outlook Express, Eudora Pro from Qualcomm supports
multiple accounts.

With multiple logins, you can tell the software to connect
to the Internet and retrieve all of your messages, from all of
your accounts. The e-mail application can deposit the mail
into the same mailbox, or create a mailbox for each of your
accounts. To add a second account in Outlook Express, follow
these steps:

1. Open Outlook Express.
2. Choose Edit | Preferences.
3. Click New Account.
4. Name the account anything you like, and leave the POP
   button selected.
5. Enter the information for the new account in the
   Preferences window, including how and when to check
   for new mail.

I keep hearing about free e-mail accounts from companies like Yahoo! and Hotmail. What's the catch?

Several companies offer free e-mail accounts. There is usually
no limit to the number of messages you can send or receive.
The catch is that you are usually asked for information about
yourself—your address, your interests, maybe even your
annual income. This information helps the provider market
products to you, through e-mail. You're guaranteed to get
some unsolicited mail from the folks who gave you the
account, and maybe even from companies your host sells
your information to.

Your e-mail account will also become a billboard for the provider. Messages from Yahoo! account holders, for example, include an advertisement for the service. You can't send a message without the "Do you Yahoo!" tag line and a URL.

If you don't mind a few (or maybe a lot of) ads, and could care less that your messages have billboards in them, go and get yourself a free e-mail account. You'll still need a full-fledged dial-up Internet account elsewhere to connect to the Internet, but a second e-mail address might be useful if you want to keep personal and business mail separate, for example.

Another approach for users who want multiple e-mail accounts is to buy them from your current provider. Some ISPs offer a second or third account for a few extra dollars a month. A few even offer a number of extra accounts free. If your extra accounts are with the same provider, your configuration chores are lessened, too.

I get lots of unsolicited e-mail. Is there a way to fight spam?

Spam is the Internet term for unsolicited e-mail that comes to you from companies who want to sell you something. Everything, from pyramid schemes to pornographic Web sites, is hawked through e-mail spam, and some people's e-mail boxes become inundated with the stuff.

Spammers get your address in a variety of ways; if you post messages to Usenet newsgroups, your address has almost certainly been added to someone's spam list. Some spammers have ways of grabbing large numbers of e-mail addresses from commercial sources, or using electronic trickery to send mail to everyone with an account in a certain domain. If you're an AOL member, you're particularly susceptible to spam if you have posted messages, participated in chats, or otherwise let the community at large know your screen name.

Here are four strategies for fighting spam:

● *Choose an Internet provider that uses spam filters.* Many spammers use particular e-mail domain names in an attempt to disguise themselves, and because these domains allow them to send bulk e-mail unopposed. Some ISPs block messages from these domains. Some write filtering routines that analyze the headers of e-mail messages and determine whether, based on the content or how many messages are being sent, the mail is likely to be spam. ISP-based filters don't catch all spam, but having them in place is an indication that the ISP is doing its part to help. After all, spam clogs the mail server, as well as your mailbox.

- *Use multiple e-mail accounts.* If you like to do the things that lead to spam—posting to newsgroups, for example— get yourself an e-mail address that is more or less public. You can ignore incoming mail or delete it all without reading it, thwarting the spammer's attempt to get your attention. Your second e-mail account should be used only to exchange mail with people you trust, and should not be given to businesses that may sell it to a spammer.

- *Create e-mail filters.* Microsoft Outlook Express and Netscape Messenger each support e-mail filtering, as do several other e-mail programs. You can set them up so that mail from certain addresses, or with certain subjects, is immediately deleted. Spammers like to use eye-catching subject lines, like "Make Money Fast," "Free Free Free," or "**Read This." After you've seen a few spam messages, you'll recognize it instantly. You can create e-mail filters that dump messages with spammy subjects.

- *Foil the newsgroup spammers.* When your e-mail address is harvested from a posting you send to a newsgroup, it's dumped into a file with the addresses of other unfortunates. The harvester rarely reads through the file, but simply sends out advertisements and other junk to the list. You may be able to stop some newsgroup spam by altering the address you use when posting to a newsgroup. Instead of *myaddress@isp*.com, change your e-mail identity to NO-SPAM*myaddress@isp*.com, and include instructions for sending your e-mail in the body of your message; for example, "To reply to this message, remove the word NO-SPAM from my address."

! *Caution:* *Though it's not a strategy for preventing spam, there is one important thing you can do to keep it from coming back: never, ever reply to spam messages, especially those that offer to remove you from a mailing list if you reply. Spammers use these replies to verify that you received and read their mail. You'll be hearing from them again!*

? ## How can I create a spam filter in Outlook Express?

To create a simple spam filter, follow these steps:

1. In Outlook Express, choose Tools | Mail Rules.

2. Click the New Rule button.

3. In the Define Rule window, give your filter a name. Leave the Apply to Incoming check box selected. Use the Criteria pop-up menu to choose an item to filter on. In our example (shown in Figure 13-5), we filter based on the Subject field of incoming messages. When you've selected a criterion, type the specific text to filter in the text field. We typed "make money fast," a subject line used by some spammers to get your attention. To add a second criterion, click check boxes in the Criteria section of the window.

4. If you choose multiple criteria, you can tell Outlook Express whether to use one or all criteria when filtering by choosing the appropriate option in the Execute Actions If pop-up menu.

5. Choose one or more actions to be taken when a message that meets your criteria appears. In our case, we will choose Move Message from the Action 1 pop-up menu.

6. In the second menu that appears, choose Deleted Messages to trash items that meet your criteria as they arrive. Figure 13-5 shows the completed filter.

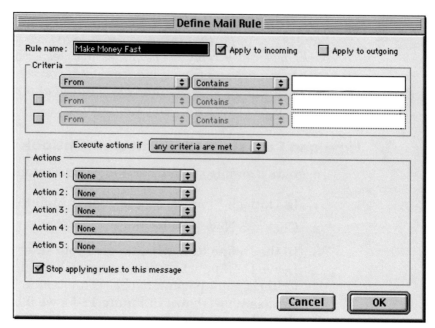

Figure 13-5 The filter will find and delete any incoming messages with the words "make money fast" in the Subject line

---

 Tip: *Filters are good for much more than thwarting spammers. You can use them to direct mail from a mailing list into a specific mailbox, assign some messages a higher priority, generate automatic replies, and more.*

How can I create a spam filter in Netscape Messenger?

To create a spam filter in Messenger, follow these steps:

1. In Netscape Communicator, choose Inbox from the launch pad window.

2. Choose Edit Message Filters.

3. Click the New button to create a filter.

4. Click in the Name field of the new filter, and type a name for it.

5. Type a description if you like.

6. Type **Make money fast** in the text box next to the Subject and Contains pop-up menus, as shown in Figure 13-6.

7. Choose an action for the filter. In this case, we'll leave Move to Folder selected, and choose Trash from the folder list.

8. To add more items to filter, click the More button. You'll be able to add more spam subjects to your filter.

9. Close the window to finish the filter.

Figure 13-6 Type the trigger for your filter, and then create an Action for it in Netscape Messenger's Message Filters window

 I don't want to filter mail directly to the Trash or Deleted Messages mailbox. I'm concerned that I will delete legitimate messages by accident. Is there a way to filter spam without losing real e-mail?

Spammers use all sorts of tricks to get you to read their mail. The "make money fast" filter we created in the previous questions will not catch most of today's spam, which can come with subject lines like "Hi;-)" and sender names like "Bill Gates."

To be rid of spam and still make sure that you don't accidentally trash a message you want, follow these steps in any e-mail program that supports filters:

1. Create a mailbox called Junk, Spam, or something similar.

2. Use other mailboxes and filters to route the mail you want to read. For example, send mail from your favorite humor mailing list to the Joke mailbox.

3. Create a filter that sends all messages that do not include your e-mail address in their To, CC, or BCC lines to the Junk mailbox. Since spammers send their mail in bulk, they usually use a fake To or CC address for everyone on their list. Since legitimate mailing lists use the same technique to send mail to their subscribers, the filters you created in step 2 are important if you receive mail that is directed to a large group of people.

4. Arrange your filters (you can usually do this by dragging within the filter window) so that mail is filtered from fine to coarse. Mail that includes your e-mail address should be filtered first, followed by mail to mailing lists you belong to. Then unrecognized mail will be filed by the spam filter.

5. Check the Junk mailbox periodically to see if you have filtered any messages you intended to keep, and then trash the spam. If messages you wanted to keep ended up in the Junk mailbox, consider creating a filter that will direct those messages to a different mailbox in the future.

Can I use styled text with e-mail?

There are two parts to the styled text equation: sending and receiving. If your e-mail program supports the creation of styled text, you can send messages with bold, italic, colored, or underlined text. Popular Mac e-mail tools, including Outlook Express, Messenger, and Eudora, all support styled text. On the receiving end, text style information is either duplicated just as you created it, or discarded if the recipient's mail program doesn't support it. Most mail programs that do support styled text allow you to disable it if you'd rather not see your mail messages in lemon yellow or orange. And since the fancy styles you put in your e-mail messages might not be seen at the other end, it is best to make sure that your message doesn't depend on the text styles and is understandable without them.

What are the rules for sending files with e-mail messages?

E-mail messages move easily from computer to computer because they are all in a format that every e-mail program and PC platform can understand—ASCII text. But when you attach a file (graphic, word processing, spreadsheet, and so on) to an e-mail message, you enter the world of MIME, BinHex, Uuencode; these are standard formats used for encoding and decoding files as they travel from one e-mail box to another. Each of these formats converts a file to text and then back to its original format when it arrives at its destination. Problems develop when the two e-mail programs don't support the same format, or when a file gets corrupted in transit.

The most common format for Mac file transfers is BinHex. All Mac e-mail programs that support attachments (and that's just about every modern offering) support BinHex transfers. That means that it's usually a piece of cake to exchange files with Mac users, whether they're using the same e-mail program or not. Since your e-mail program automatically BinHexes a file before sending it, and the Mac on the other end automatically decodes it, the process is usually a cinch.

You have two other allies in decoding attachments, whether they come from a Mac or not. First, Aladdin System's StuffIt Expander, which is free and included with Mac OS, will automatically decode and (if the file was compressed before sending) decompress BinHex files. The company's $30 DropStuff with Expander Enhancer decodes Uuencode and MIME files, too. You'll find DropStuff in the Internet | Internet Utilities folder on your Mac OS CD, or on your hard drive. Just pay your money, and the messages that ask for your serial number each time you start up will disappear.

I've heard it's a good idea to compress files before I attach them to an e-mail message. How do I go about it?

Compressing files before you transfer them can save up to two-thirds of the space of the original file. Aladdin's StuffIt is the standard compression utility for the Mac (if you've ever seen or opened a file with a .sit or .sea extension, you've used StuffIt). DropStuff, which we described in the previous question as a way to decode attachments, is mainly a compression utility. Drag a file or group of files onto the DropStuff icon to compress them. StuffIt Expander will decompress files others send to you.

If you have StuffIt Expander installed, StuffIt files will decompress automatically as they land on your hard drive, whether they're attached to an e-mail message or downloaded from the Internet. You can set StuffIt Expander to delete the compressed versions, or keep them around. We recommend keeping them until you're sure the file's decompressed version is okay.

You'll find lots of information about compressing and encoding files for PC users in Chapter 10.

What's an e-mail list?

The Internet is just about the greatest source of information there is. One way people share that information, as well as their conversations, is through an e-mail list, or mailing list. Members sign up to receive e-mail from the list: either

postings from a central source of information or messages from all the other members of the list.

Some lists distribute newsletters, like the popular TidBITS, a weekly update on happenings in the Macintosh world. (Find out more about TidBITS at http://www. tidbits.com/.) Subscribe by sending an e-mail message, and you'll get a new edition of Mac news each Monday evening.

Discussion lists are places for folks to chat about specific topics—software, music, food, motorcycles, and almost anything else you can think of. These lists typically have a leader, or list owner, who hosts the service on an Internet server, and who handles the administrative chores of adding and removing subscribers from the list. The list owner may also *moderate*, or control the discussion to keep it on topic, by restricting what can be posted on the list. When you join a mailing list, you usually receive a message explaining the list's rules for discussion, how and whether it is moderated, and how to get off the list. Here are some resources for finding mailing lists:

Apple mailing lists	http://www.lists.apple.com/lists.qry
The Internet Mailing List Network	http://www.listsnet.com/
List of Music Mailing Lists	http://www.shadow.net/~mwaas/lomml/

WEB BROWSING

Which Web browsers are included with Mac OS?

Mac OS 8.5 and later include Microsoft Internet Explorer and Netscape Navigator. In Mac OS 8.5, Netscape Navigator comes on the CD, but you must install it manually.

Which Web browser is the best?

We can narrow it down to two: Internet Explorer and Netscape Navigator. The debate over which of these two browsers is best divides Mac and PC users alike. We don't think choosing either would be a big mistake, so you'll have to decide based on the

Shelly's Scoop: Internet Explorer Site Subscriptions

I wrote the answer to the previous question, and I didn't anoint a superior Web browser because I honestly believe the choice is up to each person and that Navigator and Explorer each have points in their favor. But, as you might imagine, I do have a favorite. It's not perfect, but my browser of choice—to paraphrase Steve Jobs at the 1998 Macworld Expo in New York—is Internet Explorer.

I'll pause now while my fellow Microsoft skeptics catch their breath.

After a couple of years happily using Mosaic, MacWeb (does anyone remember MacWeb?), and early versions of Navigator, I made the switch because, gosh darn it, Microsoft built a product that was elegant and fast. One other thing convinced me to stick with Internet Explorer when version 4 came out—the site subscription feature.

If one of your favorite sites is updated frequently, you may find yourself checking every day or two for new information. Using Internet Explorer's site subscription option, you can find out what's new just by launching your browser. Internet Explorer checks the pages you've subscribed to and can notify you by e-mail or alert that a favorite site has changed since your last visit. The message will even provide the URL. Click and you're on your way. I use site subscriptions to keep track of my favorite music site, Mac news page, and others. I can have my subscription checked daily, weekly, or each time I launch the browser. To set up a subscription, follow these steps:

1. In Internet Explorer, go to a site you'd like to subscribe to.
2. Choose Favorites | Subscribe.
3. Click Subscribe to add a subscription with default preferences, or Customize to set your own.
4. If you clicked Customize, click the Subscribe tab in the window that appears.
5. Click the Check This Site for Changes check box.

6. Click the Schedule tab, and choose when you would like Internet Explorer to check this site and notify you of changes. Other options let you pick a notification method specific to this site, or a different e-mail address to receive the notices.

7. To set preferences for all site subscriptions you create, choose Edit | Preferences; then click the Subscriptions option, where you will find scheduling and notification options.

merits of the browsers themselves. And whether you get the browsers with Mac OS, or download them from Netscape or Microsoft, neither will cost you a red cent.

If you're short on memory, stick with Internet Explorer. Netscape Communicator, the complete package from Netscape, is more memory-hungry and loads and operates more slowly than Explorer.

Dynamic HTML support is a Navigator plus. While both browsers can do DHTML, Netscape does it better.

On the plus side for Internet Explorer 4.5 is the ability to review the sites you've visited over multiple sessions. Internet Explorer's History folders organize the pages you've viewed in folders that are named by date.

We could go on like this all day, but we won't. Our advice is to try both browsers and see which one you like the best.

How do I play sounds and view movies in my Web browser?

Web browsers display text, graphics, and some multimedia files without help from anyone. But many sound and video formats require special software: either a stand-alone application or a *plug-in* for your browser. Without the needed software, Web pages that include movies or sounds will load as they should, but won't play the multimedia files.

Plug-ins load when the browser is launched, much the way extensions load when you start up your Mac, and they are activated when you connect to a page that includes the

file types they're designed to open. The plug-in will either play the movie, sound, animation, or other file in your browser window, or in its own window.

Most Web sites that include files created with tools like RealNetworks' RealPlayer, Macromedia's Shockwave, or other multimedia formats will alert you that you need to download a plug-in or application. If you want to make sure you're up-to-date, go to the BrowserWatch Web site's Plug-In Plaza page at http://browserwatch.internet.com/plug-in.html. You'll find links to just about every browser helper you could ever want. To add a new browser plug-in:

1. Download the plug-in.

2. If the plug-in package includes an installer program, run it after quitting your browser.

3. If there's no installer, determine whether the software is a plug-in or an application. If it's a plug-in, copy the file into the Plug-ins folder inside your Web browser's folder.

Tip: *Navigator and Internet Explorer can use the same plug-ins. If you use both browsers, you can use the same actual set of plug-ins by creating aliases from plug-ins stored in one browser's folder and placing them in the other browser's Plug-ins folder.*

 ## Do I need to configure my Web browser before using it?

Not really. The combination of Internet Config and the Internet control panel, along with the default options set within the browser, makes Navigator and Internet Explorer Web-ready from the start. Netscape Communicator asks for your name and e-mail address when you launch the application for the first time, but that's about it.

If you launch Navigator or Internet Explorer without setting a default Web page in the Internet control panel, you'll see an Excite home page with Apple logo and links that provides a starting point for Web searching and information-gathering. It is shown in Figure 13-7.

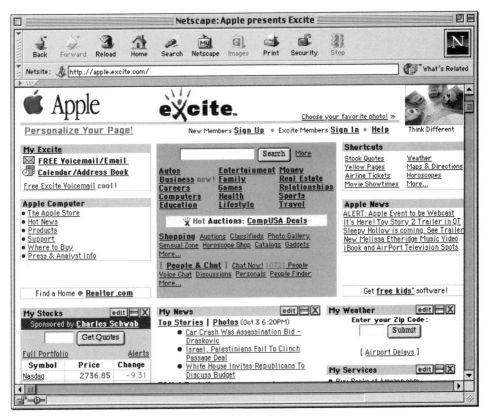

Figure 13-7 The Excite/Apple home page that appears when you open Internet Explorer or Netscape Navigator provides links to Apple resources, search engines, news, and more

Your browser also comes with URLs for a variety of useful Mac resources, available from the Favorites menu in Internet Explorer, shown in Figure 13-8, or the Bookmarks menu in Navigator.

 ## What are cookies, and should I accept them?

Cookies are small files that a Web site transfers to your computer when you visit. Cookies sit quietly on your hard drive until you visit the site again. When you do go back, the site looks to see if a cookie is present on your system and uses the information in it to determine when you visited last; what

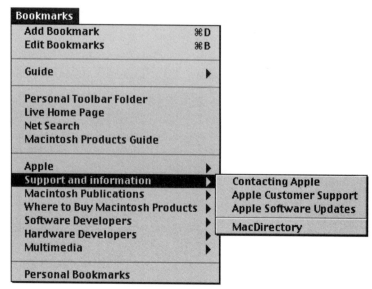

Figure 13-8 Each browser includes a list of bookmarks (Navigator) or favorites (Internet Explorer) that provide pointers to all sorts of Mac-related resources. Here is Navigator's list

pages you viewed; and, if you have a password for the site, what access privileges you should have during your current visit. Cookies do not contain detailed information about you or your computer, and they are only used by the site that left them on your computer in the first place.

If you object to the idea of cookies, however harmless they are, you can tell your browser not to accept them. If you do that, most sites will not be able to save your password or greet you by name each time you return. Whether that's a good thing or not is up to you.

In some cases, rejecting cookies will do you no good. Some Web sites use cookies to grant or deny access. In order to download files, read certain Web pages, get support, or otherwise use the site, you may be required to register or provide information about yourself. These sites typically use cookies to track their registrants' comings and goings, and to tell them apart from other site visitors. No cookie, no special perks. We don't like it, but it's the way some parts of the Web work.

To disable cookies in Netscape Navigator 4.6:

1. In Navigator, choose Edit | Preferences.

2. Click the Advanced category.

3. Click the Do Not Accept Cookies radio button or the Warn Me Before Accepting Cookies check box (see Figure 13-9).

4. Close the Preferences window. When Navigator detects a site that would like to add a cookie to your hard drive, the cookie will be rejected. If you choose to be warned before cookies are set, an alert will appear, and you'll have the chance to accept or decline the cookie.

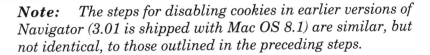

Note: *The steps for disabling cookies in earlier versions of Navigator (3.01 is shipped with Mac OS 8.1) are similar, but not identical, to those outlined in the preceding steps.*

To disable cookies in Internet Explorer:

1. In Internet Explorer, choose Edit | Preferences.

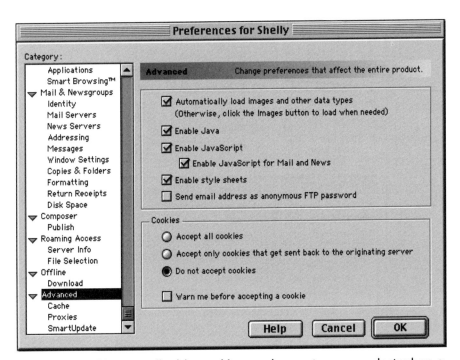

Figure 13-9 You can disable cookies or choose to see an alert when a Web site wants to set a cookie on your hard drive

2. Click the Cookies label in the left panel—it's under the
   Receiving Files label. If that's closed, click the triangle
   to open it. If you have used this browser for a while and
   have done nothing to disable cookies, those that are
   currently stored on your Mac will appear on the right
   side of the window.

   To disable an existing cookie, click its name, and then
   click Delete. To decline all cookies, choose Never Accept from
   the When Receiving Cookies pop-up menu. You can also
   choose to accept cookies only after an alert, or to accept all
   cookies. Figure 13-10 shows the Cookies panel of the Internet
   Explorer Preferences window.

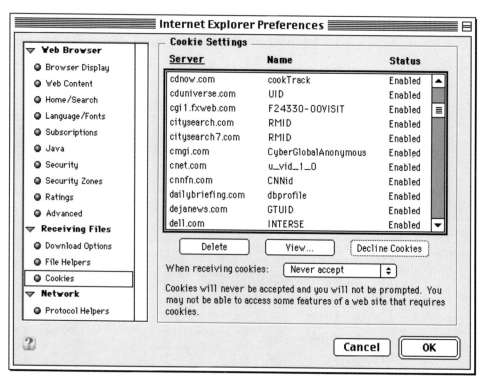

Figure 13-10   You can delete individual cookies or decline all of them in
the Cookies panel of Internet Explorer's Preferences
window

How can I make sure that my Web browser is up-to-date?

Microsoft and Netscape update their browser software frequently. If you purchased Mac OS 8.5 a year ago and haven't downloaded a new version of Navigator, you're already out of date. At this writing, the version of Internet Explorer included with Mac OS 9 is current (version 4.5). Netscape Communicator 4.61 ships with Mac OS 9. It's important to keep your browser current for a couple of reasons: the HTML standard that governs the look of Web pages is evolving, and each new browser version offers subtle tweaks to the look of the Web. The software also changes as technology evolves, and in response to pressure to integrate Web content with the rest of the software on your computer.

It's a good idea to check for new versions of your favorite browser every few months, and to keep up on technology news to find out if either vendor plans a major new release. Look for news and updates to Internet Explorer and Netscape Navigator or Communicator at the following Web sites:

Microsoft Internet Explorer	http://www.microsoft.com/mac/ie/
Netscape Navigator	http://home.netscape.com/computing/download

Netscape makes it possible for you to keep track of updates to its browser without repeatedly checking the site. Communicator includes a feature called SmartUpdate, which checks for new versions when you log onto the Internet and lets you know when a new one is available. It's enabled by default, but here's how to use or disable it:

1. In Navigator, choose Edit | Preferences.

2. Scroll down the Category list to find SmartUpdate. It's under the Advanced section (Figure 13-11).

3. To use SmartUpdate, make sure that the SmartUpdate check box is enabled. Disable it by unchecking the box.

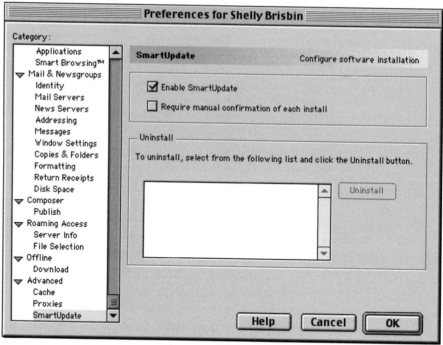

Figure 13-11 Click the SmartUpdate item under Advanced preferences to allow Netscape to automatically download updates when they are available

One more tip for those who like to be ahead of the pack: both browser makers often release beta versions of their software long before they are ready for prime time. In some cases, it's what the ever-changing Web public demands; in other cases, it's an easy way for Netscape or Microsoft to get some free testing from its customers. If you're risk-averse, wait for the shipping versions, which are usually clearly labeled as such.

WEB SHARING

Can anyone use Web Sharing to host a Web page?

Apple's Web Sharing software, which is built into Mac OS 8 and later, allows you to host Web pages on your Mac. To use it, you must be connected to the Internet when visitors want to see your Web pages. That means that if you use a dial-up Internet account, you won't be able to share pages with Web Sharing unless you first tell your visitors that you are online. People with continuous Internet access can use Web Sharing much the way they use Personal File Sharing, making a folder available to visitors, and putting Web page files inside. If your Mac is behind a company firewall, you can share Web pages with others in the office, or, if there isn't a firewall, you can share with the outside world.

Note: *You can use Web Sharing with a dial-up Internet account if you are online when visitors arrive. However, most dial-up accounts use dynamic IP addressing—where the ISP gives you a different IP address each time you dial in—so your URL does not stay the same from connection to connection. You'll need to provide the current one to anyone who should see your pages. The bottom line is that using Web Sharing from a dial-up account is usually more trouble than it is worth.*

How do I use Web Sharing to publish my own Web page?

First, set up Web Sharing, and then tell visitors where to find your pages. To set up Web Sharing, follow these steps:

1. Make sure that you are connected to the Internet.

2. Choose Apple menu I Control Panels I Web Sharing.

3. If you want to use a folder other than the Web Pages folder that is selected by default, click the Select button.

4. Choose a home page (the default page that users visiting your Web site will see). It must reside in the shared folder you just selected. It must also be an HTML file, in order for a browser to display it properly.

5. Click Start to enable Web Sharing. A URL appears next to My Address, with a numeric equivalent below. Figure 13-12 shows an active Web Sharing window.

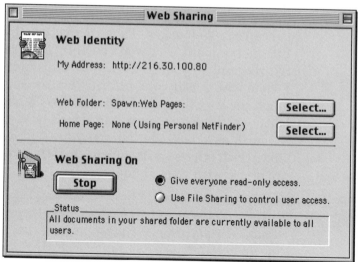

Figure 13-12 When active, Web Sharing displays your Mac's URL. Anyone with a Web browser can use it to connect to your Web pages

---

Tip: *Here's a quick way to pass your Web Sharing address along to friends, via e-mail. With the Web Sharing control panel open, and Web Sharing enabled, choose Edit | Copy My Address. Your URL is copied to the Clipboard. Just paste it into an e-mail message, and send it off.*

 How can I keep track of who visits my Web page?

Like other Web server applications, Web Sharing can keep a log of those who access your pages. To create a log, choose Edit Preferences in the Web Sharing control panel, and click the Web Sharing Log check box. Figure 13-13 shows the Web Sharing Preferences dialog box.

Can I use Personal Web Sharing to host a large Web site?

Plenty of Web sites are hosted on Macintoshes. Typically, these sites use dedicated Web server software, like StarNine's WebSTAR, or Apple's own AppleShare IP server software. These server applications are designed to accept more simultaneous users and deliver data faster than can

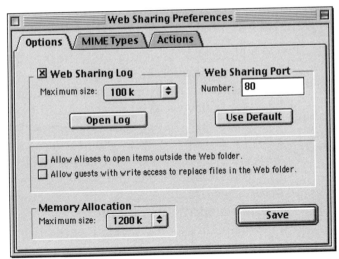

Figure 13-13 You can choose to create a log of Web page visitors and choose other options in the Web Sharing Preferences window

Personal Web Sharing. Dedicated Web servers typically reside on fast Macs with lots of memory and fast connections to the Internet. If your connection is not speedy, and/or you use your Mac for something other than a Web server, it's not a good idea to try to run a Web site with Personal Web Sharing.

Personal Web Sharing does support CGI (Common Gateway Interface) applications—external applications that make Web functions like database searching and fill-in forms possible. Configure CGI applications in the Actions tab of the Preferences window.

FILE TRANSFER

 ## What is FTP?

FTP stands for File Transfer Protocol. It's the standard method of moving files on the Internet. URLs with the format ftp://*server.company*.com, point to file servers that contain files available for download. The contents of FTP servers appear in directories (folders) or simply as links to individual files.

 Which FTP software should I use?

Both Netscape Navigator and Internet Explorer support FTP. You can click an FTP URL from within the browser and reach a directory or individual file. It's more difficult to use a browser to browse FTP directories, though. The best way to do that is with an application that specializes in FTP.

FTP software displays the contents of a server just the way the Finder displays the contents of your hard drive: in windows, with icons and names representing files and directories. Double-click to open directories, and drag files to and from the Mac Finder.

Our favorite FTP tool is Anarchie, brought to you by Stairways Software, which is also responsible for Internet Config. You'll find it at ftp://ftp.stairways.com//stairways/. To get it, enter this URL into your Web browser and click the link to Anarchie. In addition to providing a great FTP interface and compatibility with Internet Config, Anarchie features the best Archie client on the Mac. Archie is a search engine that locates files matching a text string you enter.

We mention Internet Config in relation to FTP for the same reason we discussed it in the e-mail questions. When you download a file to your Mac, it's usually compressed and encoded. If your FTP application is Internet Config–aware, and you have StuffIt Expander installed, the files you download will be decoded and expanded automatically when they arrive on your computer.

OTHER INTERNET TOOLS

What tools can I use to read Usenet newsgroups?

Newsgroups are like party-line telephones or a public bulletin board: everyone in the group can read everyone else's messages. At this writing, there are over 25,000 newsgroups devoted to an enormous breadth of subjects, from computing to bodybuilding to folk music to particle physics to pornography.

To read newsgroups, you need access to a news server (most dial-up Internet accounts include this service) and a news-reading application. Netscape Communicator and

Outlook Express can both read newsgroups, as can John Norstadt's free NewsWatcher, and many others.

To read news, you must connect to the news server (Internet Config and the Internet control panel each have a field for your news server), which is properly called an NNTP server. When you connect for the first time, your news software will download a list of all available newsgroups. This can take quite awhile, so take this opportunity to go have a cup of coffee. From the finished list, you can select groups to read. Most news-reading software requires that you "subscribe" to a group before you can read its messages. Subscribing simply places your chosen group in a different folder or list. Each time you read messages, the software marks those that have been read, and will only display new ones the next time you connect to the news server.

How can I use the Internet as a long-distance telephone?

Several vendors sell software that lets you make voice "calls" over the Internet. It works like this: with a microphone connected to your Mac and speakers to let you hear the other end of the conversation, Internet telephony software "dials" another computer using its IP address as the "phone" number. To successfully place a call, your intended recipient must be online and must have telephony software running.

When your recipient answers his or her Internet phone, both parties can talk. The voice messages you send are transmitted and played back as sound files. The quality isn't great, and there are often delays while information moves over the Internet, but neither party pays long-distance charges unless the call to your ISP is a toll call.

Internet phones work best when you're connected via a high-speed network, but are usable at 28.8 Kbps and above. Makers of Internet telephony software include NetPhone.

Can I log onto remote file servers and Macs using the Internet?

If the remote file server uses TCP/IP and has granted you access privileges, you certainly can log on. AppleShare IP server software, described more fully in Chapter 9, lets users

connect either from an AppleTalk network or using TCP/IP. To reach an AppleShare IP server or other AFP-compatible server with TCP/IP access, you use the AppleShare client software (which is available in the Chooser) and the IP address of the server you want to connect to. AFP, by the way, stands for Apple Filing Protocol. That's the network technology that allows you to see Mac file server volumes on the network. To connect to an AFP server over the Internet, follow these steps:

1. With an Internet connection active, open the Chooser.
2. Click the AppleShare icon to select it.
3. Click the Server IP Address button.
4. Type the address of the server in the field that appears, and click OK.
5. When the server's name appears in the Chooser window, double-click it to log on.
6. Type your name and password, and click OK to complete the connection. When your access is granted, the server's icon appears on the desktop. You can work with it just as you would any other server volume.

Tip: *You can save yourself a trip to the Chooser by picking up a copy of Open Door Networks' AFP Engage!, a utility that recognizes AFP servers that have URLs in the format afp://server.company.com. When you install AFP Engage! and double-click an AFP URL, the connection is launched just as it would be if you had clicked a Web (http) URL.*

Can I back up my Mac using the Internet?

There are two ways to use the Internet to back up your Mac. Dantz Development's Retrospect 4 backup software supports TCP/IP. You can use that capability to back up Macs on a local TCP/IP network, or do it via the Internet, to a server in a branch office, for example.

The second way to use the Internet for backing up your Mac is to work with a commercial service. These outfits will let you copy your stuff using TCP/IP to their server. They will

maintain a copy of the data for you and restore your stuff via the Net if anything goes wrong. BackJack is the first Mac-specific backup company we've heard about. Its Web site is at http://www.backjack.com/.

Part Four

Living with Your Mac: Troubleshooting, Upgrading, Tips, and Toys

Chapter 14

Software and Hardware Troubleshooting

Answer Topics!

Software and Hardware Troubleshooting @ a Glance

Troubleshooting Basics introduces you to Mac problems and solutions.

Startup Problems and Solutions explains how to deal with problems that appear when you start up the Mac.

Freezes, Crashes, and Error Messages provides help in dealing with a variety of problems that can occur while you're using your Mac.

Memory Problems describes how to deal with problems caused by lack of memory, or poor memory allocation.

Finding and Using Help lists help resources available on the Mac, from other users, and online.

Hardware Problems describes common hardware problems and how to diagnose and fix them.

Getting Your Mac and Peripherals Repaired suggests ways to determine whether your Mac needs repair, and details the best sources of service.

TROUBLESHOOTING BASICS

What are the most frequent causes of Mac problems?

When something changes within your Mac system, conditions are right for some sort of problem. Incompatible software is a frequent offender. Before you install a new piece of software, update or upgrade an old application, or add a hardware device, make sure you have a backup of at least your System Folder (and preferably everything important on the disk, just in case). That way you can "go back to the way things were" if the new software or hardware somehow creates a problem.

Hidden disk or directory damage can also cause lots of trouble. Mac OS uses several invisible files to keep track of what is on your hard disk. These files occasionally get damaged or "corrupted." Run Apple's Disk First Aid to fix disk directory files. See "What software will help?," later in this chapter, for more about Disk First Aid.

Bad cables are another thing to consider. A cable with a bent or broken pin, or with frayed wires, can make your whole system unstable. It's a good idea to keep some spare "known-to-be-good" cables on hand and to substitute them for your current cables if something goes haywire.

You may have sustained damage to any of the hundreds of files in your System Folder—extensions, control panels, and even preference files. Corrupted files can cause crashes and irregular behavior. The solution is often a "clean install" of Mac OS.

Finally, you may have a hardware problem: an excessive number of bad blocks on your hard drive can prevent the drive from functioning.

What steps can I take to prepare for emergencies before they occur?

The most important thing you can do is back up your data when things are working properly. There are two kinds of computer users: those who have lost data and those who are going to. It's a fact. One day your hard disk (or other storage

device) will be toast. It will almost certainly happen to you someday. If you still need convincing, think about what would happen if everything on your hard disk were suddenly gone. Now, you're ready to commit to a proper backup regimen.

You have numerous options for backup, but floppy disks are not among them. In today's world of 100+ megabyte system folders and applications, you need a high-capacity storage device like a Zip, Jaz, SuperDisk, Orb drive, CD-R (a CD-ROM burner), or tape drive.

Oh, and one backup isn't enough. You should store a recent backup off-site, in case of disaster or theft. For more detailed information about how and what to back up, see Chapter 4.

Other steps you can take to keep your Mac running happy and healthy include rebuilding the desktop. Apple says you should do it once a month, and we concur. The "desktop" in this case actually consists of several invisible files that keep track of what documents should open which programs, as well as how icons appear and which folders are inside which folders. Over time, the Desktop database can become bloated with old and unneeded information—or worse, it can become corrupted, which will cause things to go awry. So rebuild your desktop once a month. Here's how: Restart your Mac, and hold down COMMAND+OPTION at the end of the startup process (after the startup screen and the march of icons), but before the desktop appears on the screen. A dialog box will ask if you want to rebuild the desktop. You do. Click OK.

Tip: *Rebuild the desktops of floppy and removable disks every so often by holding down COMMAND+OPTION right after you insert the disk.*

What software will help?

Retrospect, shown in Figure 14-1, and its sibling Retrospect Express from Dantz Development are the backup programs we use and recommend. Both programs make it easy to automate your backup regimen and allow full and incremental backups as well as archiving. Get one. Use it.

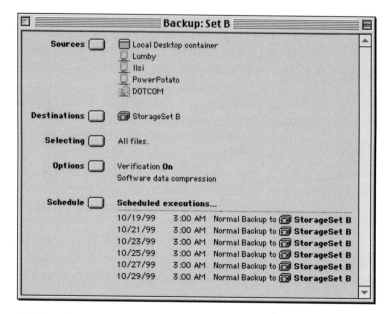

Figure 14-1 Create a schedule that will allow you to automate backups in Dantz Development's Retrospect

Apple's Disk First Aid, shown in Figure 14-2, is another program you should use if your Mac starts acting unreliably. Versions 8.2 and above are preferred for their ability to repair the startup disk. Earlier versions require you to boot from another disk or CD to repair the startup disk. We run it once a month, even if our systems seem to be working okay. Here's how to run Disk First Aid on your disks:

1. Launch the Disk First Aid application.

2. Select one or more disks at the top of the window. Hold down SHIFT to select more than one disk.

3. Click the Repair button.

If you're a so-called power user, you may want one of the diagnostic and repair programs, such as Symantec's Norton Utilities for Macintosh or TechTool Pro from MicroMat, shown in Figure 14-3. These tools can often diagnose and repair disk and directory damage that Apple's Disk First Aid cannot.

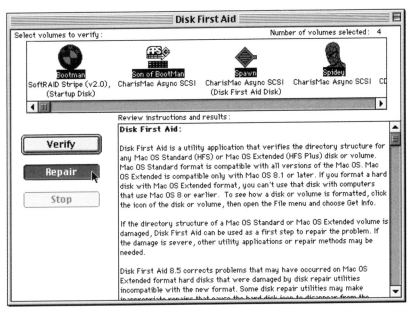

Figure 14-2 Check a drive's integrity by verifying it, and then repair it if you find problems

You may also need antivirus software. See the next question.

How do I know if I need an antivirus program?

A virus (or worm) is a malicious program or file that "infects" other files and disks it comes into contact with. Some can cause irreparable damage to your hard disk and files.

If you're at risk, you need an antivirus program, and you're at risk if you

- Download files from the Internet

- Receive e-mail with attached files

- Are on a network and share files with others

- Use floppy disks or removable media cartridges (Zip, SyQuest, Jaz, and so on) that have been inserted in anyone else's Mac

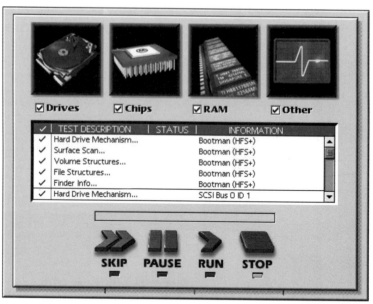

Figure 14-3 TechTool Pro from MicroMat can diagnose and repair many kinds of disk damage that Disk First Aid can't

 Caution: *Although it is rare, commercial software packages can be infected with the virus AutoStart or other viruses, passing these maladies on to you when you install the software from a CD-ROM or floppy. Don't assume that you're safe just because you only install reputable, commercial products on your Mac.*

Those are the ways viruses spread, so if any or all of the above apply to you, you'd be well advised to run an antivirus program, such as Dr. Solomon's Virex or Symantec's Norton AntiVirus. Both are easy to use, and both do the job as promised. Norton AntiVirus is a little easier to update, as shown in Figure 14-4.

However, Virex is a little less obtrusive and more convenient to use than Norton AntiVirus. The bottom line is that either commercial program is a wise investment if you are at risk.

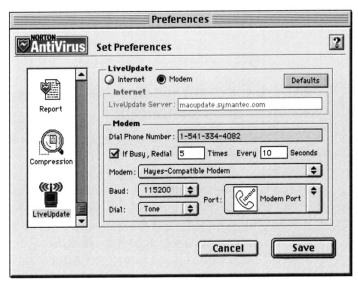

Figure 14-4 Norton AntiVirus's LiveUpdate feature allows you to automatically check for updated virus definition files and download them via the Internet

How do I know if I have a virus?

It's difficult to know if your Mac is infected. The symptoms of all known Mac viruses and worms could fill a book. Suffice it to say that if your Mac begins acting anything other than normally, it *could* be a virus.

The best way to find out if you're infected is to run the most recent version of Virex or Norton AntiVirus. Both are updated regularly to recognize and repair all known viruses and worms.

Then there are shareware and freeware virus scanners and "innoculators" and such, but none is as comprehensive or thorough as Virex or Norton AntiVirus. If you're a member of a Mac user's group, you can usually find the latest shareware or freeware virus programs in their libraries. AOL has several free antivirus programs, too. Visit the MacInTouch (http://www.macintouch.com) Web site or the MacFixIt (http://www.macfixit.com) site for news about both old and new viruses, and links to antidotes.

But the sad truth is that if you're at risk, you're probably best off springing for a commercial antivirus program that is updated regularly to combat new strains.

 Is there a difference between a worm and a virus? Which is more dangerous?

Technically there is a difference. A worm is a self-replicating, and usually malicious, program. Worms are similar to viruses. Both can be dangerous.

One particularly nasty worm, from the summer of '98, is the AutoStart 9805 worm. It can be spread by merely inserting an infected disk, and can bring your Mac to a screeching halt. Virex and Norton AntiVirus both can combat worms, including the many variants of AutoStart 9805. There are also several freeware AutoStart 9805 eradicators.

STARTUP PROBLEMS AND SOLUTIONS

What does a flashing question mark at startup mean?

It means your Mac doesn't recognize a startup disk. In other words, it can't find a valid System Folder on any of the available disks. You will not be able to boot the Mac from that disk until you solve the problem. If you're pretty sure that your hard disk *should* work—it worked last time you restarted, and/or you know that it contains a valid System Folder—try restarting with the same startup disk. If you are successful, rebuild the desktop, as described earlier in the "What steps can I take to prepare for emergencies before they occur?" question, to eliminate desktop databases as a source of the problem. If you are unable to boot with the current startup disk, insert a bootable floppy or a Mac CD-ROM (one probably came with your Mac; all retail Mac OS upgrade CDs are bootable). If you use a CD-ROM, hold down the C key during startup. When the desktop appears, run Disk First Aid, repair your startup disk, and restart.

Tip: *Use Sherlock to locate the copy of Disk First Aid on the CD.*

If that doesn't work, the next thing to try is installing new hard disk drivers. If your hard disk is an Apple-brand disk—it is if it came with your Mac—restart your Mac from a CD-ROM as described previously. Then follow these steps:

1. Launch the Drive Setup application on the Mac OS CD-ROM.
2. Choose Functions | Install Driver.
3. Update your startup disk.
4. Restart your Mac.

If your hard disk isn't an Apple-brand drive, follow the manufacturer's instructions for installing new driver software. You'll usually find the appropriate program on a floppy that came with your drive.

If installing new software doesn't work, the next thing to try is zapping the PRAM (parameter RAM). The PRAM is a little bit of memory that stores information like printer selection, sound level, monitor settings, and menu flashing. PRAM is not erased when you restart or shut down your Mac. It sometimes becomes scrambled, though, so you may need to reset it. To zap or reset your PRAM, follow these steps:

1. Hold down COMMAND+OPTION+P+R during startup.
2. Continue holding down all four keys until you hear your Mac reboot itself two times.
3. Release the four keys.

Note: *If you have a PowerBook, there is a special reset option that is intended as a last resort. See Chapter 11 or your PowerBook owner's manual for details.*

What is a sad Mac, and why should I be afraid?

A sad Mac icon at startup means there's a severe problem, usually with your Mac itself. Not all sad Macs are the same. Each comes with a code, located right below the frowning Mac face. The two-line code may (or may not) help you and your repair shop diagnose the problem. You'll find a complete,

Shelly's Scoop: Starting Up a New Mac

Apple's 1999 Mac line—the Power Mac G4s, iBook, and slot-loading iMacs—use a new restart procedure. To restart one of these Macs from an alternate disk, follow these steps:

1. When you restart the Mac, hold down the OPTION key. After a few moments, you'll see two arrow icons—a circular one and one that points to the right—and icons for each bootable disk that is connected to your Mac.

2. Click on the icon for the drive you want to boot with, and then on the arrow that points to the right.

but cryptic, list of sad Mac codes at http://til.info.apple.com/techinfo.nsf/artnum/n7748. If you ever see a sad Mac on your screen, turn your Mac off, and then follow these steps:

1. Try restarting your Mac while holding down SHIFT to disable all startup items.

2. Try restarting your Mac while holding down COMMAND+OPTION to rebuild the desktop. Try booting from the CD-ROM that came with your computer, by holding down the C key during startup. If the Mac boots successfully from the CD-ROM, follow the steps in the previous question, as though your problem had been a flashing question mark.

3. If you have recently moved your Mac, or opened it to add memory or a disk drive, shut the computer down and open it again, and make sure that all connections and cables are secure. Then try restarting.

If none of these steps works, write down the sad Mac code you've been getting, and take your Mac to an authorized service professional.

? **Why does my Mac complete most of the startup procedure and then hang at the Finder, or while the startup screen is still visible?**

That is usually the sign of a startup conflict. It means something that loads at startup—usually a control panel or extension file—isn't getting along with something else that loads at startup. Another possible reason for a crash or freeze during the startup process is a damaged preference file, usually one associated with a control panel or extension.

To determine whether your problem is indeed an extension or control panel, restart your Mac with extensions and control panels off:

1. Restart your Mac.

2. Hold down the SHIFT key immediately, and keep holding it down until the Mac OS screen appears with the words "Extensions Off" or "Extensions Disabled."

If the Mac starts up okay with extensions off, you have a problem involving an extension or control panel, or a conflict between two or more extensions and/or control panels. To resolve extension conflicts, follow these steps:

1. Choose Apple menu | Control Panels | Extensions Manager.

2. Click Edit, and choose All Off.

3. Activate half of the extensions and/or control panels you normally use.

4. Close Extensions Manager.

5. Restart your Mac.

If the problem recurs, the culprit is one of the files you just enabled. If the problem doesn't recur, follow these steps:

1. Open Extensions Manager, activate the other half of your extensions and/or control panels, and disable the ones you activated first.

2. Restart your Mac.

3. When you locate the group that contains the problem extension, activate half of the items in that group, leaving all others turned off.

Repeat these two steps until the problem recurs. The culprit is then one of the items you activated in the last batch.

 Tip: *If you don't relish keeping track of which files you've enabled and disabled, get yourself a copy of Casady & Greene's excellent Conflict Catcher. This utility replaces the Extensions Manager and includes a conflict test feature that will take you through the trial and error of resolving startup conflicts, keeping track of what's been tested and what has not, until you've been through your entire system. Conflict Catcher 8 also includes a fantastic clean-install merge function that makes the otherwise-odious clean install much easier.*

What do I do if my Mac just won't boot?

If you've tried all the suggestions so far in this chapter and still can't boot, the last thing we might suggest is that your Mac's internal battery has died. All Macs have an internal battery that is used to remember stuff like dates, even when the power is off. An Apple dealer can check and replace the battery for you. Or, if you're handy with a screwdriver, you may be able to install a new one yourself.

What should I do if I hear what sounds like a car crash when I try to boot the Mac?

Try booting from a Mac OS CD-ROM (insert the CD-ROM, restart your Mac, and hold down the C key during the restart process). If that doesn't help, take your Mac to your nearest authorized Apple service provider. That car crash sound, sometimes accompanied by the sad Mac icon, generally means you have a major hardware problem.

Note: *You may hear a sound other than the car crash—chimes of doom, the Twilight Zone theme—none of them are good news.*

FREEZES, CRASHES, AND ERROR MESSAGES

 ### What should I do if my Mac freezes while I'm working?

First, be sure that your Mac is really frozen. Check all of your cables. A disconnected keyboard or mouse cable will make it seem as if the Mac has frozen, because the keyboard or mouse no longer responds. Remember, don't plug in or unplug cables without shutting down your Mac first (with the exception of USB devices, which can be "hot swapped" and plugged in while your Mac is running). If it's not a loose cable, try these steps:

1. Press COMMAND+OPTION+ESC. This usually brings up the "Force Quit" dialog box. Click Force Quit and restart your Mac immediately.

2. If Force Quit doesn't work, press COMMAND+CONTROL, and the POWER ON key. That should force your Mac to restart.

3. If that doesn't work, press the power button on the front or back of your Mac to shut down your system. Wait a few seconds, and then press the power button again to restart.

4. If none of that works, you may, as a last resort, unplug your Mac from the wall for a few minutes, and then plug it back in and try again.

 ### What's a system bomb, and how do I recover from it?

A system bomb—usually a dialog box with a bomb icon, some text, and an ID number—means your Mac has "crashed." There is usually no way to recover from a bomb. Fortunately, they don't happen often, especially under Mac OS 8 and later.

If you get a bomb *every time* you perform a particular task (such as launch a program, use the spelling checker, click the tool palette, and so on), you should probably get out the master disks or CD-ROM and reinstall the program that's giving you trouble. You should also delete its preference file (from the Preferences folder inside your System Folder). If you're getting bombs in the Finder or during file activity, run Disk First Aid; if that doesn't solve the problem, perform a clean install of Mac OS.

My Mac froze before I could save the important document I was working on. Can I recover from a freeze without restarting my Mac?

Maybe. If the crash occurred in a program other than the one with your important document, you may be able to recover and save your work. Press COMMAND+OPTION+ESC. If the Mac hasn't completely crashed, you will see a dialog box asking you if you want to force the program in question to quit. Click the Force Quit button, and save your important document in the other program.

Caution: *After using Force Quit, it's important to restart your Mac as soon as possible, because it will probably crash again soon.*

If Force Quit doesn't do the trick, you probably can't recover the work you've done since the last time you saved that document. Press COMMAND+CONTROL+POWER ON to restart your frozen Mac.

How can I tell what those cryptic error messages mean?

You mean, how do we know that an error ID# = 1 is an "event not enabled at PostEvent" error? Or that a –35 is a "no such volume" error? There are several handy freeware and shareware programs that list the codes and ostensibly what they mean. SysErrors is one we know of ($5 shareware). Apple's Tech Info Library includes several documents that are chock full of error codes. Start at http://til.info.apple.com/techinfo.nsf/artnum/n1749, and follow the links to the rest.

Whether you use a shareware tool or dig through Apple's info, don't expect too much. The messages are usually terse and aimed at programmers.

My Mac crashes constantly. How can I figure out what's wrong?

Run Disk First Aid. If it gives your Mac a clean bill of health, try some of the other suggestions in this chapter—rebuild your desktop, scan for viruses, reinstall your hard disk drivers, zap your PRAM, and so on.

If your Mac still crashes too often, perform a clean installation of Mac OS. To perform a clean install, follow these steps:

1. Launch the Install Mac OS program from your Mac OS CD-ROM.

2. Follow the dialog boxes to the Select Destination screen.

3. Choose the appropriate hard disk (if you have more than one), and then click the Options button.

4. Click the Perform Clean Installation check box, click OK, and continue your installation.

When you perform a clean installation, your old System Folder is renamed "Previous System Folder" and deactivated. You'll find it on your hard drive when you've finished the new installation. In place of the old folder, a new System Folder, containing only Apple system software, is created. So, if the reason your Mac was acting wonky had to do with a file in your old System Folder becoming damaged or "corrupted," a clean install will probably fix you right up.

Alas, a clean install is a pain. If you use third-party control panels or extensions, you'll need to reinstall them from the floppies or CDs they came with. (You could drag them from the Previous System Folder to the shiny new System Folder you just clean installed; but if they're damaged, you're defeating the purpose of the clean install.) If you have updated your system software (from Mac OS 8.5 to 9, for example) since you got the Mac, or Mac OS CD, be sure to reinstall the update. The same

thing goes for scanners, digital cameras, removable media devices, and so on—reinstall their software, too. And your carefully configured TCP/IP and modem settings won't be preserved, either.

Tip: *To back up your TCP/IP and PPP settings (the ones you use to connect to the Internet), export them before anything goes wrong. To do this, open the TCP/IP control panel; then choose File | Configurations (COMMAND+K). With a configuration selected, click Export. In the dialog box that appears, save the exported settings to a convenient location outside your System Folder. To be really safe, put the exported configuration on a floppy, or other removable media disk. Repeat this procedure with your PPP or Remote Access settings, and save all Internet-related configuration files to the same safe place. When you've finished your clean system install, open the TCP/IP and PPP control panels, press COMMAND+K, and click Import. Locate your saved configuration files, and import their information. Now, you're ready to get back online.*

Another inconvenience associated with clean installs is that many programs store your registration information, tool positioning, macros, and other information in a preferences file that is lost when you create a clean System Folder. You may have to reenter your serial numbers and redo your tool settings and macros for some programs. If you've done extensive customization to a program, you could move its preference file from the Preferences folder in your Previous System Folder to the Preferences folder in your new System Folder. But because preference files can become damaged or corrupted, it's better not to do that unless you're sure the preference file in question is okay. We like to keep the Previous System Folder around for a few days after a clean install, just to see if we'll need any preferences the next time we run our applications. Once we've restored the System Folder to something approximating its former state, we like to copy the whole thing to a Jaz cartridge or other high-capacity removable media. That way, not only can we restore the System Folder intact if something goes wrong, but we also have another disk to boot from, in the event of trouble.

If Disk First Aid says your disks are okay, and a clean install doesn't cure your crashing problem, you need to contact Apple Tech Support for help.

 What does an "application can't be found" error mean, and how do I recover?

When you see an error message informing you that "an application can't be found for this document," it means your Mac is having trouble linking that document to a program that can open it.

The first thing to do is make sure you have an application that can open this type of document. Try this: drag the document onto the icon of the program you want it to open in. Or launch the program, and use its Open command to open the document.

Shelly's Scoop: Making Sure You Have Copies of Your Software

I like to keep my software up-to-date. When a new version of my favorite Web browser, e-mail application, text editor, or operating system becomes available on the Internet—pretty common, these days—I download and install it. I also keep a copy of the compressed installer file on my secondary hard disk in a (really big) folder called Installers. If I need to perform a clean Mac OS install, I update the system and applications, as we've described in this section, and then apply the updates from the Installers folder. In many cases, the installer files I download aren't just updates or patches, but full copies of the application and support files. All I need to restore Eudora or CD-ROM Toolkit, for example, is to run the installer from my second hard disk and enter the serial number when it's called for. How do I keep track of my serial numbers, you ask? The Installers folder includes a file called Serial Numbers. I update it each time I buy an application that requires me to enter a code to launch it.

"Application can't be found" errors are often a symptom of a desktop that needs to be rebuilt. Try that. (Restart your Mac; then hold down COMMAND+OPTION at the end of the startup process—after the startup screen and the march of icons, but before the desktop appears on the screen. Click OK when the dialog box asks if you're sure you want to rebuild the desktop.)

If that doesn't work, make sure File Exchange is enabled in the Extensions Manager, and that the control panel is set on (open Apple menu | Control Panels | File Exchange). File Exchange is the Mac OS tool that translates documents automatically so they can be opened with a program other than the one that created them. For details on configuring and using these tools, see Chapter 3.

Why are the icons on my desktop blank?

Icon pictures are among the many items stored in the Desktop database. When the database becomes damaged, the pictures can be lost. The solution is to—can you guess?—rebuild the desktop.

On rare occasions, icons associated with a specific application may go bad. This happens when the application's *bundle bit*—the portion of the application that associates icons with the program—becomes corrupted. You can use the shareware program Rebundler or a diagnostic tool, such as Norton Utilities for Macintosh, to fix the bundle bit. To fix a bundle bit with Norton, run the included Disk Doctor program. Once your bundles are in order, rebuild the desktop.

Note: *If you have recently upgraded to a newer version of Mac OS, but haven't upgraded your copy of Norton Utilities in a while, you will need to do so before you can repair damaged disks. Older versions do not support recent releases of Mac OS.*

MEMORY PROBLEMS

 I have plenty of memory installed, but I get lots of error messages that say I'm low on memory. What's wrong?

Yep. It's possible. That's because Mac OS lets you "set" the memory allocation for each and every program individually. Most programs ship with their memory allocation setting fairly low. If you work with large documents or get "not enough memory" errors, you need to increase the memory allocation for that program, so that the Mac will reserve a large enough chunk of memory for the application.

First, quit the program you want to give more memory to. You can't allocate more memory when the application is running. Then follow these steps:

1. Select the program's icon.

2. Choose File | Get Info, or press COMMAND+I. The Info window for that program appears.

3. Choose Memory from the pop-up menu.

4. Under Memory Requirements, double the amount of memory available to the application in the Preferred Size field. Figure 14-5 shows a boosted memory allocation for Myth.

If you continue to get "not enough memory" messages when working with this application, try increasing the preferred size again.

Should I use virtual memory?

For most people, the answer is yes. Virtual memory is a scheme by which your Mac uses hard disk space in place of RAM. Virtual memory (VM) can allow you to run programs

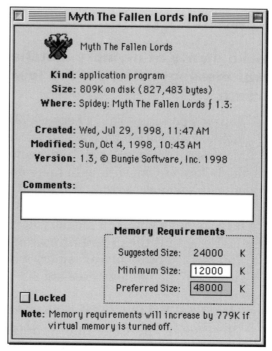

Figure 14-5 Give an application more memory by increasing its preferred size

you wouldn't ordinarily have enough RAM to run, or open more programs at once than you otherwise could. System software and applications require less real memory when virtual memory is turned on. (Note that Myth will require an additional 779K of RAM, shown in Figure 14-5, if virtual memory is turned off.)

The big disadvantages of virtual memory are that it creates a large invisible file on your hard disk and it is slower than real RAM. The reason it is slower than real RAM is because it depends on the speed of your hard disk, which is always much slower than RAM. The VM partition can be no smaller than the amount of RAM installed in your Mac. If you have 64MB of RAM, and you turn virtual memory on, you'll lose no less than 64MB of disk space. Of course, upping virtual memory takes even more of your disk space out of action. Connectix's RAM Doubler is a virtual memory replacement that works quite well and doesn't hog your hard drive. It also works with some games that won't run if virtual memory is turned on. If you're short on

disk space but want the benefits of virtual memory, check out RAM Doubler.

If you have a lot of RAM—64MB or more—set virtual memory to one megabyte more than your total installed RAM (that is, 65MB). That way, you get the benefits of having virtual memory turned on—the OS and programs will use less RAM—while wasting as little hard disk space as possible.

You may already be using virtual memory. When you install Mac OS, VM is turned on by default, using the extra memory to complete the installation and to give users with a small amount of RAM some cushion against system-related memory lapses. If you just can't abide the idea of using virtual memory, turn it off in the Memory control panel.

 ### How do I adjust the amount of virtual memory I have available?

To change your virtual memory settings, follow these steps:

1. Choose Apple menu | Control Panels | Memory.

2. If virtual memory isn't on, click the On button.

3. By default, your startup disk is selected as the location for the virtual memory partition. It's probably best to leave it that way, but this setting can be changed if you have more room on a different disk.

4. Increase your virtual memory allocation if you like, using the arrow keys.

❗ ***Caution:*** *Don't choose a Zip disk or other removable media cartridge as a storage place for the virtual memory file. VM is slow enough when it runs on your hard drive, and you'll lose VM when you eject the cartridge.*

FINDING AND USING HELP

 ### What troubleshooting help is available within Mac OS?

The built-in Mac help system is generally quite useful. Choose Help Center from the Help menu to open the Help Viewer, which is shown in Figure 14-6. Within the help system, browse or search for topics that interest you.

Figure 14-6 You can search for a topic by entering keywords in the field at the top of the Help Center window, or browse available help topics by clicking the hyperlinks

How can a user group teach me more about my Mac or help me diagnose its problems?

A Mac user group is a club made up of people like you, who have and enjoy using Macs. Most offer classes, clinics, monthly meetings and newsletters, disks-of-the-month, a Web page, and more. If you want to learn more about using a Mac, there's no better way than to join your nearest user group. To find the Mac user group near you, visit http://www.apple.com/usergroups/.

Where can I find Mac help online?

There are many good Web sites that collect and distribute Mac help. Apple offers several Web-based help pages. The Technical Information Library, at http://til.info.apple.com/, is a searchable database of many known problems and issues with Macs. Apple also provides product support pages, which start at http://www.apple.com/support/.

The Mac community has established plenty of sites with troubleshooting information and Mac help. Among the best and most reliable are MacInTouch (http://www.macintouch.com) and MacFixIt (http://www.macfixit.com).

You may also be able to find help in one of the many Mac-related Usenet newsgroups. You'll find newsgroups that specialize in hardware, software, Internet topics, communications, and much more. Look for Mac newsgroups in the comp.sys.mac hierarchy of Usenet.

Before you pose your question on the newsgroup, look around for a FAQ (Frequently Asked Questions) posting that includes questions and answers from readers of the group. Then, scan a few days' worth of messages on the newsgroup to see if your question has already popped up and been answered. If your problem is with a new piece of hardware or software, or with an upgrade to Mac OS, chances are that people online are talking about it.

In Mac OS 8.5 and later, you can search the Apple Tech Info Library from Sherlock if you have an Internet connection, as follows:

1. Open Sherlock from the Apple menu, or press COMMAND+F in the Finder.

2. Click the Search the Internet tab.

3. Click the Apple Tech Info check box and enter your search phrase.

When should I contact a hardware or software vendor for technical support?

Make that phone call when you've tried everything in this chapter and still don't have a Mac that functions properly. Then, if you suspect a particular program or hardware device,

call its manufacturer's tech support number or send e-mail to their tech support address if you can. If you suspect the problem is with your Mac hardware or Mac OS system software, call Apple (see the next question).

 **What kind of problems should I take to Apple tech support?**

If you've tried everything in this chapter and still don't have a Mac that functions properly, it would be appropriate to call Apple. If you bought your Mac from a retail store, you may want to check with them, as well.

Keep in mind that Apple can't help you with application-related problems or troubles with third-party hardware. Do your best to be sure that your problem is with the Mac or the OS before you call. We don't give this advice to reduce Apple's call volume, but to save you time. Calls to Apple usually include some time on hold, and there's nothing more frustrating than wasting 30 minutes waiting around, only to discover that Apple can't or won't help you.

What should I do if a product vendor wants to charge me for technical support?

That depends upon how badly you need the help. Most of the companies we've encountered charge a small fee—$10 to $25—but guarantee a resolution to your "incident." If it's something you must have, and you can't get it fixed any other way, pay the fee.

HARDWARE PROBLEMS

What are the telltale signs of a Mac hardware problem?

The most common is the sad Mac icon at startup, or one of the bad sounds—the "Chimes of Doom," a minor-chord arpeggio, or the car crash or breaking glass sound at startup. We covered these problems in "What is a sad Mac and why should I be afraid?" and "What should I do if I hear what sounds like a car crash when I try to boot the Mac?," earlier in this chapter. A flashing question mark is often

user-fixable; sad Macs and bad sounds at startup are usually not.

Can a dead hard disk be repaired?

That depends upon how dead it is. Utilities like MicroMat's TechTool Pro 2.5, or Norton Utilities 4 or later, can fix certain types of hard disk damage. So can reformatting and/or initializing a disk that's giving you trouble. So, you might try those things before you declare your hard disk deceased. You did back it up before it died, didn't you?

Which parts of a printer can be replaced?

That depends upon the printer you have. All printers have consumables—inks, ribbons, toner cartridges, and such—that are easily and economically replaceable. Whether you can replace other parts depends entirely on the make and model of printer. With some printers you can affordably replace the print head—the portion of the printer that adheres the image to paper; for others, it's cheaper to buy a new printer. If your printer breaks down, get a repair estimate and then decide whether it would be more prudent to replace the printer.

Which Mac cables tend to go bad?

All Mac cables will go bad over time. SCSI cables tend to be sturdy if you're not connecting and disconnecting them all the time. ADB cables and LocalTalk cables and connectors are known to go bad every so often, especially if you connect and disconnect them frequently. They're especially finicky because the connectors contain small pins that can get bent if you're not careful with them. We have drawers full of "known-to-be-good" cables of every type we use. It's nice to have extra cables around.

When should I consider opening my Macintosh?

If you're handy with a screwdriver and not afraid you'll muck things up, you can probably do simple surgery, such as adding RAM or installing a CPU upgrade, yourself. Make sure the upgrade comes with documentation that's relevant

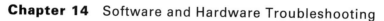

to your Mac model, and you should have no trouble. Here are a few tips for opening and working with your Mac:

1. Place your Mac on a flat, clean surface, preferably not on or near carpeting.

2. Unplug all peripherals (monitor, keyboard, mouse, and SCSI or USB devices) and the power cord.

3. Wear a grounding strap or touch the power supply of the Mac with one hand to further disperse the static field.

4. When you remove memory chips, boards, hard drives, or other components from your Mac, place them in static bags or on a clean surface, away from the computer.

 Caution: *Unless you're absolutely sure what you're doing, never open a compact Mac—that is, an SE, Plus, or Classic. Besides being difficult to work on and easy to damage, the video circuitry in these Macs remains charged long after you turn the computer off, and it could give you a nasty shock. The iMac is somewhat less challenging to open and work on, while the newest, slot-loading iMacs are pretty easy to open.*

GETTING YOUR MAC AND PERIPHERALS REPAIRED

 ### What are some common Mac problems that need repair?

One common problem is when the battery on your motherboard dies, and the Mac won't work because of it. Every Mac has a small battery inside it; replace it—an inexpensive and quick repair—and your Mac will be good as new.

Another common problem is the Mac with a fried ADB chip. If you connect and disconnect ADB devices like keyboards and mice while your Mac is powered up, you can damage your motherboard. This one can be costly, so shut down before you connect or disconnect cables, okay?

New Macs may have factory defects: some models have been shipped with cracked motherboards, faulty hard drives, dead ports, and so on. Don't think that just because your computer is new, it can't need repair. Factory defects often affect all of the computers built during a certain period of time, so you're probably not alone if your new machine needs repair. Don't be afraid to call Apple early and often until the problem is resolved. You can do a little research ahead of time by searching Apple's Tech Info Library for information about your Mac model. Just type in the name of your Mac, and wait for the list of documents to appear. Look for titles that indicate a factory defect or recall.

Apple used to include a puny 90-day warranty with its Macs. Are things any better today? How about peripherals?

Apple currently offers a one-year limited warranty on hardware and 90 days of telephone technical support (installation and basic use of your product only). Online support using the Web pages mentioned previously (see the question "Where can I find Mac help online?") is always free of charge.

Storage devices and monitors typically have two- to five-year warranties. Many printer vendors offer one-year warranties, or longer ones that don't include the print head.

Where should I take my Mac for repair?

If it's under warranty, it's usually best to go through whomever you bought it from, or from an Apple Authorized dealer of your choice. If you bought direct from Apple, try them first. If you purchased the Mac at a local computer store, try them first. If you bought via mail order, try them first.

If your Mac is out of warranty, CompUSA stores all repair Macs, but their service is hit or miss. Some stores have fine Mac repair departments; others are not so hot.

Finally, ask your friends and user-group members where they've had good repair experiences. You will find decent Mac service places in almost every city.

Can PC repair shops do a good job on my Mac?

Usually not. If they aren't familiar with the Mac, they probably won't be able to diagnose or properly repair it. Again, ask friends and user-group members for recommendations.

If you want to find out if a particular PC shop can handle your Mac, ask them about their Mac repair experience. Ask leading questions about Mac models, Mac OS, or memory. If they don't pass the test, don't waste your time.

What questions should I ask before handing over my Mac?

The most important question is "How much will you charge me to diagnose it and give me an estimate for repairs?" While a few places may do this for free, most will charge you $25–$75 just to tell you what's wrong and how much it will cost to fix it. Once you have the estimate in hand, you can decide what to do: proceed with the repairs or take it elsewhere for a second opinion.

One question you might want to ask about expensive repairs, such as a logic board replacement, is "Would it be possible to get a refurbished one for less?"

And don't forget to ask these important questions as well:

- "Will my data be destroyed?"
- "When can I have it back?"
- "What kind of warranty will I get on your work?"

How can I get referrals from other Mac users in my area?

Join your local user group. Go to their meetings. Post messages on their BBS. Put a classified ad in their newsletter. Attend their "special interest group" (SIG) meetings. If there's an appropriate Usenet newsgroup for your city (ba.computers, or austin.general, to name two), try posting a message explaining what you're looking for.

What should I expect to pay for Mac repairs?

Depending upon where you live, you can expect to pay between $35 and $75 an hour for labor. Small jobs, like installing RAM or a hard drive, will require less than an hour of labor. Don't pay for more. Larger repairs will require more labor and more expensive parts. Replacing a logic board, for

example, can cost hundreds of dollars. Replacing a bad RAM chip, on the other hand, shouldn't cost more than an hour of labor plus the cost of a new chip.

Chapter 15

Upgrading Your Mac

Answer Topics!

Upgrading Your Mac @ a Glance

Upgrading Basics explains what parts of the Mac are upgradable and how to decide which upgrades make sense for you.

Adding Memory shows how to add RAM and Video RAM to your Mac.

Accelerating Your Mac explains how to upgrade your Mac to a faster CPU.

Adding Expansion Cards describes choosing, installing, and using NuBus and PCI cards.

Upgrading Internal Modems explains how and when you can upgrade internal modems in Macs that have them.

PowerBook Upgrade Issues describes the special requirements and problems associated with choosing and installing PowerBook upgrades.

Other Ways to Upgrade Your Mac reviews the Mac peripherals that you can upgrade in order to get more speed or higher capacity from an existing Mac.

UPGRADING BASICS

 ### How do I decide if an upgrade is right for me?

This is very hard to quantify. Some upgrades provide massive and noticeable performance improvements. Others have more subtle effects that will make you more productive, such as higher screen resolution, extra storage space, or even a larger monitor. Prices for upgrades vary from under $100 to well over $1,000.

So, whether an upgrade is right for you depends entirely on how much performance you're buying, the price of the upgrade you're considering, and the cost of replacing your Mac with a newer, faster model (with or without selling your old one). For these reasons, you should always think long and hard about whether an upgrade serves your long-term needs. As you've probably figured out by now, new Macs have bigger, faster hard disks and CD-ROM drives than old Macs, and more RAM and faster processors, too. And new PowerPC G4–based Macs start at a mere $1,599. You can have an iMac for $999. The more expensive the upgrade, the more attractive the option of selling your old Mac and buying a new one.

ADDING MEMORY

 ### When should I consider adding RAM to my Mac?

If you see "not enough memory" errors often, you may be a candidate for more RAM. (Don't forget to increase the program's RAM allocation, as described in Chapter 14, before running out to buy memory, though.)

Another, perhaps even better, reason to buy more RAM is so you can run more programs at the same time. With 96 or 128MB of RAM, you can open Photoshop, Microsoft Word, a Web browser, an e-mail program, and a calendar program, all at once. Once they're all open, it takes milliseconds to switch from one program to another. So, if you find yourself quitting one program to free up enough memory to open another program, more RAM will help you, too.

Finally, if you have 16 or 32MB of RAM, a memory upgrade will make your Mac somewhat faster. That's because the less RAM you have, the more often your Mac needs to call on virtual memory, and virtual memory is slower than real RAM. As we describe in Chapter 17, you can speed things up even further by using a RAM disk to store applications.

Note: *You'll need a bare minimum of 32MB of memory if you plan to upgrade to any version of Mac OS 8 or later.*

How do I add RAM to my Mac?

You upgrade most Macs by installing small cards with the RAM chips on them into slots on the Mac's motherboard. The cards are called SIMMs (single inline memory modules) or DIMMs (dual inline memory modules). On most Mac models, you merely open the Mac, find the memory slots, and carefully snap in the SIMM or DIMM card. If you're uncomfortable opening up your Mac, any Mac dealer should be able to install your RAM upgrade for 30 minutes of labor or less (around $50 or less).

If you plan to install RAM yourself, it would behoove you to ask your memory supplier if their package includes illustrated instructions for your particular Mac model. TechWorks (http://www.techworks.com) generally offers good instructions for installing their RAM upgrades.

Newer Technologies, a manufacturer of memory and CPU upgrades, offers a handy program called "GURU" (GUide to Ram Upgrades) that tells you how much RAM your Mac can hold and what kind of RAM it requires. Download a copy from http://www.newertech.com/software/guru/.

Tip: *RAM is a commodity these days; lots of people sell it, and most, but not all, RAM is good quality. However, some companies take shortcuts on service. A good RAM seller will ask you what kind of Mac you're planning to install memory into, making sure that you've ordered the right kind of chips for the computer you have, and that your Mac has enough open slots to support what you've just purchased.*

 ## What kind of RAM should I get?

Mac memory comes in many different flavors, but there's usually only one kind that is designed to work with your particular Mac. RAM offerings vary by chip type, size, and speed, and every Mac has its own set of rules for the kind of memory it accepts. What's more, Apple keeps changing the rules, so that a full description of the memory needs of all Mac models would require much more space than we have for this topic.

The short answer is this: get the kind that's specified for your particular Mac. Fast-Page Mode (FPM), Extended-Data Out (EDO), Synchronous Dynamic Random Access Memory (SDRAM), and Synchronous Graphic Random Access Memory (SGRAM) are just some of the different types of memory used in various Macintosh computers. Be sure to get the kind Apple recommends for your Mac model. That information should be somewhere in the documentation you received with your Mac. If you can't find it, GURU has it, and so does the Apple Tech Info Library Web site (http://til.info.apple.com/); it's a bit harder to locate here, though, so check out GURU or your Mac manual first.

 ## What's Level 2 cache, and why should I care?

Level 2 cache is a small amount—usually a megabyte or less—of extremely fast memory the Mac uses to speed up processing. The cache assists PowerPC processors, allowing faster and more efficient processing. Most PowerPC Macs come with some amount of Level 2 cache pre-installed. Older 680x0 Macs usually didn't, though later models of the Mac IIci are exceptions.

 ## Can I upgrade my Mac's Level 2 cache?

Level 2 cache is upgradable in many PowerPC-based Mac models. The total amount of supported Level 2 cache varies from model to model, so check the documentation that came with your system to find out how much you have and whether yours is upgradable.

If your Mac came with no Level 2 cache or a small one (that is, 256K), a larger Level 2 cache should improve your Mac's performance noticeably. If your built-in Level 2 cache is 512K or 1MB, upgrading it will have a far less noticeable effect.

> **Caution:** *We believe that upgrading to 512K of Level 2 cache is a great idea. We can't say the same about 1MB upgrades, because they cause flakiness on some Mac models. Because we can't be more precise than this (that is, the problem is not universal), we recommend that you make sure any 1MB cache upgrade you buy can be returned for a full refund if your Mac develops any cache-related trouble.*

In Macs that have it, you'll find a Level 2 cache memory module on your Mac's motherboard, usually in a slot that looks similar to the slots your RAM cards use. To upgrade the cache, remove the old card from the slot and replace it with the new one—simple as that.

What does video RAM do?

Video RAM (VRAM) is high-speed memory used by the display subsystem—the Mac's onboard video or video card. The amount of VRAM you have governs your available screen resolutions and bit depths. The standard 6–8MB of VRAM on most Power Mac models supports up to 1024×768 resolution with millions of colors. For higher resolutions at higher bit depths, you'll need additional VRAM. If you use built-in video, you may be able to add video RAM directly to the computer's motherboard (if a slot is provided in your particular Mac). If you use a video card, VRAM is installed on the card. Adding a video card to a Mac with little VRAM will both boost the Mac's video performance and give you more resolution and color. Some Power Mac models and clones come with a video card preinstalled, making more VRAM available without redesigning the Mac's built-in video circuitry.

> **Note:** *Not all Macs use VRAM. A few older Macs use a portion of regular RAM for video.*

 Can I add more VRAM?

Yes, if your onboard video or video card supports VRAM upgrades.

If you have a multisync display and want to run your monitor at a higher resolution than you currently can—say, 1,280 × 1,024 with millions of colors—you will need to install additional VRAM. For faster performance, though, you might want to consider an accelerated video card instead of a VRAM upgrade. (See the next section for more on accelerating your Mac.)

Where do I add video RAM?

VRAM is usually upgraded by inserting a small VRAM card (or cards) into a slot on the logic board of the Mac. On most Mac models you merely open up the box, find the slot, and insert the card. If you're uncomfortable opening up your Mac, any Mac dealer should be able to install your VRAM upgrade for 30 minutes of labor or less (around $50 or less).

ACCELERATING YOUR MAC

How much faster can I make my Mac run with a hardware accelerator?

That depends on which Mac you have and what upgrade(s) you're considering. A PowerPC G3 or G4 CPU accelerator can make your pre-G3 Mac a lot faster—as much as two or three times faster than it is now. A high-performance video card can make scrolling and screen updating a lot faster. A SCSI accelerator and RAID (redundant array of independent disks) can make anything that involves reading from or writing to disk much faster. If you have enough money, it's possible to upgrade and speed up almost every part of your Mac.

But remember, if your Mac, hard disk, and CD-ROM are older and slower, and you don't have a big investment in RAM, a new Mac may be faster for not that much more than you're about to spend on upgrades. In other words, do the math first.

Finally, keep in mind that the system bus—the communications path between your Mac's CPU and all of its internal and external components—is slower on old Macs than it is on current ones. No upgrade can give your Mac a faster system bus. In other words, an old Mac with a fast CPU will not perform as well as a G4 with the same processor.

What is a CPU accelerator?

A CPU accelerator is a small card that snaps onto your Mac's motherboard and replaces your existing CPU (processor) with a faster one. A CPU accelerator can make your Mac two or three times faster for anywhere from a few hundred, to more than a thousand, dollars.

How do I choose a CPU accelerator?

The decision will be partially made for you; not all companies make accelerators for all Mac models. PowerLogix, Mactell, Sonnet, and Newer are a few of the companies that make them.

Before you buy, seek out reviews in magazines or Web sites, such as Macworld or MacWEEK.com. These publications test accelerators by putting them through real-world tests to see how fast they perform common tasks. They also use benchmarking tools, such as Ziff-Davis's MacBench, which simulate those same real-world tasks and give performance scores to the CPU and many other hardware components. You can even download MacBench, run it on your unaccelerated Mac, and compare your Mac's scores with review results for the accelerator you are considering.

If your Mac is one for which several accelerator brands and speeds are available, decide how much speed you can afford.

It's also a good idea to look for products with clear installation instructions and good packaging. Though the chips used in accelerators may be the same, each company puts its own stamp on a product by providing helpful documentation and a high-quality product. Though most vendors do a great job, we've seen a few pretty sorry accelerators in our time, so be careful.

Finally, look for a 30-day money-back guarantee and a one-year or longer warranty.

 ### Can I add a G3 or G4 processor to my Power Mac?

As we write this, most CPU upgrades are either Motorola G3 or G4 processors. All of the accelerator vendors we mentioned earlier make G3 and G4 upgrades for a wide variety of PowerMac models. To accept a G3 upgrade, your Mac must ordinarily have an upgradable CPU to begin with. Check your documentation to see if yours does, or ask the vendor about your specific Mac model when you are accelerator shopping.

 ### I have a Performa with a PowerPC processor. Can I upgrade to a G3?

Macs and clones whose processors are soldered into place can't be upgraded with daughtercard processors, like other Power Macs. These upgrade-challenged Macs include PowerPC-based Performas; and the Power Mac 4400, 5400, 5500, 6400, and 6500; along with Power Computing's PowerBase models, and Motorola StarMac 3000 and 4000 series. For these computers you can add an accelerator to the Level 2-cache slot. Vendors include PowerLogix, Newer Technologies, and Sonnet Technologies.

Because these Macs weren't designed to be upgraded, and because their system bus speeds are relatively low, these accelerators won't deliver the full speed of a new G3 or G4 Power Mac, but they are a good way of salvaging an old, low-end Power Mac or Performa.

 ### Can I upgrade my 680x0 Mac to PowerPC?

Maybe. Several companies make PowerPC upgrades for a small number of older Mac models. But are you sure you want to? Your hard disk, CD-ROM, and even your memory (RAM) are slow by today's standards; and you'd probably be better off buying a new G4 system with a fast hard disk and CD-ROM drive built-in, and with a PCI interface that can accept current expansion options.

 Tip: *If you really want to upgrade a 680x0 Mac, and can't find a vendor who still sells the upgrade you need, check out a used-Mac dealer.*

What is a ZIF accelerator?

ZIF stands for zero insertion force. Apple's Power Mac G3s (beige and blue-and-white) are designed to accept ZIF upgrade cards, which replace the original CPU. These cards are very easy to install, and they are available from most accelerator vendors.

How do I install an accelerator?

That depends on your Mac. Some Mac processors simply lift off the motherboard and can be replaced by lowering the new chip into place. Other accelerators are mounted on cards that you insert into a slot on the motherboard. Most accelerators come with illustrated instructions. Bob installed a Newer Technologies G3 upgrade in a Power Macintosh 9500 in less than 15 minutes.

What's a clock chip accelerator?

When the first Power Macs became available, some smart hobbyists figured out that they could coax higher-than-rated speeds from some PowerPC processors by tinkering with the CPU. A few vendors took up the idea and began selling clock chip accelerators—small wire assemblies that you attached to the CPU. Clock chip accelerators aren't seen much anymore, since the G3 processor became available. They were never particularly stable, and we don't recommend them.

A more modern and sometimes effective way to up the power of an accelerator is to use DIP switches or other controls provided to "overclock" the chip. When you buy an accelerator, its switches or controls are typically set for the rated CPU speed. It is sometimes possible to set the switches for a higher speed and gain a speed boost. Do this at your own risk! Many users report that they have no difficulty with overclocked CPU accelerators, but your mileage may vary. You have been warned.

What's a graphics accelerator? Do I need one?

A graphics accelerator is a PCI, NuBus, or PC (the slot on many PowerBooks, formerly known as PCMCIA) card that makes

your monitor work better and faster. ATI, Number Nine, and IXMicro are just a few makers of graphics accelerator cards. Some cards accelerate screen refreshing and updating (often referred to as QuickDraw acceleration). Others accelerate games and 3-D graphics. Some do both. Some support huge monitors at high bit depths. Others don't. Many offer upgradable VRAM. Prices go from the low hundreds to over a thousand dollars, depending on the features you get.

Do you need one? The built-in video in most Macs is good enough for all but the most discriminating users. If you use graphics or page-layout software, an accelerated video card may make your Mac feel noticeably faster.

Again, you should read reviews and lab reports before making your decision.

ADDING EXPANSION CARDS

What are NuBus, PCI, and PDS?

These are "expansion slots" inside different Mac models. NuBus and PDS aren't used anymore; all current Mac models use PCI expansion slots. PowerBooks have expansion slots, too: the PC card slots.

What can I do with an expansion card?

An expansion card is used to add additional capabilities to your Mac. Some examples of expansion cards are ones that import and digitize video from tape or camcorders, and ones that provide fast Ethernet, fast video (faster than built-in video), fast SCSI, or game acceleration. And if you want to add a second monitor, you'll need to add a video card for it.

How can I tell if my Mac supports expansion, and which card types work with my Mac?

All Power Macs have at least one PCI slot. PowerBooks include PC card slots. iMacs and iBooks don't have expansion slots. When you shop for an expansion card, the first thing you need to know is what kind of expansion slots your Mac has. You can refer to the documentation that came with your Mac, or use Apple System Profiler version 2.1.1 or above (included with Mac OS 8 and later), which, among other things, can tell you if you have expansion slots and what kind they are.

How do I add expansion cards?

In a desktop Mac, expansion cards snap into slots on the motherboard. This usually requires removing the outer casing of your Mac and snapping the card into a slot. You'll also need to remove a small metal or plastic panel on the back of the Mac so that the expansion card's ports can peek through. For most Mac models, you can do the job yourself in about five minutes. Make sure any expansion card you buy includes installation instructions for your particular Mac model.

PowerBook expansion using PC cards is a simpler matter. Just slide the PC card into the slot on the side of the portable. For more about PC cards and PowerBooks, see Chapter 11.

What software driver issues are there with expansion cards?

Many expansion cards require software drivers in order to function and come with either a CD-ROM or floppy disk that contains a software installer. Often, these are extensions or control panels that must be installed in your System Folder in order for the Mac to recognize and use the expansion card. Read the instructions for each card carefully. You may need to install software prior to installing the hardware. Or vice versa.

Can I use PCI cards designed for a PC in my Mac?

Maybe. The PCI slot in your Mac is the same as a PC's PCI slot. However, there may be no driver software to support the PCI card on the Mac. Each card is different. Some cards work on either platform and include software for Mac and Windows. Others include only Mac drivers. Still others are PC/Windows only and don't come with Mac OS drivers. If you want to use a PC PCI card, contact the vendor to find out if a Mac driver is available.

 ### Can I add expansion cards to an iMac or iBook?

iMac™

Only in iBook™

Not in the usual sense. The iMac and iBook don't have any PCI expansion slots. The slot-loading iMacs, released in October 1999, and the iBook all include a slot for an internal AirPort wireless networking card. You can have this card installed when you buy the computer, or you can buy and install the card later. If you want to add non-AirPort functionality to an iMac or iBook, you need to do it via USB expansion devices that plug into an external USB port. We cover USB storage devices in Chapter 5 and general USB issues in Chapter 7.

UPGRADING INTERNAL MODEMS

 ### Which Macs include internal modems?

Most current Macs include a 56 Kbps modem. Some Power Macs do not, but all iMacs, iBooks, and PowerBook G3s do. You'll also find internal modems in some Performa models.

 ### Can I upgrade my internal modem?

If you have a desktop Mac with an internal modem, you'll have a hard time finding a replacement. You can try Global Village, which made most of Apple's internal modems, at http://www.globalvillage.com/.

PowerPC PowerBooks include a PC card slot. So, if you have a PowerBook, you can replace a slow modem by adding a faster, PC card modem.

 ### Who sells internal modems?

If you need to replace a desktop Mac's internal modem, contact either Apple or Global Village. No other vendors we know of make these modems.

Global Village, Viking, Farallon, and others make PC card modems that are compatible with Mac OS and PowerBooks. Outpost.com (http://www.outpost.com/) usually has a good selection, as does MacConnection (http://www.macconnection.com/).

POWERBOOK UPGRADE ISSUES

Can I upgrade my PowerBook's processor?

Maybe. Some PowerBooks' processors can be upgraded, but
many cannot. Newer Technologies makes CPU upgrades for
500, 1400, and 2400 series PowerBooks. There may also be
other options available by the time you read this, from Apple
or other vendors.

Can I upgrade PowerBook memory?

Yes. PowerBooks require special memory cards, and each series
of PowerBooks uses a different kind. Fortunately, RAM cards
for most PowerBook models are available from several vendors,
including Apple, Newer Technologies, and TechWorks. Make
sure that the card you buy is actually intended for your
PowerBook model.

Like other Macs, each PowerBook model and series has
very specific rules for the kind and amount of memory you
can add. In many cases, you can add only one additional
memory card, though varying sizes are available. This means
that if you add 32MB of RAM now and want to bump that up
to 64MB later, you'll have to discard the 32MB card and buy
a 64MB card; you can't just add another 32MB card. So, it's
very important that you choose memory carefully. Even
though a 32 or 64MB memory card may seem like more than
you need, it's a better value to purchase a larger amount of
RAM now, than replacing it later.

Unlike other Macs, installing PowerBook memory is a
bit complicated. That doesn't mean that you shouldn't try it,
but it does make it very important that you feel comfortable
opening the computer and following the vendor's installation
instructions. Apple's PowerBook 5300, 1400, 2400, 3400, and
G3 series PowerBooks are significantly easier to work on
than older models.

Can I add a CD-ROM drive, Zip drive, or other storage device to my PowerBook?

Yes. Modern PowerBooks include both an expansion bay
and a port for an external storage device. The expansion bay

contains a floppy drive or CD-ROM drive, which must be removed in order to install another removable-media device. It's a piece of cake to swap out PowerBook removable media drives—no screwdriver needed. To use an external storage device with a PowerBook, you'll need a USB device or an adapter for your PowerBook that allows you to connect to a standard SCSI device. For more information about connecting external devices to your PowerBook, see Chapter 11.

We've had good luck with storage devices from VST Technologies (http://www.vsttech.com), probably the leading vendor of PowerBook peripherals. They make Zip, hard disk, and SuperDisk drives (and batteries) for PowerBooks.

Can PowerBook video be upgraded?

Most modern PowerBooks support millions of colors on their screens at maximum resolution, which is probably lower than your desktop Mac monitor's resolution. There's little need for a VRAM upgrade. A few older PowerBooks did support VRAM upgrades, but most recent models don't.

If you plan to use an external monitor, consider buying a PC card that supports video. That way, you will be able to drive the monitor at a higher resolution than your PowerBook can. For more on PowerBook video, see Chapter 11.

Can I upgrade my PowerBook screen?

Not really. Many PowerBooks include video out ports, or you can use a PC card to drive an external monitor. So, while you can't upgrade your PowerBook's built-in screen, you can use most PowerBooks with a bigger monitor.

Should I upgrade a PowerBook myself or go to an authorized Apple dealer?

It is trickier to get inside of PowerBooks than desktop and mini-tower Macs. You're probably best off having an authorized Apple technician install anything that requires opening up the case, like a RAM upgrade. And, if your PowerBook is still under warranty, you definitely don't want to do it yourself; it could void your warranty.

With that said, we've both performed RAM upgrades on PowerBooks ourselves and lived to tell about it. Things are a bit tight and somewhat fragile inside a PowerBook, so we recommend you leave it to a trained professional if you're the least bit intimidated.

OTHER WAYS TO UPGRADE YOUR MAC

Should I buy a faster CD-ROM drive?

That depends mostly on how old and slow your current CD-ROM drive is, and partly upon how fast your Mac is. If your CD-ROM drive spins at 1x to 6x, a faster drive (say 18x or more) will make some CDs run faster. But most entertainment CD-ROMs are designed to run on 4x CD-ROM drives, so faster CD-ROM drives don't necessarily make titles run faster.

The other thing to consider is your Mac itself. If you have an old 680x0-based Mac model with an equally old CD-ROM drive, replacing the CD-ROM drive with even a much faster one may not make your CDs play much faster. We have more to say about upgrading CD-ROM drives in Chapter 5.

Should I upgrade my CD-ROM to DVD?

DVD is Digital Versatile Disk (or Digital Video Disk, depending upon who you listen to)—a super-duper CD-ROM on steroids. DVD disks hold more than 5 gigabytes of data. Compare that to CD-ROMs, which can only hold 650 megabytes. DVD drives are said to be "backward-compatible," which means a DVD drive can play CD-ROMs as well as DVD disks.

Apple offers DVD as standard equipment, or as an option, on many Mac models, and we expect it won't be long before most computers include a DVD drive instead of a CD-ROM drive.

So do you want it? Maybe. Our advice is to wait until the first time you find a title that is only available on DVD and not on CD-ROM. That would be the first indication that it really makes sense to consider a DVD device. Until then, your CD-ROM drive should be all you need. Chapter 5 has more info about DVD.

 ### Will a fast AV hard drive help my Mac work faster?

If the program(s) you use are disk-intensive, like Photoshop, or FileMaker Pro database software, or a Web browser, a faster drive (possibly coupled with a SCSI accelerator card) will help speed up your work. If you are a multimedia producer and need to move audio or video quickly from disk to screen, an AV drive is essential. If you use programs that are processor-intensive, such as spreadsheets, graphing programs, and other math-intensive programs, the speed increase will be much less apparent. For more information about fast hard drives, see Chapter 5.

 ### Will a RAID help my Mac work faster?

A RAID (redundant array of independent disks) takes a pair (or more) of standard fast SCSI hard disks and uses special controller software to make the disks think they're a single disk. This makes a RAID significantly faster than a single, fast hard disk.

A RAID system requires a PCI-based PowerPC system; Mac OS 7.5 or greater; at least two available disk drives that are 1GB or larger; a PCI SCSI accelerator card; and RAID controller software, such as Conley's SoftRAID.

A RAID with a SCSI accelerator is the fastest hard disk setup you can have on a Mac.

 ### Will software tools like RAM Doubler and Speed Doubler make a significant difference in the speed of my Mac?

Yes. RAM Doubler and Speed Doubler, both from Connectix, can make your Mac feel like it's running faster.

RAM Doubler, as the name implies, can double, or even triple, the RAM available for your applications, documents, and Mac OS. RAM Doubler is, in most cases, faster than Apple's virtual memory, and it has the added advantage of not using any hard disk space. As you will recall, virtual memory places an invisible file on your hard disk, equal in

Bob Speaks: Consider a RAID System

I ordered my G3/300 from the Apple Store with a pair of internal fast SCSI drives configured as a RAID with the Apple-supplied SoftRAID RAID controller software from Conley. It has worked flawlessly since I got the system. And gosh, is it fast.

If you're about to buy a system from the Apple Store, and you're concerned with getting the maximum speed out of it, the RAID option is well worth considering.

size to the amount of virtual memory you request in the Memory control panel. Finally, RAM Doubler sometimes works with programs—especially games—that don't work with virtual memory.

Speed Doubler makes your Mac faster by speeding up disk-to-disk copies, running pre-PowerPC (680x0) software up to 100 percent faster, and speeding up disk access. It also adds two desirable features: automatic copying (that is, you can specify when a folder should be copied to another disk—like every hour or once a day) and keyboard shortcuts for opening applications, files, and menu items without using the mouse.

Both RAM Doubler and Speed Doubler are inexpensive and come with a 30-day money-back guarantee. If you're serious about enhancing your Mac's performance, you should try one or both.

Can I upgrade my mouse and keyboard?

Sure you can. For older Macs, you need ADB (Apple Desktop Bus) devices; for all current Macs, you need USB (Universal Serial Bus) devices. Any of the mail-order houses or retailers mentioned elsewhere in this chapter should have several of each for you to choose from. For more mouse info, see Chapter 7.

Bob Speaks: Mice and Trackballs

I personally don't care for Mac mice. I much prefer a good trackball. So for years I've replaced all my Apple mice with Kensington Turbo Mouse trackballs. The software that comes with them is superb; the hardware itself is excellent as well. Kensington offers both ADB and USB devices, so you can use them with any Mac you have. So, if you're looking for a trackball for your iMac, you may have to look to another vendor.

 ### Where should I shop for all this stuff?

Before you shop, read up on whatever you're considering. Look for reviews and lab reports at the following Web sites:

http://www.macworld.com/
http://www.macaddict.com/

It's important to do your homework before you buy. Upgrades get upgraded frequently, and, frankly, most retail staff will be clueless about this stuff. It's unlikely they'll be able to answer your questions. Once you have an idea of what you want, visit the manufacturer's Web site.

You may also be able to find help in one of the many Mac-related Usenet newsgroups. You'll find newsgroups that specialize in hardware, software, Internet topics, communications, and much more. Look for Mac newsgroups in the comp.sys.mac hierarchy of Usenet. Search for messages about the product and/or post a message asking if anyone has any experience with your proposed purchase.

As for where you should buy your stuff, for Apple-brand equipment visit the Apple Store at http://www.apple.com/store/ or the Apple Resource Locator at http://buy.apple.com/. The Resource Locator can direct you to an Apple retail or repair location near you.

Nationally, CompUSA, Fry's Electronics, and ComputerWare all stock and repair Macs and Mac peripherals and software. Some stores, alas, are better than others.

To avoid disappointment, we tend to buy our peripherals and software via mail order. For hardware and storage devices, we like APS Technologies (http://www.apstech.com/). For software and other peripherals and upgrades, we generally use Outpost.com (http://www.outpost.com), MacConnection (http://www.macconnection.com/), or MacZone (http://www.maczone.com).

Chapter 16

Buying a New Mac

Answer Topics!

Buying a New Mac @ a Glance

- **Deciding to Buy** suggests how you'll know when it's time for a new Mac, and what to do with your old one.

- **The State of the Mac** describes Mac choices available to you.

- **Choosing the Right Mac** includes advice for different kinds of users.

- **Getting a Good Deal** shows you where and how to choose the best Mac for your needs.

- **Buying Used Equipment** provides tips for deciding whether a used Mac is a good deal.

DECIDING TO BUY

How do I know whether to buy a new Mac or upgrade the old one?

For some people, Macs are like cars or clothes; only the newest, fastest, or prettiest ones on the market will do, whether they need them or not. For others, money and plain old common sense dictate that the old Mac stays in service until Mac OS, software, and the old age of the hardware conspire to make it unusable. It is to the latter group of people that we're talking, because the rest of you already have an iMac or a Power Mac G4 Series on your desk.

Deciding when to buy a new computer is really a question of math. It boils down to this: can I upgrade my Mac for substantially less than it would cost me to buy a new one? There's a follow-up question: if I buy a new Mac, will I lose the investment I've made in stuff that works with my old one?

We've tried to give partial answers to these questions in Chapter 15. We suggested ways to get the most out of your old Mac, and told you some of the upgrade options that are available. In this chapter, we move beyond retrofitting the old Mac, and offer suggestions for making your Mac purchase painless.

Some clues that your Mac may be past its prime are listed here:

● Mac OS updates, and new versions of software, no longer support your Mac. Every version of Mac OS, and every software tool released, include a list of system requirements. The most important of these is the Mac models or processors supported. In the days when there were only a few Mac models, vendors often listed them in the system requirements; but these days, most requirements are expressed in terms of processor speed. Mac OS 8.5 and later, for example, require a PowerPC processor. Software products sometimes state system requirements in terms of the processor supported, but also by the minimum Mac OS version supported.

- Upgrades are no longer available. Even if old Macs can be physically upgraded, new processors are often no longer available because the market isn't large enough. You can't get an upgrade for most 680x0-based Macs anymore, because there just aren't enough people out there who want them.

- Accessories or expansion options are no longer available. For the same reason you can't upgrade a Mac LC's processor—the price would be too high for too little gain—you can't easily buy expansion products to support very old computers. Fortunately, the most important accessories for a Mac (memory; SCSI peripherals; and, for PowerBooks, batteries) are easily available. But finding PDS expansion cards for that SE, or even NuBus products for a lot more Macs, is getting harder with every passing year.

For those of you who would rather have a rule of thumb than a whole lot of bullet points, try this one. If your Mac doesn't have a PowerPC processor, it's time to get a new one. All Macs released in the past four or five years have had PowerPC processors, and almost all software is designed to work with the PowerPC. Many applications and current versions of the operating system do not work with 680x0 Macs.

How can I get some use from a marginal old Mac, even after I buy a new one?

Old Macs make great typewriters. If your kid needs to type a term paper, there's no reason not to do it on an old Mac. Since all Macs can be networked, or connected directly to a printer, the kids can print the thing when they're done, or copy it to a newer machine for fancy Office 98 formatting or the HTML treatment.

Use a Mac as a cash register. We know lots of folks who use old Macs in their small businesses; some serve proudly as the receptionist's workstation, and some (including the Mac Classic at University Cyclery in Austin, Texas) can figure up your bill.

Play old games. We love the original Dark Castle, Accolade's Test Drive II, and the truly ancient Major League Baseball games. None of these have been updated in years, and Shelly still likes playing them on a Mac IIsi that's been lying around her house for several years.

Make the old Mac a file server. It may seem like a strange thing to do—servers are usually the most powerful computers in an office—but an SE/30 or IIci can make a nice file server for your home or small office. That's especially true if you only intend to store files on the server, rather than opening applications or doing lots of file copying.

If you want a little more oomph, you can replace the little 40 or 80MB hard drive that came with the Mac and add some memory for a couple hundred dollars or so. Then, network the old standby via Ethernet with your new computer and you're in business.

 ## I don't need a file server or a typewriter. How can I sell or donate my old Mac?

If you just don't have any use for your old Mac, there's probably someone in your town that does. You could sell the Mac via the local newspaper's classified ads, through a user group, or on a community bulletin board. Better yet, why not donate it to a local school or sheltered workshop program? In Austin, Goodwill Industries uses old equipment to train disabled people to repair computers. The refurbished machines are sold at the organization's thrift store, along with working computers that are donated.

Public schools, preschools, religious schools, senior centers, and other organizations may appreciate your donation. (And don't forget about them when it comes time to get rid of outdated software, printers, modems, and the like.)

If the thought of giving away a computer for which you've paid several thousand dollars bothers you, take a tax deduction when you give to a qualified non-profit organization. You'll feel better.

THE STATE OF THE MAC

 ## What Mac configurations are available, and which do you recommend?

First and foremost, all of today's Macs use the PowerPC G3 or G4 processor. In times past, Apple used different processors for different Mac products, leading to confusion about their relative performance. As of this writing, current Power Mac models include a 300, 350, 400, 450, or 500 MHz processor, while PowerBook and iBook CPUs are 300–400 MHz.

All current Macs, except the iBook, include at least 64MB of RAM (the iBook has 32MB), and you can get more memory from Apple or others, if you like. Most users will do fine with 64MB of RAM, but memory is just about the least expensive item you can add to your Mac, and one of the first you'll miss if you don't have it. You can use virtual memory in place of RAM, if money is tight or your need for lots of memory is temporary. For more on virtual memory, see Chapter 15. But never forget that virtual memory is considerably slower than real RAM.

Hard disk options today range from 3GB in the iBook to 27MB for top-of-the-line Power Mac G4s. All current desktop Macs have at least 6GB of storage, which is quite generous for most users. You can always add additional internal or external drives, which are easy to install. A built-in CD-ROM drive is a standard part of all Mac configurations, and the drive in the latest iMacs, PowerBooks, and top-of-the-line Power Macs is a DVD-ROM that can read both CDs and DVD-ROM discs. There's even a rewritable DVD-RAM in one Power Mac G4 model. Last, but not least on the storage front, you can up Power Mac or PowerBook storage with an internal Zip drive.

Video RAM is a great source of improvement in today's Macs over past ones. Each Power Mac and iMac comes with a minimum of 8MB; plenty to run most business-oriented monitors. For information about how much VRAM you'll need to operate your monitor, see Chapter 8.

Built-in Ethernet is now everywhere that LocalTalk once was. That is to say, it's on all Macs, from the little iMac all the way up the Power Mac line. In fact, you can even get 100Base-T Ethernet, which is ten times faster than the standard 10Base-T variety that every system includes.

Among the most significant recent changes in Mac configuration is the addition of FireWire for connecting high-speed peripherals. We describe FireWire in Chapter 5. You'll find FireWire ports on some Power Macs and on several iMac models. FireWire allows you to connect storage devices, digital video equipment, or other high-speed devices to the Mac.

Finally, all consumer Macs and most Power Macs, have 56 Kbps modems.

 ## Why can't I buy Mac clones anymore?

In 1997, when Steve Jobs took over the helm at Apple, one of his first initiatives was to make it difficult for companies like Power Computing, Motorola, and UMAX to compete with Apple by manufacturing Mac clones. A Mac clone is a computer that uses the same processor and motherboard design as an Apple-made Mac, and runs Mac OS, under a license agreement with Apple.

To protect Apple's position as a maker of computers, Jobs refused to grant new licenses, or drastically increased the cost of those licenses, putting the cloners out of business. Though Mac enthusiasts lament the passing of choice in the Mac market, it's worth noting that Apple has achieved a fair amount of success in the months since the end of the clone era.

Should I buy a "stripped down" Mac and buy memory, hard disks, and other items later, or should I buy a high-powered system from the start?

Apple offers Macs in various configurations, meaning that you can choose between different processors, levels of RAM and hard disk, video, and other options. Many long-time Mac users will remember the days when it made sense to buy the Mac with the lowest possible configuration, and then load up on RAM and other options from third-parties who offered these items for less money. But Apple has learned a lot in the past few years, and there's no reason to buy a system with 64MB of RAM when you really want a 128MB system in the first place.

The Apple Store (http://www.apple.com/store/ or 800-795-1000) also includes a build-to-order option that lets you configure your Mac just the way you want, making it possible to know exactly what each option you add will cost you. The Apple Store's prices are not the lowest you'll find for RAM, storage, and other add-ons, but they're not as outrageously expensive as in years past. In fact, given the fact that they'll install the stuff for you and provide a warranty for it, it's no longer a bad idea to order additional RAM and storage from Apple when you buy your Mac.

Finally, Apple's configuration options now include a choice of processor speed, with the fastest processors costing noticeably more than the slower versions. But if you plan to keep your Mac for a while, or if you do intensive work on it, spending the extra money for a middle-level or high-speed processor is probably a good idea.

CHOOSING THE RIGHT MAC

 I'm a graphic designer. Which Mac should I choose?

The Mac dominates the publishing industry, and with good reason. Its interface is pleasing to look at, software for designers is plentiful, and it's easy to share files with others in the business.

It would be easy—and accurate—to say that you need the fastest, most well equipped Mac on the market. Graphic work demands lots of processing power, disk space, and memory. Memory is especially important if you use Adobe Photoshop, a RAM-hungry powerhouse that almost everyone in the design field needs.

As we write this, the Power Mac G4, with a 500 MHz processor, is your best bet. It's fast and comes with the options and power you need to work with graphics and publishing tools. There's an internal Zip drive, as well as a

DVD-RAM drive. The base configuration includes 128MB of RAM. Double that, and you've got a great graphics machine. If you've got the dough, add an Apple Cinema Display, a 22-inch flat-panel monster that's designed specifically for this machine.

I'm a businessperson who uses a Windows computer at work, but likes the Mac better. Which Mac should I choose for home and on the road?

Get yourself a PowerBook G3. Besides its virtues as a traveling machine, it's a full-fledged Mac available with a fast 400 MHz processor, and a big 14.1-inch screen. It also includes 64MB of RAM and, if you care about such things, a DVD drive for watching movies on the airplane. When you check in at the office, plug the PowerBook into the network and copy your Microsoft Office files to the Windows computer.

I'm a parent with two kids who needs a computer to do schoolwork and play games. Which Mac should I choose?

You, and your kids, want an iMac. It sets up in no time, is easily moved (off the dining room table, for example) and is just about the most kid-friendly computer around. There's a built-in modem, CD-ROM drive, and speakers; and, while the processor speed, storage, and memory configurations are not exceptional, they'll do nicely for most home users. If you want a little more power, or would like to watch or create your own movies on the computer, try an iMac DV, which includes a faster processor, a DVD drive, and video-editing software. On second thought, your kids might have trouble getting you to let them use the iMac DV.

I'm a college student. Which Mac should I choose?

This is a tough call. A mid-range Power Mac desktop computer is a great buy with lots of power, but an iBook—now that's a note-taking, coffee-house sitting, small dorm room–lifestyle machine. You can buy either an iBook or an entry-level Power Mac G4 for the same $1,599. You'll get a little more power, storage, and memory if you choose the G4,

but both offer a modem and built-in Ethernet, which will get you connected to the campus network.

If your budget allows, the next step up in performance would be either a PowerBook G3 or the mid-range Power Mac G4. Either will cost you $2,499. The 333 MHz PowerBook G3 has 64MB of memory; a large, bright, active-matrix display; and a thin, lightweight design. If storage goodies are your thing, the $2,499 Power Mac G4's included DVD drive and Zip drive, along with a monster 20GB disk drive, will make you happy. Keep in mind that the Power Mac G4 prices we've mentioned don't include a monitor.

Another option for students on a budget is to buy a used PowerBook. You are at some risk when you go this route (PowerBooks are more fragile, and susceptible to damage than desktops that stay in one place), but you can save a lot of money. We'll have more to say about used computers in the section "Buying Used Equipment," later in this chapter.

Our final piece of advice about PowerBooks is to be careful. Portable computers are hot items for thieves, and the fast-paced, highly mobile college life could make your computer a tempting target.

Many colleges have computer stores on campus that have made deals with Apple and other manufacturers allowing the stores to sell you a Mac and software at a discount. Before you buy your college computer, check to see whether your school offers such a program.

GETTING A GOOD DEAL

 ### How do I find the best Mac price and configuration?

It's a lot harder to shop for Macs by price than it used to be. You can buy Macs via mail-order, from dealers like CompUSA, or directly from Apple, but the difference in price won't be great unless you buy from someone who will throw in software, RAM, or some other add-on for the same price Apple or CompUSA charges for the same system.

We would suggest beginning your shopping trip at the Apple Store, since the company's Mac prices are included

with the various configurations available. Then, armed with the Apple baseline, go to your dealer, or to a mail order/online company, such as Outpost.com (http://www.outpost.com), The Mac Zone (http://www.maczone.com), or MacMall (http://www.macmall.com), for a little comparison shopping. By the way, that shopping trip will be valuable if you plan to buy software or peripherals for your new Mac, as those prices vary noticeably.

 ## Where should I buy my Mac?

We're going to interpret this question as "who do you trust?" If you need a lot of advice about your Mac purchase or would like to test drive a computer before plunking down cash, a dealer may be your best bet. Apple made a deal with the national computer store chain, CompUSA not long ago, getting Macs (and a section devoted to them) added to the chain's stores. That improves the chances that your experience there will be pleasant, and that you will actually connect with a knowledgeable salesperson. Late in 1998, Apple announced that Best Buy will carry the iMac line (but not other Mac models, at least at this writing), so that may be an option if you're looking for an iMac. If not, consider talking with members of your local user group. They may be able to suggest smaller outlets in your community with good Mac product selection and service.

If you're shopping strictly on price, and know exactly what you want, give the mail order/online dealers a try. We've had good luck with the companies we've mentioned in this and other chapters, and there are often special deals available on peripherals and software when you buy your computer.

Is it safe to buy a Mac via mail order?

Many people used to be justifiably fearful of buying computers through mail order, either because they weren't sure what they were getting, or because the companies involved were fly-by-night operations. But as the business of buying long-distance has grown, the good companies have edged out the bad ones, and we can recommend it. Of course,

you'll pay shipping charges, which can be pretty significant when you're buying a computer, but you will probably also save the state or local sales tax you'd pay on purchases from dealers. Because computers are much pricier than most mail-order items, those shipping and handling charges may also include insurance. Do the math before making the purchase, though, to make sure that shipping costs aren't inflating the price of your new computer.

As to the physical safety of shipping equipment by mail, we've been fortunate. Apple and other companies we've dealt with pack their equipment securely, with lots of padding, and include warnings to handlers about the fragility of the box's contents.

See the question, "What are some caveats for buying via mail order or online?" in Chapter 17, where we discuss the steps you should take to protect yourself when buying anything by mail.

 Apple offers lots of cables, network adapters, and other accessories through the online store. Are these a good buy?

How can we put this? No, they are not a good buy. Most of the items you'll find under the Accessories link or that are available from Apple dealers are grossly over-priced and most are available from other sources. Large computer stores, and even office superstores, have computer accessories like cables and network adapters. Mail order Mac outlets will also give you a good deal and are usually the best source of Mac-specific stuff, like PowerBook batteries and Ethernet cards.

BUYING USED EQUIPMENT

 Should I buy a used Mac?

Since we suggested that you could sell your old Mac in an earlier question, you can obviously buy a used one. But buying a used computer can be both a great way to get yourself or your kids a great deal, and an opportunity for caution.

You need to know two things when considering a used Mac or used peripherals: what is the configuration and what is it worth.

The United Computer Exchange (http://www.uce.com/) maintains a list of prices of used Mac models, as do lots of businesses that sell used equipment. You may have to pay more, but the list gives you a starting point.

Used Mac price lists describe the ideal price for a Mac configured as it was when it left Apple. Many users upgrade their Macs before finally selling them, or include software and peripherals. First, get the seller to write down the Mac's configuration. To be on the safe side, get a shareware utility like TattleTech, and run it on the Mac in question. TattleTech will give you a list of all components, tell you how much memory the Mac has, what version of system software it has, and what applications are loaded. You can print the report or view it onscreen.

 Note: *If the Mac you plan to buy includes a copy of Mac OS 8 or above, you can use Apple System Profiler to get configuration information about the Mac.*

If the Mac has upgrades, the price will probably be higher, and your job is to figure out whether that faster CPU, increased memory, or bigger hard disk are worth the money. You can start by doing some price shopping online. Let's say, for example, that a Mac IIfx has 128MB of RAM, rather than the 4MB it probably came with. Price IIfx memory before taking your new old computer home.

On the software front, keep in mind that it is only legal for you to buy used software if the seller isn't using a later version of the same program. Get the boxes, serial numbers, and so on, when you acquire a system that includes software, especially if you're paying part of the purchase price for the software.

How can I test the used Mac to make sure it's in working order?

First and foremost, be sure that the Mac you're buying is the Mac you think you're getting. Run TattleTech to get a listing

of components and configuration information, and look on the back, or inside the Mac to see if expansion cards and/or accelerators are where they should be. Make sure that you agree with the seller about included cabling, mouse, keyboard, monitor, printer, or other items. If, for example, you're getting a StyleWriter as part of the deal, be sure that you locate the power and serial cables that go with it.

Boot the Mac with everything that you're supposed to get attached to it: monitor, keyboard, and so on, and turn on any peripherals (printers, modems, and external SCSI devices) that are part of the deal. Run Disk First Aid on all hard disks to see that they are undamaged. If you can, run Symantec's Norton Utilities, too, for a more thorough evaluation of the hard drive. Rebuild the desktop, just to make sure that the process goes smoothly.

Note the operating system version and software included. Before you buy, make sure you're comfortable with the existing system software, or that the Mac can be upgraded to the current version or one that is downloadable from Apple's Software Updates Web site.

Be sure you get original disks for software that is included, especially a set of system disks. At minimum, you need a bootable Disk Tools floppy or a Mac OS CD-ROM that can boot the Mac in case of trouble.

Is there anything I should avoid when buying used equipment?

A thing is not worthless if the price is low enough. If you get a monitor with your new old Mac, don't pay very much for it. Monitors do die after a few years, and they are never worth fixing.

Hard drives, too, are suspect, because they are subject to damage and old age. It might even be a good idea to replace the old Mac's hard drive with a new, faster and larger one.

Are there special issues with used PowerBooks?

PowerBooks are more fragile than desktop Macs, so used ones bear especially careful scrutiny. Whether it's a careless user who dropped the computer or a factory defect, used PowerBooks are no bed of roses.

A significant problem for potential buyers of used PowerBooks is the fact that they're often overpriced. Just off the assembly line, PowerBooks with the same configuration are always much more expensive than a desktop equivalent, and that disparity continues into a PowerBook's "previously owned" years. But since technology changes quickly and the entry price of PowerBooks has come down significantly, we think that sellers often get away with outrageous prices.

When you consider a used PowerBook, examine it very carefully. Make sure that the case is not cracked, that nothing inside rattles, that cables plug securely into each and every port, and that the rear door is not broken or missing.

Turn on the computer and, after following our testing suggestions in the previous questions, switch to an all-white desktop pattern and look for pixels that are "on." Many PowerBooks with passive-matrix displays have bad pixels, and a couple are not a disaster, but too many can spoil things in a hurry. For more information about pixel anomalies, see Chapter 11.

Use the modem. Does it connect regularly, and at the speed it should? Is the software installed properly?

Next, check out the battery or batteries. Charge them fully and work with the computer for a couple of hours to see how long the batteries hold their charge. You can get specifics about how long batteries should last from Apple. Since batteries are consumables—they wear out eventually—you should count on buying one or more new batteries for a used PowerBook, even if everything seems to be OK with the ones that come with the computer. New batteries cost around $100–$150.

Be sure to get the full complement of accessories, including a power adapter, spare batteries (if available), and any adapter cables that connect the computer to SCSI devices or external monitors. Test these cables while connected to the PowerBook you're buying.

Even if the PowerBook looks okay to you, there may be trouble. Apple recalled a number of PowerBook 5300 series computers because of defects in the case, motherboard, and batteries. Today, there's a repair program available for PowerBook 5300s that have one of several problems listed by

Apple. For more information, see Chapter 11. Our advice is to be very careful when purchasing a PowerBook 5300. Given their many reported problems, it might be a good idea to pass the 5300 by, in favor of another model.

Chapter 17

Tips for Making Your Mac Easier to Use

Answer Topics!

Tips For Making Your Mac Easier to Use @ a Glance

Boosting Mac Performance offers tips for making your Mac run faster and more efficiently.

Shortcuts, Timesavers, and Productivity provides pointers on how to use shortcuts and automation to make your computing more productive.

Cheap and Free Stuff to Make Your Mac Better tells you where to find quality utilities for a low price.

Saving Money When You Buy Software and Peripherals discusses the pinnacles and pitfalls of peripheral and software shopping.

BOOSTING MAC PERFORMANCE

? How can I speed up my Mac?

There are two main ways to speed up your Mac: add hardware that makes it go faster, and circumvent those processes that keep your beloved computer from performing at its peak. The next question addresses the hardware issues (you can find more information about hardware choices in Chapter 15), and the following questions in this section deal with software options.

? What sort of hardware can I use to make my Mac go faster?

Elsewhere in this book, we have addressed upgrades and peripherals for your Mac. Here is a comprehensive list of the parts of your computer that can be replaced or made faster.

● **A new processor**   The processor (also called the CPU or Central Processing Unit) is the brain of your Mac, and it ultimately determines how fast your computer runs. Even the most powerful processors have their limits, and if your processor is too slow for your taste—and if your Mac can accommodate a faster one—you might want to upgrade to a faster CPU. Processor upgrades come in the form of third-party accelerator cards and are available from companies including Newer Technologies, PowerLogix, and Sonnet. These cards can contain either a faster version of the processor you currently have—say a 400MHz G3 or 450 MHz G4—or a newer and faster type of processor than the one that now lives in your Mac. In the old days of 680x0 Macs, you sometimes had to pry out your original processor and replace it with a faster chip. These days, processors are mounted on cards that can be easily removed and replaced. Some Power Mac models have a special slot designed to hold an accelerator card.

● **Accelerate your current processor**   We mention this only because it's possible, not because we think it's a swell idea. Most processors can actually run a little faster than

the speed they're set to at the factory. For example, a processor rated at 400 MHz may actually be able to go as fast as 433 MHz. By adjusting DIP switches on the processor card, you can attempt to boost your processor's speed beyond its current setting. Although this works most of the time, the degree to which you can accelerate a CPU varies from processor to processor, and running a processor at accelerated clock speeds causes the chip to work harder and generate more heat. Excess heat can shorten the life of the processor and strain your power supply, which means you may be buying a new Mac before you would normally care to. As mentioned in Chapter 15, boosting your processor's clock speed is not recommended.

- **A faster hard drive**   The faster a hard drive can transfer data to your Mac, the zippier your Mac will seem. With a fast hard drive installed, you'll notice that applications launch more quickly and files open in an instant. In addition, a fast hard drive will play audio and QuickTime movies more smoothly—adding to the impression that your Mac is one hot little number. The *AV* label is usually slapped on high-performance hard drives that spin at 7200 RPM or faster. RAID (redundant array of independent disks) systems—a group of hard drives configured to impersonate a single drive—are faster still.

- **A fast SCSI card**   Another way to move data more quickly between your hard drive and Mac—and, therefore, speed up performance—is to buy a SCSI card that supports faster transfer rates. With a SCSI card and hard drive that support Fast and Wide SCSI, data will move like the wind (see Chapter 5 for more information about fast hard drives and SCSI options).

- **A faster CD-ROM drive**   Although a faster CD-ROM drive won't make your games run more quickly, it will certainly send data to your Mac in a sprightlier fashion. That's helpful when you're installing very large applications or copying lots of files from a CD-ROM disc to your hard drive. Of course, if the rest of your components—hard disk, the Mac itself, and so on—are old and tired, a faster CD-ROM drive won't do much for you.

● **A graphics accelerator** If you've purchased a Mac in the past four or five years, your Mac probably includes all the video power you'll need to work with a large-screen monitor. If, however, you need more video performance to develop QuickTime movies, work in Photoshop, or perform other professional graphics tasks, adding a graphics accelerator can give your system the kick in the butt it needs. Accelerated video cards blast pixels to your screen more quickly than the Mac's onboard video can, and the added VRAM (video RAM) they include gives your Mac access to more, and richer, color.

● **More RAM** For general computing, additional RAM won't do a thing to speed up your Mac. But in very specific circumstances, such as when you're using Adobe Photoshop or other memory-hungry graphics and 3-D applications, you'll see significant speed improvements in certain operations when the Mac has been outfitted with lots of RAM. Adding RAM can also speed up your Mac by eliminating the need for virtual memory, which is slower than real RAM.

What can I do to speed up my Mac without buying hardware?

Try these little tune-ups:

● *Turn off extraneous extensions and control panels.* We realize that it's lots of fun to load up on control panels that make your Mac burp whenever you eject a disk, and extensions that make your Mac's windows and dialog boxes look like they were created in the Roaring 20s, but these doodads can slow your Mac to a crawl. Give your Mac's processor a fighting chance by eliminating those extensions and control panels you can live without. Use Apple's Extensions Manager (Apple menu | Control Panels | Extensions Manager) to turn off extensions and control panels you don't need.

● *Use a RAM disk.* With the Mac's Memory control panel, shown in Figure 17-1, you can create a RAM disk—a portion of the Mac's memory that is configured to act like

a virtual hard drive. The Mac accesses RAM much more quickly than a hard drive, so any data stored on a RAM disk can be retrieved almost instantly. To get the most out of a RAM disk, copy slow applications there. Another good use is to put your Internet browser's "cache" folder on a RAM disk. Remember that the RAM disk will lose everything you store there on restart. Also keep in mind that a RAM disk is barely useful unless you have at least 64MB of RAM, because a low-RAM Mac needs all of its resources just to run applications and Mac OS.

● *Increase the size of the disk cache in the Memory control panel.* The Mac's disk cache stores frequently used bits of data in RAM. As with a RAM disk, this data can be accessed very quickly. Unlike a RAM disk, the Mac OS—not you—determines which bits and bytes to store in RAM. The old rule of thumb was to assign 32K of cache for every megabyte of memory you had installed in the Mac. While this advice is a reasonable starting

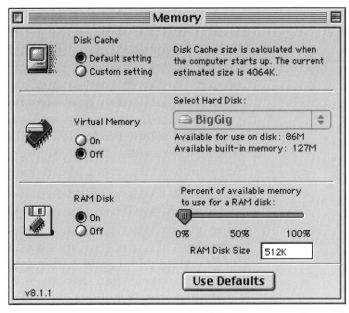

Figure 17-1 Switch RAM Disk on in the Memory control panel, configure the size of the disk, close the control panel, and restart the Mac

point, it shouldn't be considered a hard and fast rule.
In these days, when people have dozens and dozens of
megabytes of RAM onboard, this scheme breaks down
after you reach a certain limit. We have plenty of RAM
in our Macs, but we still set our disk caches no higher
than 1,024K. Up to that point you'll see some performance
benefits, but beyond 1,024K, you're just wasting perfectly
good RAM. Also, since RAM used for the disk cache
is not available for other stuff—like your system
software or applications, you shouldn't just crank it
up indiscriminately.

● *Use Speed Doubler if you have a PowerPC-based
Macintosh.* With the introduction of the Power
Macintosh, both hardware and software changed
drastically. New applications were written to take
advantage of this PowerPC processor— employing
technology unlike anything used with Apple's earlier
680x0-based Macs. To be backward-compatible with
programs that didn't use this new code, Apple found
a way for Power Macs to understand the old code by
"emulating" a 680x0 Mac. Unfortunately, this emulation
process tends to slow down the performance of Power
Macs, and Apple couldn't seem to make emulation
work any faster. Thankfully, a software company called
Connectix could. This faster emulation scheme can
be found in Connectix's Speed Doubler program. With
Speed Doubler installed, Power Macs run old code
much faster than with Apple's emulation scheme. Speed
Doubler works with all Macs that use the PowerPC chip.
That includes all current Mac models.

● *Don't use the Calculate Folder Sizes option.* In Mac
OS 8 and 8.5, you'll find this setting in the View Options
dialog box. In Mac OS 8.6 and later, choose Edit |
Preferences to locate the window shown in Figure 17-2.
The Calculate folder sizes option appears when a Finder
window is active. When this option is switched on, the
Mac determines and displays just how much space files
and folders take up on your hard drive. This process
takes time and slows down your Mac. Under System 7,
this used to be a universal option—either it was off

Bob Speaks: Choosing a Disk Cache Size

Here's how to feel the effect of different disk cache sizes so you can choose the best one for you:

1. Open the Memory control panel.

2. Crank the Disk Cache down to its lowest setting.

3. Restart your Mac.

4. Open the System Folder.

5. Close the System Folder.

6. Open the System Folder again. The reason you open the System Folder twice is that it's a good indicator of how much effect the Disk Cache is having. The first time you open it after you restart, the cache is empty and the folder will open more slowly than the second time, when some of the information about your System Folder is stored in disk cache.

7. Increase the Cache Size by two clicks.

8. Restart your Mac.

Repeat this procedure five times, noting how quickly the System Folder opens the second time after each restart. Now choose the setting that felt fastest to you. If several settings felt about the same, what you do depends upon how much RAM you have installed: if you have 64MB or more, choose the higher setting; if you have less than 64MB of RAM, choose the lower setting.

completely or the size of every file, folder, and volume was calculated. Mac OS 8 allows you to turn this option on for only those folders you select. If you use Personal File Sharing, be sure to turn off this option. It's a drain on the shared Mac and on the network.

- *Optimize your hard drive.* As you add and trash items on your Mac, space opens up on your hard drive and files become *fragmented*—meaning that part of a file may be

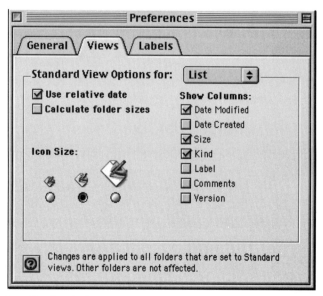

Figure 17-2 Uncheck Calculate Folder Sizes to speed up your Mac

written on one section of the drive, a second piece may be on another section of the drive, and yet a third may be somewhere else altogether. When your hard drive's read head looks for a file on a heavily fragmented disk, it may need to take a few extra turns around the neighborhood to locate all of a file's parts. This can slow down hard drive access, which, in turn, slows down your Mac. You can use a software program to put all these scattered pieces back together again. This is called *optimizing* your drive. In theory, optimizing your drive should speed up your Mac. But we're here to give you the facts, not the theory. Despite the claims you may have heard from software manufacturers who, coincidentally, make optimization software, optimizing your hard drive increases performance only when a drive is horribly, painfully fragmented.

Can I make applications load faster?

It just so happens that this is the perfect use for a RAM disk. If you have an application that you use all the time, and if it's

small enough to fit, toss it onto a RAM disk. It will launch in no time at all.

Another trick you can use that won't actually make your application load any faster but will add convenience to your computing is to drop an alias of applications you routinely use into the Startup Items folder (found inside your System Folder). Items placed in this folder will launch on startup. Sure, they'll take just as long to launch, but they'll be ready for use as soon as your Mac finishes booting up. To prevent the startup items from loading (along with your extensions and control panels, by the way) hold the SHIFT key while restarting your Mac.

How can I speed up file copying?

We mentioned Speed Doubler earlier for running programs under emulation more quickly. Speed Doubler 8, the current version as we go to press, has another nifty option: it copies files on the desktop and across networks more quickly. In addition, it empties the Trash more speedily than the Finder does.

What can I do to conserve memory?

The very first thing you can do is turn on virtual memory or install Connectix's RAM Doubler. With either of these methods in use on a Power Mac, your applications require less physical memory to run. For more about virtual memory, see Chapter 14.

You might also follow our advice about weeding out extraneous extensions and control panels. These items may or may not slow down your Mac, but they definitely eat up memory.

If you have Casady & Greene's Conflict Catcher 8 installed, it can tell you just how much memory each of these items consumes. This information can be very helpful when you're trying to determine which items to switch off. To use this view, follow these steps:

1. Choose Apple menu | Control Panels | Conflict Catcher from the Apple menu (or simply select Open Conflict Catcher under the Conflict Catcher icon in the menu bar).

2. Click and hold the Listed By menu item in the Conflict Catcher window.

3. Select By Memory Use from the resulting pull-down list.

Your extensions and control panels will now be listed in descending order of memory usage, as shown in Figure 17-3. From here, you can simply switch off those items whose memory demands outweigh their usefulness.

Can I do anything to speed up games on my Mac?

Games may seem like innocent diversions, but they are among the most processor-hungry applications around. You may think that you have a robust Mac, but until you challenge it with a game like MacSoft's Unreal, you'll never know for sure. Here are our gaming speed tweaks:

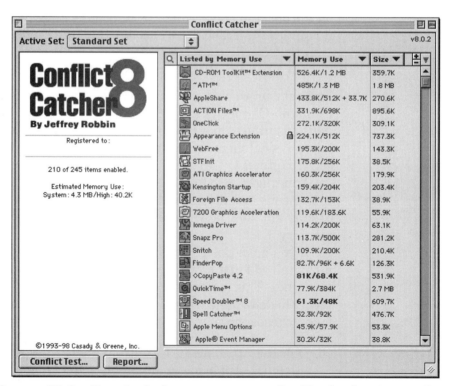

Figure 17-3 If you're losing your memory, Conflict Catcher 8 can tell you where it has gone

● *Quit other applications.* Most games require your Mac's full attention. Quit other programs and put a stop to any background processes that might interfere with game play. This includes background optimization, virus checking, diagnostic utilities, networking (don't switch off networking if you're playing a network game, of course), and fax software.

● *Use the game options wisely.* Because games are so needy, game designers build in options that allow players to switch off certain features in order to increase the speed of the game. For example, high-resolution audio and graphics take their toll on performance and, therefore, many games allow you to play with lower-quality sounds and with fewer colors. Likewise, you can play the game in a smaller window—at a resolution of 320 × 240 rather than 640 × 480, for example. In some cases, you can even have the game draw only every other line onscreen. These compromises detract from the game's presentation, but at least they allow you to run the game on a Mac that otherwise might not be hardy enough to do so.

● *Use a video card with 3-D hardware acceleration.* Earlier, we mentioned that you can use a fast video card to speed up your Mac's overall performance. There are also video cards whose sole purpose in life is to speed up performance in certain types of games. These cards support something called 3-D hardware acceleration, a process whereby a game's graphic duties are assumed by the special chips on one of these cards. These chips can draw pixels and polygons very, very quickly, leaving your Mac's processor to take care of less taxing gaming duties, such as keeping track of where you've moved your joystick or playing the horrifying shriek that results when you've blasted a Neptunian cootie into space debris. With the proper video card, your games can play much faster than before. And because these cards can draw textures unavailable with software rendering, the games will look a lot better too—like Nintendo 64 or Sony PlayStation games.

 How can I get the most out of my slow modem?

The best way to get the most from your slow modem is to limit the amount of data coming through it. This means configuring your e-mail program and browser so that your modem only has to download the information you need. Here are some hints for doing so:

- Most e-mail applications can be configured so that messages larger than a certain size will be left on the server until you're ready to download them. This is helpful if you tend to receive large e-mail attachments and you want to see what these attachments contain before you go through the trouble of downloading them. You can delete those that are unworthy of your attention from the server.

- Web pages are littered with graphics. Although attractive, these pictures can take a long time to appear if you're using a slow modem. Both Internet Explorer and Navigator give you the option to turn off the display of these graphics.

- If a Web site offers a "low-bandwidth" version, use it. These sites are usually uncluttered, and text appears quickly.

- As soon as the text on a Web page begins to appear, look for hypertext navigation controls at the bottom of the page. You can quickly move from page to page by using these links, without waiting for the rest of the page graphics to load. If you make extensive use of this tip, consider making Internet Explorer your Web browser of choice. Unlike Netscape's offerings, Internet Explorer loads all of the text and tables on a Web page before going back for the graphics. So, the stuff you're interested in comes on screen more quickly.

If you've visited a Web page that doesn't interest you, don't wait around while it downloads. Just click the Stop button in your browser (or press COMMAND+PERIOD) and move on to the next site.

SHORTCUTS, TIMESAVERS, AND PRODUCTIVITY

How can I get quick access to important documents and applications?

In case you haven't noticed, the Mac is a wonderfully flexible computer. Apple provides many ways for you to quickly access documents and applications. Here are some examples:

● *Look to the Launcher.* For some time now, Apple has included the Launcher control panel with Mac OS. It's disabled by default. You can use the Launcher to quickly get at your often-used applications and documents. Just open the control panel by selecting Apple menu | Control Panels | Launcher, and turn the Launcher on. Next, drag and drop application and document icons into the Launcher window when it appears. When placed in the Launcher window, items are miraculously transformed into buttons. If the button represents an application, a single click launches the program. If the button is a document, the file opens in its proper application. You can also drag and drop a document onto an application Launcher button to open the document in that application.

● *Use the Recent Applications and Recent Documents folders.* The Apple menu contains folders labeled Recent Applications and Recent Documents. These folders hold exactly what they claim—the names of the applications and documents you've recently launched or opened. These folders are mighty handy when you want to access an item that you've used recently. Just select an item in one of these folders, and it automatically launches. To set the number of items displayed in these folders, open the Apple Menu Options control panel, shown in Figure 17-4, and enter the number of items you'd like these folders to remember.

● *Maintain an alias.* There's almost no easier way to get to your favorite application than making an alias of it and placing that alias in the Apple menu. We said

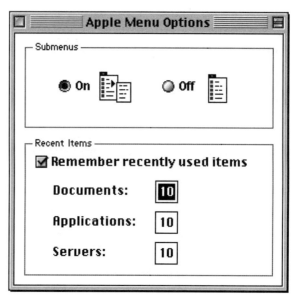

Figure 17-4 The Apple Menu Options control panel is where you choose the number of recent applications, documents, and servers to view on the Apple Menu

almost. Here's the easiest way. Click your favorite application's icon once, and select Apple menu | Automated Tasks | Add Alias to Apple Menu. An alias of this application will automatically be created and placed in the Apple menu. Whenever you want to use that application in the future, it's close at hand.

● *Maintain an alias II.* Make aliases of your favorite applications and current documents, and place them on your Mac's desktop.

● *Maintain an alias III.* Creating a desktop full of aliases can lead to clutter, so pull the clutter off the desktop by creating a pop-up window and placing your aliases in it. While in the Mac OS 8 Finder, press COMMAND+N to create an empty folder, name the folder something like My Favorite Apps, drop your aliases into the folder, and click and drag the window's title bar (and the window) to the bottom of the screen. Poof! The open window turns into a pop-up window as indicated by the small tab that peeks up from below. To easily access your aliases, just

click the tab, double-click the alias you want, and you're on your way. When applications launch and documents open, the window pops back down automatically.

● *Use a third-party utility.* There are a wealth of third-party launcher utilities and macro programs that you can use to keep your favorite applications and files close at hand. We love James Thomson's DragThing. Check your favorite software source for this and other shareware options.

How can I keep my Mac's date and time accurate?

All versions of Mac OS allow you to set the computer's date and the correct time, but Mac OS 8.5 and later add the ability to keep the setting accurate, using a date and time server. Using one of several atomic clocks around the world, a time server makes the correct time available online to any application that can connect to the server. When you set the Date & Time control panel to connect to a network time server, it will acquire the correct time and update your Mac at an interval you choose. To set the correct time using a network time server, follow these steps:

1. Choose Apple menu | Control Panels | Date & Time.

2. Click Use a Network Time Server.

3. Click Server Options to choose a time server on your continent.

4. Choose an option that tells the control panel how often to check the time. The default option compares your system clock to the time server and updates it when there is a difference.

Are there ways to automate tasks I perform frequently?

Apple provides one way. It's called AppleScript, and it is a system that allows you to automate a number of tasks on your Mac. We mentioned one automated task earlier—the Add Alias to Apple Menu AppleScript. AppleScript comes with the Script Editor, an application you can use to write

your own AppleScripts. Although it helps to know the syntax for writing AppleScripts, the commands are very English-like and with a little effort can be mastered by those who've never scripted or programmed before. You can also create simple AppleScripts without knowing a single AppleScript command. Here's an example:

1. Drag a file you no longer want into the Trash.

2. Launch the Script Editor application (found inside the AppleScript folder inside the Apple Extras folder).

3. Click the Record button in the Untitled window.

4. Go to the Finder by clicking the desktop and, while pressing the OPTION key, select Special | Empty Trash.

5. Go back to the Script Editor, and click the Stop button. You'll see that some words have appeared in the window, as shown in Figure 17-5. Those words and command structure are AppleScript's way of saying "Empty the Trash when I execute this script."

6. Select Save As from Script Editor's File menu, name your script something like Empty Now, and save it to the desktop. While you're there, pull down the Kind menu and save the script as an application, and click the Never Show Startup Screen check box so that you won't have to see a display screen every time you double-click the script.

7. Quit the Script Editor.

8. Place the Empty Now script on your desktop, and place another useless file in the Trash.

9. Double-click the Empty Now script, and watch as your Trash empties automatically. Congratulations, you're now an AppleScripter!

AppleScript is a powerful but often unexplored part of the Mac OS. If you're interested in learning more about it, start at ScriptWeb (http://www.scriptweb.com/), a Web site with scripting resources related to AppleScript, HyperCard, UserLand Frontier, and lots more. Apple's own AppleScript pages (http://www.apple.com/applescript/) are good sources to try as well.

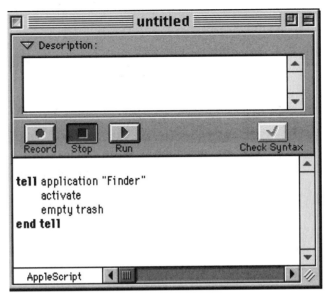

Figure 17-5 AppleScript's Script Editor

Are there utilities other than AppleScript that I can use to automate my Mac?

Yes, you can use a more powerful (and more complex) scripting application from UserLand Software called Frontier to automate just about any task you can think of on your Mac. You can also use a macro program such as WestCode Software's OneClick or CE Software's QuicKeys to create shortcuts for tasks you routinely perform.

Some application programs, such as AppleWorks (formerly ClarisWorks), Nisus Writer, and Microsoft Office, have macro functions built in. You can use these macros to automate common tasks you perform from within these applications.

Can I use menu commands without having to drag my mouse to the menu bar?

The easiest way is to use the keyboard command that appears next to the menu item they correspond to. Here are keyboard shortcuts that work in most Mac applications you're likely to encounter:

Shortcut	Function
COMMAND+N	New (can mean new document, new folder, or new window)
COMMAND+O	Open
COMMAND+W	Close (window)
COMMAND+S	Save
COMMAND+P	Print
COMMAND+Q	Quit
COMMAND+Z	Undo (also the F1 key)
COMMAND+X	Cut (also the F2 key)
COMMAND+C	Copy (also the F3 key)
COMMAND+V	Paste (also the F4 key)

Every application has its own set of keyboard commands that you'll become familiar with as you use the applications. Learn and use them—they're better and faster than reaching for the mouse all the time.

Using the macro programs that we discussed in the previous question, you can also assign keyboard commands to menu items. For example, you can create a macro that empties the Trash when you press COMMAND+T in the Finder.

 How can I use keyboard shortcuts to navigate around the screen?

The Mac supports a number of keyboard shortcuts and commands for moving around the desktop. Here are some examples that you may find useful:

- Click in a Finder window and type the first letter of a file's name to highlight that file. If there is more than one item on the desktop that starts with that letter, type the first couple of letters of a file's name to select it.

- In an open dialog box, you can move to any file or folder by typing the first letter or letters of its name. If you type "gro" really fast, you should be able to locate the grocery list in a dialog box that also contains your German lesson.

- With nothing highlighted on the desktop, press the LEFT ARROW or UP ARROW key to highlight the icon nearest the upper-left corner of the screen. Pressing the RIGHT ARROW

or DOWN ARROW key highlights the icon nearest the bottom-right corner of the screen.

- With an icon highlighted, press the arrow keys to jump to the nearest icon in that direction; the RIGHT ARROW key highlights the nearest icon to the right, for example.

- Pressing TAB highlights the next icon in alphabetical order. If no icon is highlighted, TAB highlights the first numbered icon on the desktop (1 or 2, for example). If there are no numbered icons, the first icon in alphabetical order is highlighted.

- Highlight a folder or volume, and press COMMAND+DOWN ARROW to open that folder. COMMAND+DOWN ARROW will also open any document that's highlighted.

- Press RETURN to click the highlighted button in a dialog box. Press ESC or COMMAND+PERIOD to choose Cancel in a dialog box.

Can I use a keyboard shortcut to switch between applications, as Windows users can with ALT+TAB?

It depends on the system software version you use. Under Mac OS 8.5 and later, pressing COMMAND+TAB switches to the next application, and COMMAND+SHIFT+TAB switches to the previous application. Earlier versions of Mac OS don't have this feature built in, but the COMMAND+TAB key combination may work for you anyway, because a few popular applications provide you with this shortcut. Microsoft Office 98's Microsoft Office Manager control panel and the excellent shareware program GoMac, for example, allow you to switch applications using the COMMAND+TAB shortcut.

Can I launch Internet URLs without first opening my browser?

Yes, and you can do so in a number of ways:

- *Drag Links.* Select a URL in an application and drag it into an open browser or on top of an alias to your browser.

- *Use the Connect To item.* If you have Mac OS 8 or 8.1, select the Connect To item from the Apple menu. When the Connect To dialog box appears, enter an Internet

address and press the Connect button to be whisked to that site. If you have Mac OS 8.5 or 8.6, you'll find the Connect To item inside the Internet Access folder in your Apple menu. Connect To is not included with Mac OS 9.

- *Use Apple Data Detectors.* Apple has created software that allows you to quickly launch a URL from just about anywhere on your Mac. This software is called Apple Data Detectors (ADD), and, once installed, ADD places a number of new options inside Mac OS 8's contextual menus. While holding down the CONTROL key, click and hold a Web address, e-mail address, FTP address, or newsgroup name. A contextual menu appears that offers you many options. If the item you've selected is a Web URL, you can go to that site with the browser of your choice. Or if it's an e-mail address, you can have your e-mail client create a new message addressed to this recipient. ADD is an add-on for Mac OS 8 and later. You can find it at http://asu.info.apple.com/ swupdates.nsf/artnum/.

- *Save bookmarks as Favorites.* In Mac OS 8.5 and later, the Apple menu contains a folder called Favorites. You can save bookmarks there by copying them or by clicking a link while you press the CONTROL key. Choose Add Link to Favorites from the contextual menu. From then on, you can launch the URL by choosing it from the Favorites submenu of the Apple menu.

- *Look for live links.* Most e-mail clients and some newer applications now support *live links*—hypertext links that, when double-clicked, launch your browser. Microsoft Office 98 also supports live links. By default, when you type a URL into a Word 98 document, it's automatically converted to a live link (you can turn this option off). Double-clicking this link launches your browser and takes you to that site. Live links are almost always blue.

How can I manage large numbers of Internet bookmarks?

Netscape Navigator/Communicator and Microsoft Internet Explorer allow you to create folders within the Bookmarks or

Favorites menu, and these folders are the first step toward organizing your bookmarks. Do you like to visit sites dedicated to music? Great. In your browser, create a new folder, call it Music Links, and drop all your music-related bookmarks into it. Do you consistently visit the same bunch of sites on Monday morning? Create another folder, call it Monday Browsing, and drop the bookmarks for these sites in there.

Here's how to create a new folder in Communicator 4.6:

1. Select Bookmarks | Edit Bookmarks (COMMAND+B).

2. Select New Folder from the File menu.

3. Type a name for your new folder in the dialog box. If you like, add a description in the appropriate field.

4. In the Bookmarks window, SHIFT+click to select the items you'd like to move, and drag and drop these highlighted items into the new folder.

5. To move the folder up or down in the list, simply drag and drop it into position.

And here's the Internet Explorer (4.5) way:

1. Select Favorites | New Folder.

2. The Favorites window appears to the left of the browser window. The new folder's name will be highlighted, ready for naming. Name it.

3. SHIFT+click the items you want to place in the folder, and then drag and drop them into place.

4. As with Communicator, click and drag the new folder into any position on the menu you like.

There are also a number of very capable bookmark utilities available on the Web. We like Alco Bloom's URL Manager Pro quite a bit, and there are other shareware and commercial utilities to choose from.

 How can I install fonts temporarily?

There are font management utilities that allow you to temporarily activate fonts, as well as create special font sets

that work with particular applications. For example, you can create a huge font set for use with Adobe PageMaker and a smaller set to use with AppleWorks. Font Reserve, from DiamondSoft, provides these capabilities as do Insider Software's FontAgent (formerly known as Font Box), Alsoft's MasterJuggler Pro, and Symantec's Suitcase. Before you buy a font utility, be sure that it is compatible with the version of Mac OS you are using.

If you have the patience, you can also temporarily install fonts manually. Just select the fonts you want, and drag them to the closed System Folder. The fonts will be installed but won't be available to any open applications. Just quit and relaunch any open applications to start using the new fonts. When you no longer care to use those fonts, open the Fonts folder inside the System Folder and remove the fonts you no longer need.

Installing fonts temporarily makes sense if you only need certain ones occasionally. Fonts require RAM, and long lists of fonts on a menu can become difficult to manage. Though the problem is less pronounced in recent versions of Mac OS, fonts are also subject to conflicts, which may make one or more unusable when combined.

How can I locate invisible files on my hard disk?

Apple hid the function for finding invisible files, but nothing escapes our eagle eyes. Here's how to find these files:

1. Select Sherlock from the Apple menu, or press COMMAND+F while in the Finder.

2. Choose Find | More Options (COMMAND+M).

3. Under the Advanced Options section of the More Options window, click the Is check box.

4. The pop-up menu gives you the option to select Invisible items, as shown in Figure 17-6.

5. Click OK to close the More Search Options dialog box.

6. Choose which disks to search.

7. Click the Find button to gather a list of all the invisible items on your hard disk.

Figure 17-6   Click Is to see the option that allows you to search for invisible files, using Sherlock

---

Caution: *Invisible items are usually invisible for a good reason. If you don't know what an invisible item is for, don't mess around with it. Moving or trashing certain invisible items is a formula for disaster.*

CHEAP AND FREE STUFF TO MAKE YOUR MAC BETTER

 How can I find good Mac shareware and freeware?

If you have a connection to the Internet, you have access to more Mac shareware and freeware than you could use in a lifetime. There are a number of wonderful Mac software archives on the Net. These are some of our favorites:

●   **Info-Mac HyperArchive**   This site probably has the most extensive collection of Mac shareware and freeware

in the world. Because the collection is so extensive, this site tends to be busy much of the time. Look for HyperArchive mirror sites, and try to log on during late evening hours when the site is likely to be less busy. The HyperArchive site is at

http://hyperarchive.lcs.mit.edu/HyperArchive.html

● **MacDownload** This is ZDNet's Macintosh file library, and it includes a fine collection of Mac shareware and freeware. The site features special "files of the day" and offers profiles of shareware and freeware authors. The MacDownload site is at

http://www.macdownload.com

● **Shareware.com** C I Net was thinking ahead when it grabbed this domain name. Shareware.com is popular for two reasons: the name is a cinch to remember, and the site has a reasonably fast search engine that tracks down much of the Mac freeware and shareware you're looking for. Shareware.com is at

http://www.shareware.com

● **VersionTracker** If you're seeking the latest update to just about any application on your Mac, check the VersionTracker site. The folks behind VersionTracker are fanatical about maintaining an up-to-date archive. The latest and greatest can always be found here. The VersionTracker site is at

http://www.versiontracker.com/

If you're an AOL member, you can also find a fair amount of Mac shareware and software simply by clicking the Software Search button in AOL's graphic menu bar. Once the Software Search window opens, enter a search term to start your hunt.

Should I join a "disk of the month" club?

If you have access to the Internet or a good newsstand, we don't recommend it. After all, if you only want a few pieces of shareware or freeware every couple of weeks, it's pretty easy to download them. And if you want a slew of software on

CD-ROM once a month, you'll find that the popular Mac magazines—*Mac Home Journal, MacAddict,* and *Macworld Magazine*—bundle software-laden CD-ROMs with their newsstand issues. (If you subscribe to *MacAddict*, you'll receive a CD-ROM full of useful software with each issue.)

Is shareware word-processing software available?

Better yet, as we write this there's a *free* word processing program available. Nisus is giving away free copies of Nisus Writer 4.1, a very robust word processing application. This isn't the current version of Nisus Writer, and we're not sure if it will still be available by the time you read this, but it's worth checking http://www.nisus.com to find out. To download the program, you must fill out an extensive questionnaire and have cookies turned on in your browser.

If Nisus Writer is no longer free, and you're interested in an excellent shareware word processing application, give Mariner Software's Mariner Write Lite a test drive. It's a full-featured word processor at the bargain price of $20. We know several pros who use Mariner Write exclusively. You can get more information at http://www.marinersoft.com.

If you don't need a complete word processing application, there are a number of text editing programs that will do in a pinch. Tom Bender's shareware program Tex-Edit Plus is one of our favorites, and Bare Bones Software's BBEdit Lite is another good option. You can find both of these in any good online software archive.

What are some good shareware productivity tools?

There are enough good shareware productivity tools that we could easily write a book on just this subject. But in the interest of saving space, we'll try to narrow it down to a choice few that you can find easily. Most, if not all, of these tools can be found at major Mac archive sites, such as Info-Mac, Umich (University of Michigan), and others. The appendix to this book includes a number of these sources under the "Software Archives" heading.

● **AlwaysONline**   Alex Rampell's $12 shareware program keeps AOL from severing your connection if

you're away from your computer when one of AOL's "Hey, you've been on for 46 minutes, what say we kick you off if you don't respond really soon?" dialog boxes appears. Best of all, AlwaysONline takes care of these warnings even when they appear in the background—for instance, when you're browsing the Internet and can't see AOL's main window. Alex is a good guy and needs the money for college.

● **CopyPaste**   This awesome utility does many things, but what we like most about it is that it allows you to transfer multiple items in and out of the Clipboard. No more copy one item, paste it somewhere, copy another item, paste it somewhere else. With this $20 gem, you can copy ten items, if you like, and then paste them one after the other, any place you like.

● **DropStuff with Expander Enhancer**   Apple bundles Aladdin's StuffIt Expander with its system software (you can find it in the Aladdin folder inside the Internet Utilities folder inside the Internet Folder at the root level of your hard drive), and this same folder carries a copy of the DropStuff with Expander Enhancer installer. But it's shareware and Aladdin would like $30 for its use, if you please. Why use this version over the regular StuffIt Expander? The Expander Enhancer allows you to expand far more file types than StuffIt Expander—AppleLink Packages (.pkg), ARC (.arc), gzip (.gz), TAR (.tar), Unix Compress (.z), Uucode (.uu), and ZIP files (.zip).

● **FinderPop**   Turlough O'Connor's free FinderPop extends the capabilities of Apple's contextual menus in a number of ways. One of the nicest options is the Processes menu that allows you to easily switch from one open application to another.

● **GraphicConverter**   If you ever have to convert a graphic document from one type to another—PICT to GIF, for example—you need this $35 graphics conversion utility from Thorsten Lemke. You can also use it as a graphics viewer.

● **Prestisimo**   PolyMorph Software's free Mac OS 8.5 and later interface helper allows you to customize the tear-off application palette and application switcher.

- **Snapz Pro**   It may be that we like Ambrosia's $20 screen capture utility, Snapz Pro, so much because our jobs require that we take lots and lots of screenshots and this is the best utility for doing just that. Even if you take only one tenth the number of screenshots we do, you'll still appreciate its elegance and versatility.

- **Snitch**   Does Apple's Get Info command leave you craving more information? Do you occasionally need to change a document's file type or creator code? If so, Mitch Jones' $20 Snitch is for you. Using Snitch, not only can you get way more information than you need on a file, you can make that file invisible as well.

- **SoundApp**   Norman Franke's free SoundApp is the audio equivalent to GraphicConverter. Use it to play and convert just about any audio file type.

- **WebFree**   Thank goodness this book is being printed on paper rather than on the Web. That way we won't make anyone angry when we suggest that those who have little tolerance for Web page advertising try WebFree, Steve Falkenburg's $20 cookie- and ad-blocking control panel.

Is buying used software a violation of copyright laws?

We're not lawyers, nor have we read every copyright statute on the books, but we can pass along the common wisdom on the subject: The person giving away software (for money or for free) is also passing along the license to that software. This means that person may no longer use that software because he or she no longer has the license to do so. So, for example, if you give away SuperWizPaint 2 after you've received the SuperWizPaint 3 upgrade, and you continue to use SuperWizPaint 2, your action is in violation of the license agreement. When you give away SuperWizPaint 2, you forsake your license and must, therefore, refrain from using other copies of the program unless and until you purchase a new copy.

But let's say you've given up every copy of SuperWizPaint you have. Do you have to contact the company that produced the software and tell them that you have transferred the license to another individual? It depends. Some license agreements

demand written notification of transfer and others don't. Either way, most companies won't honor upgrade or technical support agreements once a license has been transferred.

A basic rule of thumb: If you have even the slightest suspicion that your actions might violate common copyright practices, stop whatever you're doing. Piracy is bad. Don't do it.

SAVING MONEY WHEN YOU BUY SOFTWARE AND PERIPHERALS

Where can I get the best deal on Mac peripherals?

If you happen to live in an area with an abundance of computer stores, you can usually find what you're looking for at a bargain price. But it requires a fair amount of looking, and a thorough knowledge of what's worth having and what isn't.

For most people, mail order and online shopping is the best way to save a buck. These outfits usually buy in bulk and don't have to worry about the kind of overhead inherent in a local retail store. This bulk pricing and lower cost of doing business translate into savings for you.

If you don't mind used peripherals, user groups are another excellent source for inexpensive hardware. We've seen some great deals on good gear at user-group sponsored swap meets. The newspaper classifieds are another reasonable source if you know what you're looking for and what it's worth.

Finally, if you go to Macworld Expo, the Macintosh trade show that's held twice a year (in San Francisco in January, and in Boston in August), check out the show prices. Peripherals are often offered at deep discounts.

Where can I get the best deal on Mac software?

Become a software reviewer for one of the major Macintosh magazines. The savings you realize will make your head spin.

Of course, then you'd be competing for our jobs, so never mind. Instead, check mail order catalogs and online sources, such as Outpost.com. Also, if you're looking for a deal on a particular program, surf over to the site of the company that makes that program. Sometimes companies will offer special prices if you buy direct. You can realize even greater savings

if you buy your software electronically and download the software over a secure connection, rather than asking the company to ship you the boxed and shrink-wrapped version.

Remember our little advice about copyright issues earlier in this chapter? When buying used software, make sure you get the complete package—original disks, original manuals, and any warranty information the former owner may have. Steer clear if you see a couple of floppies with homemade labels.

What are some caveats for buying via mail order or online?

If you have a problem with the products you receive—say the monitor you order catches fire when you plug it in—you usually don't have the option to take it back to a local retailer. Instead, you have to pack it up, ship it off to heaven knows where, and pray that you see it again before the end of the year.

Some mail order and online companies are better about returns, repairs, and exchanges than others. Although you can find bargain prices in the back of the major Mac magazines, it's a good idea to ask around on newsgroups, bulletin boards, and at local Macintosh users' groups to see who provides good prices as well as reputable service.

Also, be aware that these remote dealers offer good prices on some gear and terrible prices on others. For example, MacWarehouse, MacConnection, MacZone, and MacMall—all of whom sell products online and through mail-order catalogs—are fine places to order CPUs and software, but their RAM and hard drive prices are no bargain. For such items as memory and hard drives, shop with dealers who specialize in these areas.

Finally, always pay by credit card. That way, if you don't get the items you want, or if the product arrives in a dozen pieces and the seller is reluctant to put things right, you can ask your credit card company to withhold payment until matters are resolved to your satisfaction.

What are some caveats for buying from a retail store?

In a perfect world, all salespeople would know more about the products they're selling than the name and price. If you've ever shopped at one of those cavernous electronics

emporiums, you've probably come to realize that it's not a perfect world. So, before you go shopping, it's a good idea to educate yourself by skimming through a few appropriate Web sites or reading an authoritative tome such as this. That way, you won't have to depend on the dubious opinions of a salesperson who can't tell a Mac from a large block of cheese.

This point applies to just about any big-ticket item these days: Beware the extended warranty. Margins are pretty thin on computers and peripherals, so many places try to make their money on service contracts. For the most part, they're not worth the dough. Macs are now covered for a year by Apple, and if your Mac makes it through that year without any trouble, it's not likely to start acting up on day 366.

Chapter 18

Mac Fun and Games: Spending Your Disposable Income

Answer Topics!

Mac Fun and Games @ a Glance

- **Games and Gaming** describes games and game information available for the Mac.

- **Hardware for Games** discusses hardware accessories for Mac gamers.

- **Other Fun Stuff** suggests some non-game fun you can have with your Mac.

GAMES AND GAMING

 What are some cool games for the Mac?

Bob likes bloody, violent stuff like Myth: The Fallen Lords, Myth II: Soulblighter (both from Bungie), and Unreal (from MacSoft). The Myth duo are unique strategy/battle games played on three-dimensional battlefields. Unreal is a traditional first-person shooter with lots of style.

Bob also liked both Myst and Riven from brothers Rand and Robyn Miller, published by Broderbund/Red Orb. These are slower-paced "thinking-persons" games set in a beautiful universe far, far away.

For what it's worth, Bob thinks Myth and Myth II are the best multi-player games ever invented. You can join games with friends and strangers on the Internet, for free, via Bungie's Internet server (dubbed "BungieNet").

 Caution: *Playing Myth online is extremely addictive!*

Bob's wife, Lisa, is partial to Patrick Fournier's old Tetris knock-off, Pentris ($15 shareware); KidPix Studio Deluxe (both kids love it too...); and Loony Labyrinth, a pinball-simulation from StarPlay.

We both like the You Don't Know Jack series from Sierra.

Shelly seems to be working, even when she's gaming. SimCity 3000 from Maxis was her passion, until the music took up permanent residence in her head, and the pursuit of the perfect route from her downtown commercial district to the new airport took over her waking moments. SimCity lets you plan and run a city with punishment and reward for raising taxes and building a good educational system, respectively. Because Shelly is a rabid public transportation activist, it stands to reason that her other gaming passion is a driving game. That would be NASCAR Racing II, from Sierra. Shelly still misses the late lamented Test Drive II, from Accolade, but its demise is something she's learning to live with.

It's important before buying any game to check its system requirements and make sure your Mac is up to the task.

Many of the best action games require massive computing resources. MacSoft recommends a whopping 64MB of RAM for Unreal! So if your Mac sports an older PowerPC processor (like the 601 or even 603), has less than 32MB of RAM, and/or less than 100MB of available hard disk space, you may not be able to run many popular games. (That's yet another reason to get a new, faster Mac, eh?)

What games are good for kids?

Bob's almost ten-year-old daughter, Allison, is in fourth grade. She says her favorite Mac games are ClueFinders 4th Grade from the Learning Company; Rugrats Adventure Game from Broderbund; and an oldie-but-goodie, PowerPete, from MacPlay.

Her brother, Jacob, is a six-year-old kindergartner who likes to play SpyFox in Dry Cereal from Humongous, The Incredible Machine from Sierra, and Nanosaur, which came with our iMac.

We get a lot of free software, so these titles represent what they're playing with today. A month from now, they'll be in love with something totally different. Overall, we have found that Humongous, The Learning Company, and Broderbund make excellent software for kids. You almost can't go wrong with any of these three publishers.

Can I play network games with PC users?

It depends mostly on the game. For example, Marathon I and III are Mac-only games, and even Marathon II, which did come out on the PC, is not playable across platforms. While you can play them on a Mac-only LAN or via TCP/IP, you can't play them with PC users.

Myth I and II, on the other hand, are totally platform-indifferent. Each is available for Mac and PC, and once you log onto BungieNet, there's no way to tell which computer you're using, and everyone is equal. Macs and PCs can also coexist nicely for the local area network games of Myth.

Other games, including Quake and Unreal, allow Macs and PCs to play on local area networks, as well as via the Internet, but don't include a free matchmaking service where you can find games, as Myth does.

The bottom line is to read the package carefully and make sure the games you buy support the type of network gaming you desire—against Macs, PCs, or both.

I have trouble finding Mac games at my local computer store. Where can I find them?

CompUSA generally has a pretty good selection in the Apple "Store within a Store." If there's a CompUSA nearby, check it out. However, the best selections of Mac games come from mail-order vendors. Check out the following companies: Outpost.com (http://www.outpost.com) and MacWarehouse (http://www.warehouse.com/MacWarehouse/).

Why aren't more PC games on the Mac?

The main reason is that there are four or five times more PCs in the world than Macs. That means a PC game has a larger potential market available. As a result, most game makers choose to publish for the PC exclusively, or to release their game for the PC before they offer a Mac version.

Also, for a long time the Mac wasn't considered a "consumer" machine. This also led many game companies to focus their resources on the Windows world.

There is a bright side: though computer stores and catalogs are full of PC games, many of them are awful. The games that do make it to the Mac are usually the best and/or most popular ones. You may have to wait for the Mac version of this month's hottest PC game, but what you get when you open the box will probably be worth your money.

There's even more reason to feel cautiously optimistic about the state of Mac games: many game companies today, including MacSoft, Aspyr, Changeling, Varcon, and others, make games only for the Mac. The status quo is starting to change, with a big push from the iMac. Apple recently upgraded the iMac's video and added a chipset designed to make game-playing easier and faster.

What publications, zines, and sites cover Mac games?

MacAddict (http://www.macaddict.com) is probably the most game-oriented magazine, followed closely by *MacHome*

(http://www.machome.com). One nice thing about *MacAddict* is that every issue comes with a CD-ROM, and every disc includes several demos of new games. *Macworld* (http://www.macworld.com) has recently added a game column, "The Game Room," penned by our esteemed technical editor, Chris Breen.

If you're a serious gamer, *Inside Mac Games* is what you want. It's a magazine on CD-ROM that reviews the latest games and provides news, information, rumors, and gossip about Mac games, plus a CD-ROM packed with updaters, cheats, maps, levels, strategy guides, QuickTime movies, and more. It'll cost you $39 a year for 10 CDs.

If you're not a serious gamer and don't want to spring for a subscription, there's still plenty of neat game-related stuff on Inside Mac Games' site (http://www.imgmagazine.com/).

How can I make games run faster?

First and foremost, make sure you quit all other applications before launching a game. Having anything running in the background will slow down the game.

If you're using virtual memory, turn it off and restart your Mac. Next, allocate as much RAM as you can spare to the game by following these steps:

1. From the Finder, choose Apple menu | About This Computer. (About This Macintosh in pre-Mac OS 8 systems.)

2. Note the "Largest Unused Block." This is how much RAM you have available for the game.

3. Set the game's preferred memory size: select the game's icon; then choose File | Get Info (or use the keyboard shortcut COMMAND+I) to 2 or 3MB less than the largest unused block.

If you use lots of third-party extensions and/or control panels, consider restarting your Mac using the "Mac OS Base" set of extensions in Extensions Manager (in Mac OS 8 and later, only). To do so, follow these steps:

1. Choose Apple menu | Control Panels | Extensions Manager.

2. Choose Mac OS Base from the pop-up Selected Set menu at the top of the window.

3. Restart your Mac.

You can copy some games entirely to your hard disk from the CD-ROM. If you have enough disk space, copying the game and its data files is a good idea. Doing so will make games run significantly faster, at a cost of several hundred megabytes of disk space. If that doesn't work with your particular game, you might try using Apple's Disk Copy program to make an "image" of the CD-ROM, and then mount the image and try again.

Finally, some games can be "accelerated" by adding a PCI card, called a 3-D or game accelerator, to your Mac (see the next section).

HARDWARE FOR GAMES

Will a wicked fast CD-ROM drive make my games run faster?

Probably not. Most CD-ROM games are optimized for a 4x CD-ROM drive. Unless your drive is much slower than 4x (not likely), a faster drive won't do that much for most games, though it may speed up encyclopedias and other reference works on CD.

The easiest thing you can do to speed up a game is to run it on a Mac with a G3 processor. All G3s are great game machines.

What are some cool accessories I can get for my gaming Mac?

There are joysticks, steering wheels, pedals, gamepads, and more available from companies including CH Products, ThrustMaster, Advanced Gravis, Saitek, and others. Depending upon your game, one of these optional controllers may be just the ticket. Flying games, for example, beg for a joystick and pedals.

You also need a great set of speakers, preferably ones with a big, booming subwoofer. Games sound better over good speakers.

Finally, many games look better and play faster if you install a "3Dfx", "Voodoo" card or ATI's Rage Orion. These

game accelerating PCI cards start at around $100. Recently, 3Dfx released Mac drivers for its Voodoo2 and Voodoo3 cards—allowing Mac users to finally buy the same game acceleration cards favored by PC users (at PC prices!).

How about for my iMac?

iMac™

iMacs have built-in 3-D acceleration that will speed up many games. The first iMacs—those without slot-loading CD-ROM and DVD-ROM drives—have pretty weak graphics chips. The latest slot-loading iMacs use the same high-performance graphics chipset found inside the Power Mac G4s—the Rage 128. Although these iMacs' graphics chipsets have less VRAM than their G4 counterparts—8- rather than 16MB—the Rage 128 is a vast improvement over the chipset the iMacs' used to carry. As far as controllers go, all of the major manufacturers mentioned earlier have announced USB versions of their products.

Can I use PC compatibility cards to play PC games?

You could. But whether or not it's any fun depends mostly upon the game and the speed of your Mac. With first-person shooters, flying games, driving games, and other 3-D games, you probably won't be happy. With less-demanding software it'll work better.

The bottom line, though, is that unless you get a PC compatibility card with a beefy and fast Pentium II or Pentium Pro processor, the latest greatest games won't run all that well. Furthermore, for what that card is going to cost you, you could almost buy a full-fledged Pentium PC with the latest SoundBlaster audio, a big fast hard disk, and a fast CD-ROM drive, too.

In other words, we don't think a PC compatibility card in a Mac is a very good way to play PC games.

Can I use Virtual PC or SoftWindows to play PC games?

That depends mostly upon the game and the speed of your Mac. On a fast Mac with lots of RAM, some PC games will play tolerably under Virtual PC or SoftWindows. But

fast-paced shooting, flying, driving, and other sports games will be too sluggish to enjoy, even on the fastest Mac.

Once again, we don't think Virtual PC or SoftWindows is a very good way to play PC games. Keep in mind that these software emulators are much slower than a PC compatibility card, and games are a category of software where speed is absolutely crucial.

Speaking of virtual game playing, there's another way to play non-Mac games on your computer. It's called Virtual Game Station. With it, you can play Sony PlayStation games on your Mac. Like Virtual PC, it comes from Connectix.

To use Virtual Game Station, you'll need at least a PowerPC G3 processor (not a G3 upgrade). You'll probably also want to seek out a USB game controller of some kind, though you can use your keyboard. Of course, you'll also need some games to play. Many well-known game vendors offer titles for Virtual Game Station. There's a list on the Connectix Web site (http://www.connectix.com).

Note, however, that depending on the outcome of litigation between Sony and Connectix, you may not be able to find Virtual Game Station in the future. Sony, the owners of PlayStation, have sued Connectix to stop production of VGS, claiming that the program illegally emulates its product. As we go to press, no final determination has been made on the matter.

Can I get better speakers for my iMac?

iMac™

Sure. The original iMac's built-in speaker system, while better than most Macs, is still a little anemic. There's a speaker jack inside the little door on the right side, where your keyboard plugs in. It has a little picture of a speaker next to it. Just plug your speaker or speaker system into that jack.

The newest iMacs—the iMac DV and DV Special Edition, include enhanced speakers from Harman Kardon. If you don't like them, you can still attach external speakers.

OTHER FUN STUFF

How do I get photos onto my Mac so I can e-mail them to my friends?

To bring photos or other images into your computer, you need to convert the image on paper to a graphics file. You have three options:

- A digital camera
- A scanner
- Kodak PhotoCD process

A basic digital camera costs several hundred dollars and allows you to take "filmless" pictures and transfer them by cable to your Mac. Unfortunately, the image quality of inexpensive digital cameras leaves a lot to be desired. Before you commit to one, make sure you're happy with the quality of the pictures it takes. You'll find more info about digital cameras in Chapter 7.

For better-quality images, you can use a scanner to "scan" photos and create Mac files out of them. A scanner is like a color copier except that instead of making copies, it creates Mac files that you can manipulate and send via e-mail, or place on a Web page. Scanners usually connect to the Mac's SCSI chain and cost anywhere from $200 on up. Again, Chapter 7 has more to say about scanners.

Finally, the least expensive solution is to find a photo shop that will create a Kodak PhotoCD from your pictures. You can get an entire roll of film on CD-ROM for around $20.

❓ What do I need in order to create and edit video on my Mac?

Unless you have a late-model Power Macintosh, PowerBook, or iMac with a FireWire port, the first thing you need is a card that will import (digitize) video onto your Mac. Most of these are PCI cards, whose prices start at just over $300 and go up to thousands of dollars, depending on the quality of video you want to create. Vendors include Iomega, Miro, and Truevision. Power Macintosh G3 AV systems include a video capture card, as did the Power Macintosh 8500 and several Power Computing clones.

The next thing you need is video-editing software. The best-known titles are Apple Final Cut Pro, Adobe Premiere, and Avid Cinema. Some video-editing cards are bundled with a "light" version of Premiere, or some other editing package.

iMac™

If you have an iMac DV or iMac Special Edition, you've got all you need. These systems include the hardware and an Apple software application called iMovie. With these tools, you can connect the computer to a video source, capture footage, and edit it.

Make sure that the bundled software doesn't have the features you want before buying a separate—usually expensive—alternative.

Finally, you will need a substantial amount of hard disk space—5 to 20MB per second—to store your digitized video.

If you have a blue-and-white or graphite Power Mac with a FireWire port, all you need is a digital camcorder with a FireWire connection and some video-editing software, such as Apple's Final Cut Pro or Adobe's Premiere. You don't need a video capture card.

The bottom line is that for less than $1,000, you can turn most Macs into video-editing systems capable of creating VHS-quality videotapes.

Bob Speaks: The Beloved Talking Moose

There's no way we can complete a chapter about fun on your Mac without at least a mention of the Talking Moose.

It all began back in 1990 when I wrote these words in the preface to *Stupid Mac Tricks* (Reading, MA: Addison-Wesley, 1990):

> *"If you're wondering why a serious, dedicated, and well-known Macintosh journalist such as myself would embark on such a wacky project, all I can say in my defense is, 'The moose made me do it.'"*

The Talking Moose was an animated moose that popped up on your screen and talked to you, saying things like "How come we never go out anymore?" and "The pessimist says the glass is half-empty; the optimist drinks it anyway." And so on. Technically, he was nothing more than a control panel, but he was fun and spawned an entire generation of Stupid books.

Anyway, System 7 came around and the moose stopped working. His creator, Steve Halls, had gone on to become a brain surgeon in Canada, or something, and the moose, alas, was dead.

Or so I thought. Just a few days ago, my friend (hi Deb!) directed me to a Web site (http://www.weblayout.com/witness/Moose.htm) where I found the following:

> *"After Steve Halls left his moose to become a famous doctor in Canada, I thought I'd simply import some mooses from Sweden and start my own moose ranch. And now you can hear their witty comments on your Mac, too! Fully System 7 compatible (Mac OS 8 is perfectly fine, too) and wackier than ever. These crazy elks know more than 250 phrases! And you can add more using the phrase editor! And if that isn't enough, there are also three different moose animations you can choose from: a nostalgic one that resembles Steve Hall's design, a cartoony one that was hand-drawn by myself, and a Swedish 'Mooses Crossing' traffic sign.*
>
> *So, if you have a Mac with Mac OS 7.1 or higher and the Speech Manager installed, get your copy of Uli's Talking Moose now!!!"*

Guess what? Uli's Talking Moose is just as much fun as Steve Halls' original and works with Mac OS 8.5 and later! You probably won't keep it on your Mac for long, but it's worth checking out.

Appendix A

Mac Resources on the Internet

This appendix is a categorical listing of Web sites and their uniform resource locators (URLs), where you can find even more Mac answers than those provided in this book. We've included our "Top Ten" list of favorites, as well as Apple sites, sites for games, graphics and multimedia, the iMac, Internet resources, Mac advocacy, news, online Mac periodicals (sometimes referred to as *e-zines,* short for *electronic magazines*), PowerBooks, product guides, shareware, shopping, support, technical issues, and vendors.

TOP TEN MAC SITES

Here are our favorite Macintosh sites and the reasons why we love them. Some of these sites are also listed under the specific categories throughout this appendix.

Site	URL	Comments
Apple Tech Info Library	http://til.info.apple.com/	Searchable database of technical information, detailed product descriptions, and answers to frequently asked questions
Info-Mac HyperArchive	http://hyperarchive.lcs.mit.edu/HyperArchive.html	The most respected shareware archive around, with a searchable interface
MacCentral	http://www.maccentral.com/	News, reviews, and columns; updated daily
MacConnection	http://www.macconnection.com/	A well-organized site for buyers of Macs, peripherals, and software
MacFixIt	http://www.macfixit.com/	Indispensable and in-depth trouble-shooting site
MacInTouch	http://www.macintouch.com/	The most straightforward and authoritative Mac news site on the Web
MacOS Rumors	http://www.macosrumors.com/	A place to dish the Apple dirt

Site	URL	Comments
Mac Resource Page	http://www.macresource.com/	Loads of links to all kinds of Mac information
MacSurfer's Headline News	http://www.macsurfer.com/	Collection of news stories from both the Mac press and other sources
MacWorks	http://www.macworks.com/	Dealer in new and used Macs and accessories; great source of upgrades for older Macs

APPLE SITES

Apple's collection of Web pages do much more than promote the Mac and sell products, though some of them do these things. You'll find lots of technical information, as well as software updates and details about Apple technology.

Site	URL
Apple Computer (main)	http://www.apple.com/
Apple Contacts Information	http://www.apple.com/about/phonenumbers.html
Apple Developer connection	http://www.apple.com/developer/
AppleFacts Online (Apple product data sheets)	http://product.info.apple.com/productinfo/datasheets/
Apple QuickTime page	http://www.apple.com/quicktime/
AppleShare IP	http://www.apple.com/appleshareip/
Apple Software Updates	http://horton.austin.apple.com/alphalist/alpha_swupdates.new.html
The Apple Store	http://www.apple.com/store/
Apple Support	http://www.apple.com/support/
Apple Technical Publications	http://developer.apple.com/techpubs/
Apple User Groups page	http://www.apple.com/usergroups/

FUN AND GAMES

Game sites include news, reviews, and sometimes games themselves for download. The sites we've labeled as "fun" are those that include Mac lore, images, and system enhancements.

Site	URL
Flight Simulators for Macintosh	http://www.shirenet.com/~crusader/html/Flight_Simulators.html
Inside Mac Games	http://www.insidemacgames.com/
The Mac Game Gate	http://www.macgate.torget.se/
Mac Gamers' Ledge	http://www.macledge.com/
MacGaming.Com	http://www.macgaming.com/
The Macinspired GIF Gallery	http://www.geocities.com/SiliconValley/Bay/1228/gallery.html
Moof! in Mind!	http://www.storybytes.com/moof.html
ResExcellence	http://www.resexcellence.com/

GRAPHICS AND MULTIMEDIA

These Mac graphics and font compendia will point you toward resources for specific software, as well as to images, fonts, and other applications available for download.

Site	URL
Fontaholics Anonymous	http://www.flash.net/~fontahol/
The Macintosh Font Vault	http://www.erik.co.uk/font/
Macintosh MIDI User's Internet Guide	http://www.aitech.ac.jp/~ckelly/mmuig.html
Postforum (digital video resources)	http://www.postforum.com/
Macintosh Graphics Resources	http://www.users.interport.net/~jashear/mac_graphics.html

iBOOK

Only in iBook™

Apple's newest portable computer isn't a PowerBook. It's kind of like a portable iMac, and it's already gotten its share of attention from Web page authors. Here are some sites for iBook fans and users.

Site	URL
Everything iBook	http://www.everythingimac.com/ibook/
iBook Planet	http://www.ibookplanet.com/index.shtml
iBook User	http://www.ibook-user.com/
iBook Zone	http://www.ibookzone.com/

iMAC

iMac™

Lots of sites cover the iMac, but these do it exclusively.

Site	URL
Daily iMac	http://www.dailyimac.com/
iMac Floppy	http://www.imacfloppy.com/
iMac Linux	http://www.imaclinux.net/
iMac2Day	http://www.imac2day.com/
iMacCentral	http://www.imaccentral.com/
iMacworld	http://www.imacworld.com/
The iMac News Channel	http://www.mactimes.com/newspage/

INTERNET-RELATED RESOURCES

We've provided a number of Internet resources throughout this book, but here are some we didn't get to that we find very useful.

Site	URL
BrowserWatch	http://browserwatch.internet.com/
Fight Spam on the Internet	http://spam.abuse.net/
Jon Wiederspan's MacLand	http://www.comvista.com/index.html
The Mac Orchard	http://www.macorchard.com/

Site	URL
Mac WWW FAQ	http://www.nisto.com/mac/
Webintosh	http://www.webintosh.com/

MAC ADVOCACY

Many Mac users feel very strongly about their computers, and don't hesitate to say so online. But these sites do more than just exhort the faithful. Many offer strategies for preserving Macs in corporate environments or provide fuel for those who argue that Macs are better than their "Wintel" competitors.

Site	URL
As the Apple Turns	http://www.infoXczar.com/atat/
Macs Only!	http://www.macsonly.com/

NEWS SITES

News about the Mac comes in several flavors. Some sites cover Apple's position in the business world, while others detail new product offerings or the state of the Macintosh in the corporate world.

Site	URL
Apple Recon	http://www.pelagius.com/AppleRecon/
Apple's Orchard	http://www.enigmaworks.com/orchard/
MacCentral	http://www.maccentral.com/
The Macintosh News Network	http://www.macnn.com/
MacInTouch	http://www.macintouch.com/
MacSurfer's Headline News	http://www.macsurfer.com/
O'Grady's PowerPage	http://www.ogrady.com/

PERIODICALS

The Mac magazines have all taken to the Web, and a few publications exist only online. Some of these sites contain the complete print edition, while others are a tease for the paper versions. The online-only periodicals include news, reviews, links, and opinion columns.

Site	URL
Mac Today	http://www.mactoday.com/
MacAddict	http://www.macaddict.com/
MacHome	http://www.machome.com/
MacTech	http://www.mactech.com/
MacTimes	http://www.mactimes.com/
MacWEEK.com	http://www.macweek.com/
Macworld Online	http://www.macworld.com/
TidBITS	http://www.tidbits.com/

POWERBOOKS

PowerBooks are Macs, all right, but they have a special set of tools, joys, and perils. These sites are very much on the go.

Site	URL
PowerBook Army	http://www.powerbook.org/
The PowerBook Source	http://www.pbsource.com/
The PowerBook Zone	http://www.pbzone.com

PRODUCT GUIDES

Looking for a new Mac, a piece of software, or a peripheral? These independent product guides can help you find it and keep up with current software versions.

Site	URL
Apple Tech Info Library	http://til.info.apple.com/
EveryMac	http://www.everymac.com/
MacDirectory	http://www.macdirectory.com/
Macintosh Products Guide	http://www.macsoftware.apple.com/
MacSense Reviews	http://www.macsense.com/

SHAREWARE ARCHIVES

Shareware archives include a surprisingly wide array of applications, utilities, Internet tools, toys, and more. Though these archives include many of the same files, there are gems to be found in each of them.

Site	URL
Info-Mac HyperArchive	http://hyperarchive.lcs.mit.edu/HyperArchive.html
Macdownload.com	http://www.macdownload.com/
MacUpdate	http://www.macupdate.com/
University of Michigan Archive	http://www-personal.umich.edu/~sdamask/umich-mirrors/
University of Texas Mac Archive	http://wwwhost.ots.utexas.edu/mac/main.html

SHOPPING ONLINE

Looking for a new Mac? Wondering where to find a PowerBook battery? Mail order and online-only sites let you buy just about everything for the Mac. You can also find deals on used Macs, and even accessories for outdated Macs.

Site	URL
Outpost.com	http://www.outpost.com/
deal-mac	http://www.deal-mac.com/
The Mac Zone	http://www.zones.com/Mac_Zone/
MacConnection	http://www.macconnection.com/
MacMall	http://www.macmall.com/
MacWarehouse	http://www.warehouse.com/MacWarehouse/
MacWorks	http://www.macworks.com/
USBStuff	http://www.usbstuff.com/

SUPPORT AND HELP

Help comes from lots of places in the Mac community. Companies support their products, to be sure, but plenty of individuals and organizations also have set up sites that

are intended to help you buy, use, or fix your Mac, of whatever vintage.

Site	URL
Accelerate Your Mac	http://www.xlr8yourmac.com/
Apple Tech Info Library	http://til.info.apple.com/
Macintosh audiovisual FAQ	http://www.sims.berkeley.edu/~jwang/cgi/av-faq/
Digital Camera Resource Page	http://www.dcresource.com/
The DVD Resource Page	http://www.dvdresource.com/
Extensions & Control Panels database	http://www.casadyg.com/Tango/Tango.acgi$/CC4/file.qry?function=form
LowEnd Mac	http://lowendmac.com/
The Mac Conflict Solution Site	http://www.quillserv.com/www/c3/c3.html
MacAssistant	http://www.macassistant.com/
MacFixIt	http://www.macfixit.com/
MacPC	http://www.macpconline.com/
MacWindows	http://www.macwindows.com/
Net Monitor Database	http://www.nashville.net/~griffin/monitor.html
PC<->Mac Networking	http://wcic.cioe.com/~galanti/
PCI Cards for Macintosh	http://msproul.rutgers.edu/macintosh/PCIcards.html
starmax.net	http://www.starmax.net/
VersionTracker Online	http://www.versiontracker.com/

TECHNICAL RESOURCES

Mac nerds can call several Web sites home.

Site	URL
Apple Tech Info Library	http://til.info.apple.com/
Macintosh Evolution	http://www.macevolution.com/
Mac Online Technical Journal	http://www.mactimes.com/lowend/tech/

VENDORS

Vendor sites usually include news and software updates, and they'll often allow you to buy software online, as well.

Site	URL
Adobe	http://www.adobe.com/
Aladdin Systems	http://www.aladdinsys.com/
APS Technologies	http://www.apstech.com/
Bungie	http://www.bungie.com/
Casady & Greene	http://www.casadyg.com/
Connectix	http://www.connectix.com/
Dantz	http://www.dantz.com/
Edmark	http://www.edmark.com/
Extensis	http://www.extensis.com/
Farallon	http://www.farallon.com/
FileMaker	http://www.filemaker.com/
Intuit	http://www.intuit.com/
Macromedia	http://www.macromedia.com/
MacSoft	http://www.wizworks.com/macsoft/
MetaCreations	http://www.metacreations.com/
Metrowerks	http://www.metrowerks.com/
Microsoft Internet Explorer	http://www.microsoft.com/mac/ie/
Microsoft Office for Macintosh	http://www.microsoft.com/macoffice/
Netopia	http://www.netopia.com/
SuperKids	http://www.superkids.com/
Symantec	http://www.symantec.com/
TechWorks	http://www.techworks.com/
The Learning Company	http://www.learningco.com/
Wolfram	http://www.wolfram.com/

Index

NOTE: Page numbers in *italics* refer to illustrations or charts.